Temple of our Fathers:
St. James Church

(1729-2004)

Susan Taylor Block

This book is dedicated to all the quiet saints of St. James,
unheralded individuals whose prayers and steady work
have made a good and lasting difference.

ISBN 0-9761594-0-6
Printed by Friesens
Canada

Edited by Suzanne Nash Ruffin
Book production, visual concepts, and cover design
by Jane L. Baldridge
Photo selection and captions by the author

Endsheets: The silhouette of St. James was created by Charles Gault, a 14-year-old communicant, in 1925. A student of artist Elisabeth Chant, the young man crafted this work while rooming with the Cranmer family at 311 Market Street. The image frames the church symbolically, representing ties to the old covenant with the Temple of Israel — and family, hearth, and home through the Burgwin-Wright House. (Courtesy of the Lower Cape Fear Historical Society.)

Here Charles Gault poses with the Rev. Edward Wootten, about 1935. (Courtesy of Mary M. Wootten)

Foreword

The 275th anniversary of this noble parish church celebrates more than history. It is also a new beginning of her ministry, which began in 1729. Countless thousands have been made whole in this place, and countless thousands have contributed to her welfare. Our congregation is grateful for all who have gone before us and prays that we, too, will be good stewards of this glorious tradition.

All of us have special memories about St. James. It is irreplaceable for us. There is no single person who stands out for everyone. Here, for example, are three whose contributions to the church are permanent: Dr. William H. Milton, rector for twenty-five years; J. V. Grainger, senior warden for forty years; and Bishop Wright, our native son who was baptized, confirmed, ordained, consecrated bishop and buried in St. James Church.

But St. James is not for us alone. Our responsibility to those who do not belong, to those whose hearts are broken, to those who suffer the ills of this world, is continuous and will not cease. Friendship with our neighboring churches is an enduring thing for which we are most grateful; no church is an island unto itself.

May God's grace grant us a new beginning and a proper gratitude for those who planted this part of Christ's church here 275 years ago. And may our hearts be always grateful for those unnumbered souls who carried it forward for our benefit.

I am deeply thankful that this book has been written. It is a much-needed chronicle of an enduring congregation.

Walker Taylor III
Chairman, History Committee

Preface

In the history of the American Episcopal Church and of the United States of America, certain people and places illumine our understanding of the faith and freedom passed down from generation to generation. The rich and vibrant history of St. James Parish is a wonderful example of such a place.

From its humble beginnings in 1729 when the Society for the Propagation of the Gospel sent missionaries from England to minister to the growing Carolina colonies, to its present-day status as the largest Episcopal parish in eastern North Carolina, St. James Parish has continued to be a sacred community of faith and a witness to God's love and compassion for all who pass through her doors.

St. James has been a pivotal force in the lives of countless people – from the occupation of the church by British troops led by General Cornwallis during the Revolutionary War, to Bishop Atkinson's fervent labors to keep the Episcopal Church unified during the Civil War, to Dr. Milton's revolutionary "Every Member Canvass," and to our efforts to house the homeless in our community.

Susan Taylor Block's marvelous book *Temple of Our Fathers* eloquently captures the interconnections between our national history and the events and challenges encountered by the people of St. James and the Wilmington community.

May the words of this book be a living legacy of the faithful lives and ministries that make St. James Parish the joyful and exciting church it is today.

Photo by the Author

The Rev. Ronald G. Abrams
XXVI Rector of St. James Parish

Author's Introduction

In the course of writing this book, I have sat in St. James Church more than once thinking, "If Gothic arches could only talk...." Though immense, the records of St. James contain baffling omissions, archival black holes that leave one wondering about such things as the origins of the various stained glass windows and the whereabouts of some of St. James's lost treasures. The absence of vestry minutes from 1729 until 1811 makes the earliest history of St. James a particular challenge. Among other things, *Temple of our Fathers* is designed to offer answers to some of the mysteries

This book is not meant to be a comprehensive history of St. James Church. That would take years to write and many volumes to contain. For, figuratively speaking, the story of St. James Church is a baroque tapestry too large to drape across anything but a palace wall. However, this 275th anniversary history is an effort to chronicle a portion of the collective life of a body of believers, the buildings in which they worship, and the ties St. James holds with the greater community.

The title comes from a letter the Rev. Mr. Alfred Watson wrote to President Abraham Lincoln on April 12, 1865. Bemoaning the "Yankees'" treatment of St. James Church during the Civil War, Watson wrote, "The principal church of the Diocese has, with every circumstance of irreverence, been torn to pieces with pickaxes and hammers...the Temple of our Fathers where the present generation has been baptized, married, and received to the Communion, and whence the dead have been buried."

In that context, Watson used the word Fathers in a genealogical sense, but that is not the whole reason for adopting it as a title. For that would leave out the many treasured members of St. James who have no family history within the church.

The title also hearkens back to Christianity's spiritual fathers and the encouragement we receive by examining their lives. We draw inspiration from the faith of Abraham, devotion of Ruth, spiritual ardor of David, courage of the prophets; the penitence of John the Baptist, discretion of Mary, the stability that came to Peter, the spiritual conviction of Paul — and a host of other saints.

In addition, within the church, we admire the giants among our ecclesiastical fathers because, for the most part, men with spiritual vision, intellectual acuity, and strong leadership skills have occupied the pulpit of St. James. Many have risen to high places in this diocese or others and a few have held distinguished national positions.

And lastly, there are those mighty oaks among us: fellow church members who delight our spiritual senses. Whether they be layreaders, Sunday School teachers, friends who offer up prayers and encouragement, or the widow happily giving her mite; all of them raise us to a higher place.

Susan Taylor Block
August 3, 2004

Table of Contents

Artist Jocelyn Strange Lynch painted this image of Mount Lebanon Chapel.

"Immoderate light scatters the thoughts." —Thomas More. The horizontal west window, delightful in hue and subtle detail, sits above the double doors of St. James. (Photo by the author)

"When Michael saw his host, he first grew pale,
As angels can; next, like Italian twilight,
He turn'd all colours – as a peacock's tail,
Or sunset streaming through a Gothic skylight
In some old abbey."

—Byron (George Gordon, Lord Byron, 1788-1824),
Vision of Judgment.

A Bureaucratic Beginning

St. James Parish was born November 27, 1729, before there was even a boundary between North and South Carolina. The North Carolina legislature created both the parish and New Hanover Precinct with the passing of a single law entitled, "An Act for Regulating Vestries in this Government, and for the better inspecting the Vestrymen and Church Wardens' Accompts of each and every Parish in this Government." Grammar aside, the General Assembly knew what they were doing, for in one fell swoop they claimed a large and lucrative hunk of real estate that was hanging in the borderless balance for North Carolina. The official establishment of the Church of England came with the territory, for the Crown would own New Hanover province for the next 47 years — and every shilling in the Sunday offering plate went back to England.[1]

But the act that created St. James Parish also directed that the "Church, Court House, and Gaol (jail)" be built in Brunswick. At the time, Brunswick was more civilized than the area that would become Wilmington. But even so, settlement on the western side of the Cape Fear River was described in 1731 as "a poor, hungry, unprovided Place, consisting of not above 10 or 12 scattering mean Houses, hardly worth the name of a Village."[2]

Brunswick was also the seat of the "Family," a politically powerful group of 35 individuals who accounted for the ownership of 115,000 acres of land. Many of the "Family" members were related, and the rolls of St. James Church include a host of their descendants. The original "Family" included, among others, Roger Moore, Maurice Moore, Nathaniel Moore, John Porter, John Baptista Ashe, Samuel Swann, Jehu Davis, John Grange, and Thomas Jones.[3]

Professor Charles M. Andrews of Yale University wrote of the early settlers of St. James Parish in his 1921 book *Colonial Folkways.* "No people in the Southern colonies were more devoted than they to their plantation life or took greater pride in the beauty and wholesomeness of their country. They raised corn and provisions, bred stock — notably the famous black cattle of North Carolina — and made tar, pitch, and turpentine from their lighter trees, and these, together with lumber, frames and houses, and shingles, they shipped to England and to the West Indies."[4]

The establishment of the parish necessitated boundaries and the naming of leaders. The bounds were described as being "from Haul over between Little and New River Inlett & Southernmost Boundary of this Province." The vestrymen were: John Baptista Ashe, John Grange, Cornelius Harnett, Edward Hyrne, Col. Maurice Moore, Nathaniel Moore, "King" Roger Moore, Richard Nixon, John Porter, John Swann, Samuel Swann, and Joseph Watters.[5]

Though there has been some confusion over the matter, the official story is that St. James is named for James the Less, also known as James the Little and James the Young. If there is evidence of this fact before the formation of St. Philip's Parish in 1741, it has not surfaced. It is possible that James the son of Zebedee, who was a brother of the disciple named John, was the intended disciple. The two of them were known as the "Sons of Thunder." Apparently the scholarly Dr. Robert Brent Drane believed the intended disciple was James the Greater. He chose the name St. John's for the 1853 church because he wanted the congregations to be as close as brothers. Perhaps in their eagerness to bond St. James to the new parish, Colonial authorities chose the name St. Philip because he shares a feast day with St. James. But May 1st is the feast day of James the Less, not James the Greater. James the Less seems an odd choice for a parish established originally as much for reasons of power as religion.

Biblical and historical writers record that James the Less was the son of Alpheus, one of Christ's apostles. A cousin of Jesus, he was the second man named James to be called as a disciple — therefore the name. James the Less is the patron saint of pharmacists, hatters, and Uruguay. The crest seen on the east side of the balcony railing has been said to be a symbol of St. James the Less who, tradition states, was the first bishop of Jerusalem.[6]

Mary Grady Koonce, an eleventh generation descendant of John LaPierre, unveiling a historical marker in Brunswick Town, 1968. (Courtesy of N.C. Dept of Cultural Resources.)

By the time St. James Parish was created, an Anglican clergyman, John LaPierre, had been laboring in Wilmington for nearly a year, officiating at services held both in Brunswick and in New Hanover County. He also managed his small plantation, Sandy Bay, on the western side of the Cape Fear River.

On October 25, 1728, LaPierre wrote to the secretary of the SPG that he would like an appointment to "edify a poor dispersed multitude of People residing up and down Cape Fear. I have been already with them at my own Cost to baptize Several of the Children and to preach to them at three several times."

The Reverend John LaPierre, a 1706 graduate of Trinity College in Dublin, Ireland, was a Frenchman by birth. Ordained by the

Bishop of London in 1707, he came to Cape Fear from the South Carolina parish of St. Denis. According to historian Edward S. Barnhill, LaPierre was a Huguenot who converted to the Anglican faith. He came to America "recommended to the Governor of South Carolina to preach in a parish called St. Denis in the French Colony to serve until the death of the old Settlers who did not understand the English tongue."[7] He moved to Brunswick Town in December 1728 and labored for the Crown in the future parish of St. James.

LaPierre's relocation from an ecclesiastical position in South Carolina would prove an unusual path to St. James. The preponderance of ecclesiastical moves would be to and from points north. St. James had many bonds with Christ Church in New Bern — and various Episcopal churches in Richmond. Many came from north of the Mason-Dixon line, and 8% of the rectors, to date, have come from Hempstead, New York.

Although LaPierre was a zealous minister, he had little means of support for himself, his blind wife, and his three children. Often he was paid in rice. Even after the parish was established, Governor George Burrington refused to recommend him for financial aid from the venerable Society for the Propagation of the Gospel in Foreign Parts, or SPG.

Founded in London in 1701, the SPG was the missionary society of the Church of England, answerable to the Crown and to the Archbishop of Canterbury. The SPG held meetings once a month at the Church of St. Martin-in-the-Fields in London to read letters from representatives in the colonies and to respond in kind. The crown sometimes paid the missionary's passage to America, and always provided a library and meager salary. In their effort to establish the Church of England in America, the SPG sent some less than attractive candidates who had burned their ecclesiastical bridges in the Old Country. One missionary who was sent to N. C. was a convicted felon.

But the SPG also sponsored many dedicated souls, a few of whom were highly educated and had places of privilege in Britain. Once they reached coastal N.C., they faced painful adjustments to climate, mosquitoes, "fevers" to which they had no natural immunity — and a decreased amount of academic stimulation. They were truly missionaries in an untamed land.

Despite the bureaucratic beginnings of St. James, parishioners quickly exhibited a yearning for spiritual food and a shepherd to feed them. The vestry of St. James Parish met on Easter Monday, 1730, near the foot of Market Street and drew up a petition addressed to the "Rt. Rev. Father in God Edmund Lord Bishop of London." They praised the "Worthy" LaPierre for his "great goodness and pious concern," then requested the Crown provide LaPierre with a salary and other provisions appropriate for a minister of the Gospel. hired

If St. James Parish, at its own expense, had provided LaPierre with a rectory and glebe, Gov. Burrington would have also recommended LaPierre to the SPG. However, the new parish refused both and quit paying the meager salary they had once allowed LaPierre. The young minister resigned almost four years after his arrival at the place he called "Cape Fear alias New Hanover."[8]

John LaPierre sold Sandy Bay Plantation, a tract that abutted Lilliput. The land passed through the hands of several owners including Roger Moore, George Moore, and John Nutt — and is now incorporated into Pleasant Oaks, a riverfront property that once belonged to John D. Taylor and Frank B. Adams. After World War II, Hargrove Bellamy purchased Pleasant Oaks. It is now the home of Brian and Lyell Bellamy McMerty.

In 1734, LaPierre wrote to the Bishop of London, Edmund Gibson: "I was a minister of the Church of England, that came to this place to preach which I did during three years and a half and at last frustrated of the best part of my salary was obliged to ask for my discharge, then forced to work in the field to help maintain my family, afterwards compelled by necessity to sell my house and land and lastly my movables so that at this time I am no better than a mendicant…"[9]

Even while John LaPierre waged his struggle to gain financial support, another minister was making inroads for the popular vote as the parish priest. Richard Marsden, a native of Yorkshire, England, arrived in the Cape Fear area about 1729, and was recipient of a 1,000-acre land grant on Prince George Creek on which he built a home he called The Hermitage. Located in what is now called Castle Hayne, his residence was situated about where the modern subdivision Castle Estates lies.

At first, Marsden was willing to preach gratis, a condition that did not aid LaPierre in his battle for a salary. Not only did he hold services during LaPierre's term, but also he fed the worshippers afterward with a Colonial style "dinner on the grounds." Fine wines accompanied the repast, making the feasts especially popular.[10]

Mr. Marsden was well acquainted with hospitality on a large scale, having previously served as private chaplain to William Bentinke, the first Duke of Portland; the post began in England and eventually led Marsden to live in Jamaica. While there, Marsden wed a wealthy Jamaican widow, an odd move considering he was already married. Apparently, Marsden divorced his Jamaican wife, or had the marriage annulled. Either way, he apologized to the Bishop of London in 1733.[11]

When the Duke of Portland returned to England, Marsden sailed for Charleston where he had been promised a church position. However, by the time he arrived, the post was already filled and the venerable Society for the Propagation of the Gospel in Foreign Parts suggested they might cooperate if Marsden would try to find work in Newton, or "New Town," known later as Wilmington.

Even though the SPG refused to pay him, Richard Marsden acted the role of minister, even traveling to Onslow County to hold Anglican services. Marsden's ministry was marred by what seemed to be his almost irresistible urge to borrow money on false pretenses, with no apparent intention of repayment. But he had one sterling accomplishment in the eyes of St. James: he helped lead the first campaign for a church building.

Meanwhile, John LaPierre ended his emotional and financial struggles in the Lower Cape Fear by moving to New Bern about 1735. He had been preaching in Onslow County for about a year before moving north. New Bern must have been kinder to him, for LaPierre purchased a 360-acre tract on the Neuse River and a lot on Jones Street. He was associated with Christ Church, but was also the chaplain of the N. C. Assembly when it met in the old capital. He even preached for the famous evangelist George Whitefield in 1737. LaPierre died in New Bern, in 1755.

Richard Marsden's personal charisma attracted many admirers, but he did not have the blessing of the Bishop of London, titular head of the SPG. Marsden also gained an adversary named Alexander Garden who was commissary for the Carolinas. Garden wrote to the Bishop of London complaining of Marsden's refusal to pay some of his debts.

Because there was no bishop in the colonies, a fact that lent more power to the Crown, all official business of the SPG had to be done in London. Richard Marsden traveled there to gain official status as minister of the Parish of St. James. A series of dizzying events followed in which the Bishop of London reviewed numerous character references unfavorable to Marsden.

People from different parts of the world had reported Marsden for using the integrity of his office to borrow money, and then refusing to pay back his loans. One letter from Dublin even contained a description: "Mr. Marsden is a full bodied man between 60 and 70 years of Age near Six Foot high a Stoop in his Shoulders a Swarthy Complexion."[12]

Despite a glowing recommendation from the vestry of St. James, the Bishop denied him an audience. However the SPG gave him official appointment to the very post he desired. But before Richard Marsden could return to the Hermitage, church officials reversed their decision and his appointment was axed. Unfortunately, he had to hear the news of his career's demise from his successor, James Moir, who would be minister from 1740-1748.

Disappointed and financially compromised, Marsden died in 1742, leaving the Hermitage to his daughter, Mrs. Roger Haynes. Castle Hayne gained its name from Roger Haynes, who built a "fine building called by him Castle Haynes." But the name now seems to be permanently misspelled.[13]

Castle Haynes and the Hermitage would have another St. James connection in 1753, when a Welsh businessman named John Burgwin married Roger Haynes's daughter, Margaret. Burgwin, a member of St. James Parish, purchased a lot across the street from the church about 1769, and built a house there upon the stone foundation of an old jail.

In 1740, when Mr. Moir arrived, the place called Wilmington was an infant city. The geographic moniker "Cape Fear" had covered Newton and Brunswick, but the river sat between them: an active liquid symbol of their division and rivalry. Ships were the cars, trucks, and trains of that era and the Cape Fear was usually full of them. They were the lifeblood of the local economy.

At a point near Sunset Park, an ancient cypress that sat out at least 50' in the river marked the place at which all outgoing ships unfurled their sails. The natural marker created a good time for all hands to enjoy a drink before continuing upriver or downriver, thus the name "Dram Tree." For a time, the Dram Tree itself became a symbol of the rivalry between the towns.

Trade was the chief contention and rivalry pervaded almost every aspect of both towns. With the incorporation of Wilmington on February 25, 1739/1740, the seat of power began to shift. The name evolved from Spencer Compton, the Earl of Wilmington, who was a patron of Governor Gabriel Johnston. After a series of conflicts with the Brunswick "Family," Gov. Johnston not only renamed the city after his most celebrated supporter, but also put his heart and considerable power into making the new town a success.[14]

This image of the Dram Tree was created by Henry G. Latimer who underwrote the cost of the reredos. (Courtesy of the Lower Cape Fear Historical Society)

Mr. Moir, who also journeyed to London, preached on the Sermon on the Mount and was approved by the church fathers. He won partial support, a library, a Bible and Book of Common Prayer, "five pounds worth of Small Tracts," and a dozen catechisms. The SPG gave him responsibility for five counties, but he made the new town of Wilmington his home. His charges, positioned along a hundred miles of coastline, included townspeople and rural dwellers. Though he annually baptized hundreds of people, both blacks and whites, he found few were willing to be communicants. He blamed the situation on the "people being ignorant of religion to the last degree."[15]

In 1741, St. James Parish lost its Brunswick territory when St. Philip's Parish was created. The new domain included Eagles Island and everything on the western side of the Cape Fear River. As stated, the names of the parishes were connected: both were disciples and they share the same feast day, May 1. The existence of the new parish caused the St. James vestry to increase Mr. Moir's salary in hopes of keeping him on the eastern side of the river. However, in 1742, a new vestry decreased his salary and Moir went to St. Philip's. But the Society could find no one to take the position at St. James so it unofficially united the parishes of St. James and St. Philip.

The rivalry created mirror experiences for Moir. While at St. James, Wilmington churchmen complained when he ventured into Brunswick. After he moved to Brunswick, his journeys to Wilmington exasperated the parishioners who were paying his salary. The perpetual voyages and tension prompted Moir to write complaining of the "fatigue and hazard of travelling" and the "malice and perverseness of those with whom he had to do."[16]

"A Missionary in this River has a most difficult part to act, for by obliging one of the Towns he must of course disoblige the other, each of them opposing the other at the utmost of their Power."[17]

And apparently some parishioners didn't limit their Sunday morning alcohol consumption to what they sipped at the Communion rail. In 1745, laws were enacted in Brunswick forbidding "any person to get drunk in his house on the Sabbath." Those caught breaking the law were fined ten shillings. But for those "drunker offenders" who disturbed worship services at St. Philip's, the bill was 2.5 pounds.[18]

In 1746, Moir ended his unhappy rectorship in Brunswick by moving to Wilmington where he requested St. James provide him lodging. The church declined and Moir, believing the local environment was beginning to affect his health, moved to Edgecombe County in 1747.

Despite Mr. Moir's frustrations, members of St. James summed up his work with praise and humility. "He hath, to the great comfort and edification of our families, and these dark and distant regions of the world, prosecuted the duties of his calling with utmost application and diligence, adorned his character with an exemplary life and conversation, shewing uncorruptness, gravity, and sound speech, so that they who are of the contrary part have no evil thing to say of him."[19]

Mr. Moir served St. Mary's Church at Chapel Bridge on the Tar River. In 1760, Moir was one of a handful of citizens who purchased land to create the town of Tarboro. At least as late as 1765, the SPG employed him as an itinerant missionary. But perhaps he was not terribly active. Gov. Tryon wrote to London, "It would be better if he were fixed in a parish, as it is reported that he seldom preaches anywhere."[20]

From 1746 until his death, about 1750, the Rev. Mr. Christopher Bevis, a Cambridge graduate, served St. Philip's Parish. But from 1747 until 1754, St. James had no minister. However it was during that very period that an unlikely event spurred construction of the first St. James church building.

Francisco Pacheco, an artist, scholar, and the father-in-law of Valezquez, painted *Ecce Homo.* Salvage from a skirmish with the Spanish, it was given to St. James by the state – just when the parish needed cash. Now considered a sacred blessing, the painting is the most ancient possession of the church. (Photo from the brochure, *Ecce Homo*, published by St. James Church)

Ecce Homo

"To write history properly has always been difficult." – Francesco Pacheco

Despite the structure of the upcoming American constitution, it was the *lack* of separation between church and state that opened the doors of St. James Parish to one of its most celebrated treasures. *Ecce Homo*, proudly displayed in St. James, was a gift to the church of state, from the state. It was during the 1740s that Spanish privateers paid stealthy visits to Brunswick. As if civilizing raw territory weren't enough of a challenge, residents had to endure thieves gliding upriver to purloin the very objects that gave their new homes distinction and meaning.

Technically, the villains were not pirates but robbers sanctioned by international rules of war. The powers of Europe continued to fight one another for control of trade, property, and power in America. Spain still ruled St. Augustine and orchestrated attacks on the colonists from the heavily fortified city that lay menacingly close to Cape Fear. The English and the Spanish fought the War of Jenkins Ear from 1739-1741. Then in 1744, after the French sided with the Spanish, the English fought King George's War until 1748.

The international conflicts that affected Cape Fear endangered the lives and possessions of some early members of St. James Parish. In 1741, the crew of a Spanish man-of-war that had already seized several vessels plotted to attack and plunder Orton, the treasure-filled home of Roger Moore (1694-1759), a charter vestryman. But distracted by a departing brigantine, the pirates confiscated the vessel and vacated their watery hunting blind near the mouth of the Cape Fear. They sailed away leaving the residents of Orton blissfully unaware of the dangers that had hovered nearby.[21]

During the summer of 1747, Spanish privateers who sporadically vandalized property, kidnapped slaves, and killed colonists terrorized Cape Fear residents. But on Saturday, September 3, 1748, the most frightening visitors arrived. Two Spanish vessels from Havana, the *Fortuna* and the *Loretta*, plus a sloop confiscated from South Carolina sat in the river, awaiting unsuspecting Brunswick pilots who would come aboard the following morning to navigate them through the tricky waters of the Cape Fear River.

Like taxi drivers with pistols to their heads, the pilots led the privateers to Fort Johnston, in what is now the town of Southport. Intent on stealing slaves, the Spaniards were angered when they realized the slaves had the day off — it was Sunday. So they ordered their guides to lead them upriver where Spanish scouts disembarked and made their way through snake-infested thickets to descend upon the town. Deafening gunfire from the ships further terrified Brunswick citizens who fled from their homes, leaving their precious treasures to the rowdy rogues.

Two days later, on September 6, the Spaniards were still making their way through Brunswick, plundering houses and celebrating their uncontested takeover, when Capt. William Dry (III) and his local militia launched their own surprise attack. The Brunswick group included men from neighboring communities, as well as a few from the confiscated vessel and a number of slaves. There were 80 men, but only about 60 were armed because many had left their weapons when they rushed to flee the Spanish.

Under the direction of Capt. Dry, a justice and assemblyman, local men killed ten Spaniards and captured 30 more. The remainder of the fleeing privateers took refuge on the *Fortuna*, a 24-gun ship that began shelling the town. As Brunswick forces watched from cover, suddenly a fire broke out aboard the vessel, followed quickly by a catastrophic explosion. When the gunpowder settled, 90 bodies were discovered including those of the captain and his crew. A portion of the ship was partially visible and some of the loot survived the explosion. About 40 prisoners, both privateers and slaves, were taken to Wilmington for incarceration. Dr. Samuel Green, the man from whom Greenfield Lake derives its name, treated them for their injuries.[22]

Meanwhile the remaining privateers fired on Orton and shelled Brunswick. William Dry and Wilmingtonian Major John Swann, another member of the original St. James Parish vestry, fought to gain release of Cape Fear residents being held prisoner on the Spanish ships, and to force the enemy to return property stolen. Nothing seemed to come together and the villains sailed away — but not before being spotted pursuing a hapless brigantine that came within its sight. Though the residents of Brunswick suffered materially, none was killed and only two were injured. The handful taken away as prisoners were probably integrated into the slippery fold.

Ecce Homo, an oil-on-wood painting of Jesus, was among the items salvaged from the captain's cabin of the *Fortuna*. Based on John 19:5, Jesus is pictured wearing a crown of thorns and a scarlet robe. The name applies to all such depictions and derives from the words of Pilate, "Behold the man." Early members of St. James Parish believed that the painting was probably stolen from a church in South America or the West Indies. However the possibility always remains that the captain was a religious man who saw his role as privateer merely as patriotic service. He could have carried *Ecce Homo* in the same spirit that soldiers carry pocket Bibles into battle.

In 1950, it emerged that Francesco Pacheco (1564-1654) most likely painted *Ecce Homo*. Pacheco, a resident of Seville, was a teacher and the father-in-law of Velazquez — and art tutor to Alonso Cano, the "Spanish Michelangelo." The artist was identified through the efforts of Mrs. Cecil Appleberry of Wilmington. She received the following information from art historian Stephen Bourgeois, of New York, a family friend.

Pacheco was born San Luccer de Barrameda in Andalusia, in 1564. *Ecce Homo* was painted early in his career, when he used a "rather cool color." His style varied throughout his career as he was influenced by the artists he met. His best picture was "The Embarkment of St. Peter Nolasco." However, Pacheco achieved much more fame for writing several definitive volumes on leading

Spanish painters of his era. By the time he died, at age 90, Pacheco had outlived many of those he taught and wrote about.[23]

The painting has moved about the church through the years. In 1874, it resided in the vestry room. In 1886, it hung where the reredos now stands. Today it is a rare and treasured piece of church and area history. *Ecce Homo* has now been resituated on the southern side of the chancel, protected as much as possible from light and modern day pirates.[24]

A 1753 law dictated that the proceeds of the sale of objects and of captured slaves were to be divided equally between those who experienced loss during the invasion and those who fought against it. In 1760, apparently feeling that adequate compensation had been paid, the legislature ordered that the profit from any additional sale of effects and from the captured slaves go for the completion of St. James and St. Philip's churches, with two thirds going to Brunswick and one third allotted to Wilmington.

A largely ineffective lottery was also bundled into the law entitled, "An Act for raising Money by a Lottery, towards finishing the Churches at Wilmington and Brunswick; and for applying the Produce of the Slaves, and other Effects taken from the Spaniards at Cape Fear, in the Year of our Lord One Thousand Seven Hundred and Forty Eight, to the same Purposes."[25]

Before construction of the 1751-1770 St. James building was completed, church services were held in the bright yellow courthouse that sat in the intersection of Front and Market streets. (Sketch by E. V. Richards from *Cornelius Harnett, Revolutionary Patriot*, by Andrew J. Howell.)

The House of the Lord

By the time work began on the first St. James church building, the congregation had been worshipping in the New Hanover County Courthouse for over twenty years. Under British rule, it wasn't so odd. Church and state were entwined. And fewer events happened in churches at that time. Weddings and funerals usually took place in parishioners' homes, leaving only the Sunday services for the courthouse.

However, the desire to build a church on the sea side of the river had been there almost from the beginning. Local businessman William Flavell included St. James Parish in his will, written in 1737 and proved in 1739. He left 200 pounds and other proceeds towards the construction of an "English Church in Newton," and the purchase of communion silver. (If the silver was purchased, it was probably stolen by the British forty years later.) But other donations were slow in coming and the congregation continued to coexist with the ever-increasing bureaucracy of government.

Finally, things were set in motion when Michael Higgins donated a parcel of land at the corner of Fourth and Market streets to St. James Parish. His gift, which determined the site of the church, provided beautiful high-and-dry ground in a city still beset with unharnessed streams that wreaked havoc on rainy days. Not only would the church building be well positioned; those buried in the intended graveyard would most likely be spared the indignity of being disinterred by occasional floods.

The parish established the graveyard first and money raised from the sale of plots was saved to help finance construction of the church. But by the time there was money to erect the church, the graveyard, soon to be known by the quaint name "God's Acre," had exceeded the proposed building's grounds. So when the cornerstone was about to be laid, the provincial legislature allowed the church to jut out into Market Street a full thirty feet.

"Old St. James Church was formerly located 1/2 in the street, 1/2 in the burying yard," wrote Nicholas Schenck, a nephew of St. James vestryman Phineas Fanning. "In the old days, walking the sidewalk straight east carried you into the church."[26]

But mid-18th century, it didn't seem quite so peculiar. The street was 99 feet wide, there was little traffic, and St. James was on the far side of town. Also, the protuberance was not unusual. The market sat in the middle of the foot of Market Street. The courthouse sat in the middle of the intersection of Front and Market streets — and the "Mud Market" was in the intersection of Second and Market streets.[27]

Officials appointed a commission to oversee the affairs of the new church. John Ashe, Joseph Blake, Lewis deRosset, William Faris, John Sampson, and Samuel Swann were to decide on a style for the building, choose laborers and materials, and assign pews to those who purchased them. Glass arrived from England and bricks were probably made on the site. Masons shaped the walls, but the work moved as slowly as an aged sloth.[28]

The problem wasn't workmen because the same fine craftsmen that created St. Philip's probably also built St. James. Thomas Dick was chief carpenter for the Brunswick church. He built the roof, finished the interior, and put in doors, windows, and pews. The brickmason for St. Philip's who crafted the three-foot-thick walls was Richard Price.[29]

From 1751 to 1753, merely the glassless walls were completed. Like St. Philip's Church today, St. James sat there, defined but roofless. In 1757, in hopes of spurring action, a new commission was appointed consisting of Cornelius Harnett, John DuBois, and George Wakely. They answered to the vestry of St. James Parish and were empowered to collect unpaid taxes and subscriptions to fund completion of St. James Church.[30]

A St. James parishioner who witnessed the building process, William Faris, has provided us with an interesting cameo of what life was like in Wilmington in 1749/50. He wrote the following letter to Arthur Dobbs (1689-1765), an Irish aristocrat who purchased 1.3 million acres of land in North Carolina, sight unseen. Dobbs's dream was to successfully relocate poor Protestant Irishmen in the province. Though little of his land was inhabited during his lifetime, he did manage to encourage many hundreds of emigrations, including that of the Andrew Jackson family in 1765. In 1754, Dobbs sailed to North Carolina where, on November 1, he began an eleven-year term of office as Royal Governor of the Province.[31]

"I heard you had thought of seeing this country this year yourself," wrote Faris in 1749/50, "but I fear this settlement is yet too much in its infancy to give you much satisfaction and the accommodations in many parts are so bad. A number of the settlers meet with disappointment and become unhappy. Your land on Black River would be very fit for sugar. Cattle and hogs are easily raised under careful industrious people.

"Mr. John Rutherford is a worthy neighbor of mine and returns in this fall probably with a vessel of his own. It would be a fine opportunity (for you to travel) as she is a good vessel, and his commander a remarkably good seafarer and a sober man, which is of no small importance.

"The fall is the best time. October particularly."[32]

William Faris died in 1757, leaving his estate, after the payment of debt and legacies, to "be used to finishing the church – St. James Parish."[33]

During the early days of St. James, there were many different accents within the congregation. Immigrants from Scotland, Ireland, Ulster, and England all brought their own twists of the tongue and colloquialisms. Some of those from England, "the Descendants of Ancient Britons," celebrated their heritage on St. David's Day with an annual banquet. In fact, on the first of March, 1807, members of the Giles and Burgwin families led a series of ten toasts to the old country.

From 1754 until 1757, the Rev. Mr. John McDowell served St. James, at the request of Governor Arthur Dobbs. Even though McDowell would continue to serve St. James on demand, in 1758 he became minister of St. Philip's and its most celebrated member. Governor Dobbs, who had chosen to live at Brunswick rather than in New Bern, brought fresh attention to the Province and the Lower Cape Fear — and a new ferocity to Anglicanism at St. Philip's and St. James.

Erudite and wealthy, the Irish gentleman was already considered elderly when he left his home, Castle Dobbs in Carrickfergus, Northern Ireland, to move to North Carolina. His Irish residence, known for its private library and other dazzling treasures, still exists, but a much grander castle has replaced the one Gov. Dobbs inhabited. Lord Byron and Jonathan Swift were both captivated by the books and wonders found in Governor Dobbs's home on Belfast Lough. Additionally Dobbs's political ties in London, gained through holding high office in protestant Ireland and working to establish the Northwest Passage to India and China, also gave him advantages.[34]

It is probably no accident that soon after Dobbs arrived, St. James Parish owned a fine library. Not only did he love books and probably bring some from home, but also he requested them from the SPG. Since the congregation was still worshipping in the courthouse, the collection served from 1755 until 1760 as the St. James Parish Public Library as well. As late as 1874, the library at St. James contained hundreds of books that were already considered rare. They were vestiges of the first parish library. Two of the books bore the stamp of "His Royal Highness George, Prince of Wales." The Prince of Wales, the grandson of George II, would become George III in 1760 and reign until 1820. He was the very Hanoverian who would make trouble for St. James during the Revolutionary War.[35]

Though Dobbs's critics considered him autocratic and nepotistic, he had endearing attributes. One was his unusually fervent brand of Christianity, deeply rooted in Anglicanism. He made several attempts to jumpstart religious fervor throughout the Province. In 1758 he proclaimed June 7 a day of "fasting and supplication" in seeking forgiveness from sins he felt caused God to harshly discipline "Britain and these colonies" with sufferings caused by the French and Indian War (1754-1760.)

Then in October 1758, he declared the first Wednesday in December to be a day of Thanksgiving. And again in 1759, in honor of the British victory at Quebec, he set aside a special day to thank the Lord. Not only did parishioners attend a Thanksgiving service, they also sang a 12-stanza hymn composed by Governor Dobbs for the occasion. Dobbs insisted on at least two more days of religious thanksgiving: December 23, 1760, and May 4, 1762. Fifteen years later, in 1777, the U. S. Congress recommended all colonies set apart a day of general thanksgiving.[36]

It was McDowell who led the first crusade to recruit lay readers in local congregations. Since it was impossible to serve all the needs of large parishes, lay persons proved invaluable in both remote areas and in churches without their own rector.

In 1759, the Rev. Mr. Michael Smith moved to Wilmington from Johnston County. It was during this period that the General Assembly authorized certain proceeds from the Spanish privateer that was blown up September 6, 1748, to be used for construction costs at St. James and St. Philip's. Assemblymen also approved plans for a lottery to finance completion of the two churches. The lottery was to be held at the Courthouse and managed by Marmaduke Jones, Alexander Duncan, Jehu Davis, and John Paine. However no provisions were made to augment the rector's salary and personal financial difficulties dogged Michael Smith during his brief ministry at St. James. He left the parish in 1762 to become a chaplain in the British Navy.[37]

In 1760 the roof was put on St. Philip's. Governor Dobbs requested the completed church be designated "His Majesty's Chapel in North Carolina." The honor would mean that St. Philip's would not only have the most prestige in the province, but also would receive communion silver, garments, and church furniture, an imposing Bible, and Books of Common Prayer from the Crown. It is thought that the communion plate at St. Philip's was removed during the Revolutionary War to keep the British from confiscating it. It is possible that the plate at St. Paul's Church in Edenton is part of the St. Philip's collection.[38]

But in July of 1760, nature suddenly interrupted the building process at St. Philip's. Lightning struck the new roof and it fell in, along with the beams and belfry tower.[39]

By this time, Brunswick had lost many citizens to Wilmington, making it a town of almost 800 residents. Author Peter du Bois wrote of Wilmington in 1757: "The regularity of its streets is equal to that of Philadelphia and the buildings are in general very good. Many of brick, two or three stories high with double piazzas, which made a good appearance."[40]

Governor Dobbs's lobbying efforts helped both St. James and St. Philip's when the state legislature voted in December 1760 to give proceeds from the *Fortuna* cargo and a lottery to both churches. An earlier lottery failed for lack of ticket sales, but this one was a mild success. Managed by Cornelius Harnett, Alexander Duncan, Thomas Davis, and John Payne, the lottery benefited both churches. A thousand tickets were sold for 3 pounds apiece. Each read:

"Cape Fear Church Lottery. This Ticket entitles the Bearer to whatever Prize may be drawn against this Number, deducting Fifteen per Cent. as by Act of Assembly passed in December, 1760."[41]

Meanwhile John McDowell continued his work at St. Philip's, battling financial difficulties and successfully winning approval as a missionary of the SPG. He also became chaplain to the family of Governor Arthur Dobbs, succeeding the Rev. Mr. Alexander Stewart, Dobbs's cousin who had become happily ensconced in Beaufort Parish. Apparently it was McDowell, in 1762, who officiated at the wedding of Arthur Dobbs, 73, and a young Brunswick County citizen named Justina Davis, age 15. It must have tested McDowell's ministerial fortitude when he pronounced the 73-year-old governor and the fifteen-year-old girl "man and wife."

McDowell developed a disease that left him infirm by 1763. He died in 1764. Survived by a young son, the Rev. Mr. McDowell was buried next to his wife in the St. Philip's Churchyard.

Governor Dobbs, who lived in Wilmington for most of the year 1763, almost certainly worshiped with the congregation of St. James.[42]

In 1764, Gov. Dobbs reported to the Lords Commissioners of Trade and Plantations that, because of the "absence of [contrary] northern members of the assembly," he had successfully gotten new ecclesiastical laws passed. A schoolmaster would be provided for each parish, and each rector would automatically become a member of his own vestry. Dobbs blamed the lack of sufficient Anglican clergymen for the numbers of North Carolinians who were turning away from the state church. "We abound in Sectaries, and turn Profligates and Deists," he wrote.[43]

Ironically, there still was no minister in the area to perform the funeral of Arthur Dobbs when he died March 28, 1765. Weakened by a series of strokes, the aged governor died in the arms of his dear Justina. The passionate Anglican who had pressed hard for more missionaries for North Carolina was buried by a Justice of the Peace. Dobbs, remembered later as a "sincere adorer of God," was interred "in the new church of Brunswick."

Governor Dobbs's cousin, the Rev. Mr. Alexander Stewart of Bath, eulogized him in a letter to the SPG. "[He was] a worthy member of the Venerable Society's and a true friend to the Established Religion and the few clergy of this Province. The many good Laws that he took care to have Pass'd in this Province, for the encouragement of religion will make his memory ever esteemed by the clergy. Mr. Dobbs was to have embarked in a few days for London, but I hope in God he has had a better remove."[44]

Back at St. James, John Barnett, a highly acclaimed minister, followed the Rev. Mr. McDowell, in 1765. Mr. Barnett established a residence in Wilmington for his work at St. James, and lodged at the home of the new governor, William Tryon, while in Brunswick.

His time in Cape Fear was marked by growing numbers of non-Anglican assemblies. McDowell complained more than once, and on one occasion wrote to London from Castle Tryon, citing the example of a "Scotch" minister who had "several times preach'd here in a lawyer's old gown given him in Wilmington."[45]

It was also in 1765 that discontent with the Crown hit the Cape Fear area hard and early. After November 1, when the Stamp Act went into effect, all contracts, licenses, maritime papers, newspapers, and playing cards required a stamp purchased with specie. With gold and silver coins about as scarce as affection for King George, locals began to protest even before the Stamp Act was enforceable.

Mr. Barnett wrote of widespread public disturbances, and he was a good one to know. The churchyard was the scene of a quirky patriotic demonstration on All Hallows Eve, 1765. The following day, November 1, the Stamp Act was due to go into effect.

In the darkness, a mock funeral procession, accompanied by the sounds of a mournful drummer and the town bell, moved through the streets of Wilmington. The bereaved finally reached

St. James Graveyard where a unique drama unfolded — for the body was actually an effigy of "Liberty," created by local patriots.

Sadly no copy of the eulogy survived, but it almost certainly was a combination of the sweet praise for freedom and vitriol for the Mother Country. Soon the time came to commit Liberty to the soil of St. James. But just as it was about to be interred, the participants "felt it advisable to feel its pulse." In a scene that evokes in reverse the eerie tragedy of Samuel Jocelyn's unfortunate premature interment in 1810, a faint beat was detected in Liberty's chest — and it was decided that full recovery was a possibility.

Mourning quickly turned to joy, and perhaps a few of Wilmington's most prominent citizens were dancing a jig. But the strangest sight was yet to come. The participants lit a bonfire just outside the graveyard, then placed the effigy in a "large two-armed chair" where it sat "watching" the fire's hot wonder.[46]

As it evolved, the Stamp Act affected the minister directly. Barnett sent a note to Governor Tryon's residence, on February 1, 1766, announcing that his vestry had agreed to pay him his salary, but that no contract could be drawn "without a stamp."[47]

Apparently, it was also John Barnett who had one of the most unusual ecclesiastical tasks in the history of St. James Parish. The story began near St. Philip's Church where two members of His Majesty's Navy dueled over their mutual affection for a local girl. After a messy fray that involved skull cracking in addition to gunshot, Lieutenant Thomas Whitehurst lay dead and Captain Alexander Simpson fled the scene. Simpson eventually turned himself in and was tried in local court in October 1765. After he was convicted of manslaughter, he made the unusual request of a minister's presence at his sentencing. Perhaps the sight of Barnett in vestments conjured up images of mercy, for Simpson was merely ordered to pay a fee and have the letter "M," for murder, branded on his thumb.[48]

In March of 1765, St. James played host to a famous guest: the Rev. Mr. George Whitefield, the Anglican who launched The Great Revival in 1740, and subsequently became one of the founders of Methodism. Whitefield had been concerned about North Carolina since at least 1741 when he wrote the Bishop of Oxford, "[there are] but two settled Missionaries in all North-Carolina and one of those viz. Mr. Garzia [at Bath], can scarcely speak English. Does not this look too much like making a Party of Religion?"

Whitefield also had voiced outrage with the leaders of the state and their reluctance to offer the best in Christian teachers to the slave population. "Governours" of North Carolina, Whitefield wrote, were "so exceedingly jealous over any that shall undertake publickly to teach them."

Nevertheless, Whitefield's message to Wilmington in 1765 was well received. Governor Tryon wrote to the S P G, "Whitefield preached a sermon in Wilmington...which would have done him credit in St. James." The inspiration from Whitefield's sermon may have spurred construction activity at St. James a few months later. And, no doubt, the competition from a growing splinter group of revivalists from New England known as the New Lights, also added impetus.

In September of 1765, the vestry reached an agreement with a carpenter named Ebenezer Bunting to "raise, shingle, finish, and complete" the church roof within six months.

The SPG wanted Barnett to serve St. James and St. Philip's, but a new law barring ministers from serving more than one church interfered. Barnett, who had complained to the Bishop of London that many members of St. James drank too much on Saturday nights, left Wilmington to minister to the parishioners of Brunswick until he also fell ill.

Anglicans still didn't have enough active shepherds, a fact exhibited by a Mr. Stevens who was a shamed Presbyterian minister. "He has offended the governor and council," wrote Barnett shortly before leaving the area, "and is alleged to have boasted that he could obtain Episcopal orders for the price of a good beaver hat."[49]

On Easter Monday 1766, St. James Parish had a new rector: the Rev. Mr. John Wills. He was originally contracted to earn 185 pounds and free rent for a year's service. But he would officiate in St. James Church only eighteen Sundays a year. The balance of the Sabbaths would be spent at the "Sound,"Rocky Point, Welsh Tract, Black River, and Long Creek. Mr. Wills shepherded St. James Parish from 1766 until 1777, after Colonial government ended in Wilmington.[50]

In 1768, John Barnett left Brunswick, which he considered dangerously hot in the summer, and moved to Northampton County. But before doing so, he participated in the consecration of St. Philip's Church, a more imposing structure than the first St. James building. Even though St. Philip's was probably not entirely finished, Barnett and St. James rector John Wills blessed the building that was the largest church in North Carolina, on March 24, 1768.

But William Tryon was already at work on a new residence in New Bern and soon St. Philip's Church would no longer have a governor in regular attendance. The dissension between St. James and St. Philip's began to vanish. As

Architect Thomas U. Walter, famous for painting watercolors for potential clients, could have created this image of old St. James when he first met with the vestry. Years later, the painting was presented to the church by Clayton Giles (1844-1917). (Photo by John Bankson)

Historian Elizabeth McKoy created this model of St. James Church for the "new" building's centennial in 1939. (Courtesy of Mary Wootten)

to administer the rites of baptism, communion, and matrimony; to visit the sick and bury the dead. At times, on horseback, they spent long and tiresome hours on lonely country roads. Sometimes small boats, usually steered by a slave, carried them along the river and tributary streams to the scattered homes of the people. In either event they were constantly exposed to the elements."[57]

On January 29, 1781, Major James Craig and his British soldiers occupied Wilmington. Predictably Craig commandeered the imposing Burgwin House, an unfortunate situation for the church. Apparently looking for a nearby source of fireplace fuel, they tore down and burned the fencing around St. James Graveyard. Then British soldiers tore out the pews of the church with pickaxes and possibly burned them for heat as well. They also removed the other church furniture, and perforated the walls to make loopholes for armed defense. The building was used as a hospital first and a defense post second.[58]

But a lowlier use was to come. On April 7, 1781, General Cornwallis arrived in Wilmington with about 2000 troops, half of whom were ill or wounded. Cornwallis occupied the Burgwin House, a situation that would lead eventually to the house's being called after the aristocratic trespasser. Cornwallis sent Craig to stay at the home of Richard Bradley on South Second Street. But it was Cornwallis's flamboyant assistant, Lt. Col. Banastre Tarleton, who was the bane of St. James's Revolutionary War existence.

Artist E. V. Richards created this sketch in 1896, when there were still people who remembered the Burgwin-Wright House before the alterations. (Sketch from *Cornelius Harnett, Revolutionary Patriot*, by Andrew J.Howell.)

Like some sort of twisted Bethlehem tale, Tarleton, who arrived a day earlier than Cornwallis, turned the sacred building into a stable. The actions of Tarleton's green-coated dragoons, who would eventually get their comeuppance at Cowpens, would have grieved many of the communicants— but most church members had already taken refuge in inland areas.

Tarleton had freshly lost two fingers from his right hand and some of his fighting spirit in the Battle of Guilford Courthouse at Greensboro. He requested retirement leave, but Gen. Cornwallis refused, saying that "Ban Tarleton with one hand was better than most of his other officers with two." Tarleton, who would later become famous in England for his personal life, was known to entertain party guests by waving about his wounded hand in fits of bravado.[59]

There is no evidence that Tarleton ever suffered pangs of remorse for his pillage of St. James Church. He spent his time in Cape Fear resting, nursing his wound, learning to use a saber and a quill with his left hand — and writing letters to his siblings in England.

Tarleton wrote to his brother in London, "I thought of coming home; upon reflection I find it impracticable at present, as there will be nobody to command the light Troops of Lord Cornwallis' army."[60]

Sir Joshua Reynolds painted this portrait of Banastre Tarleton, the 18th-century bane of St. James Parish. (Reprinted from *Redcoats and Rebels: The American Revolution Through British Eyes,* by Christopher Hibbert.)

Cornwallis used his time in Wilmington to rest and to plan his next move. The general considered whether he should retreat to South Carolina or travel to Virginia. With Tarleton leading the way, Cornwallis and all of his men left Wilmington by ferry on April 25, just 18 days after the general arrived.[61]

The question of how Cornwallis, the nephew of Frederick Cornwallis, the Archbishop of Canterbury (1768-1783), could have allowed the molestation of the church has intrigued many. The Rev. Mr. Mortimer Glover mused on the subject two hundred years after the event. "I asked [someone] how Cornwallis, a perfectly good churchman, could have made the church a stable."

Other than the old adage "War is Hell" there are few answers. But it is certain that the British saw the entire Anglican Church in America as property of the Crown, therefore available as a resource for war needs. Tarleton, famous for his wartime brutality, displayed his disdain for the colonists by misusing the edifice. But, on the other hand, Loyalists, associating St. James with British rule, lost some of their own warm feeling for the church during the war. For a time, the little brick building fell between the proverbial cracks.

By 1784, Wilmington was a town of about 150 "framed houses,…most of them of good appearance," according to German traveler Johann David Schoepf. The blistering trade Wilmington had enjoyed with the West Indies had cooled, and most merchant ships went to and from Charleston. Larger ships, challenged by the shallow river, lightened their cargo at the old wharves of ghostly Brunswick Town. Bridges to Wilmington from South Carolina were still in disrepair from the war. It was a time of heightened isolation for the Lower Cape Fear — and a period of ministerial drought for St. James Parish.[62]

On June 11, 1787, the town mourned when Major Samuel Swann, a vestryman at St. James, was killed in a duel on Fourth Street, just a few feet east of the Churchyard. Swann had had an argument with John Bradley over the integrity of a shipwrecked British naval officer. Bradley, a successful merchant and trustee of the Presbyterian Church, claimed that the stranger stole some jewelry from his store. Swann stood by the bereft but cultured gentleman.

Swann, a veteran of seven years of military service, aimed and purposefully inflicted a mere flesh wound, but John Bradley subsequently killed his opponent with a shot to the head. Sentiment ran deep over the tragic event and it cast a shadow of "sadness over the town from which it did not emerge for many months."[63]

In 1788, about eleven years after the previous rector, John Wills, resigned, deacon Adam Boyd (1738-1803) began to serve St. James. A Pennsylvania native of Presbyterian forebears, Boyd moved to Wilmington where he purchased the state's first printing press from Andrew Stuart, about 1769. Boyd established the *Cape Fear Mercury* and published it until about 1776. In 1788, Bishop Samuel Seabury presided when Boyd was ordained a deacon in the Protestant Episcopal Church. In 1790, after his brief stint at St. James, Boyd moved to Georgia —and then to Natchez where he died in 1803.[64]

During that era, the Rev. Mr. William Bingham, a Presbyterian minister, performed services at St. James and opened a classical school. Bingham, a native of County Down in Ireland and a graduate of Glasgow University, was progenitor of the well-known Bingham family of Louisville. At that time, the vestry allowed not only Presbyterians but also Methodists to conduct their own services at St. James. The church's generosity was repaid by Bingham's interim services.

However harmonious the arrangement, local Scots were still eager to have their own house of worship. In 1817, John Hill, John Bradley, Col. Thomas Wright, John Huske, Robert Wells, and Thomas MacLaine, all communicants of St. James Parish, sponsored a petition to the Fayetteville Presbytery to establish the first official Presbyterian congregation in Wilmington. In 1818, the

Prestyterians met at St. James Church, listened to a sermon delivered by a Methodist minister, James O. Andrews, and processed to the 100 block of South Front Street where a cornerstone was laid for the town's first church for Scots.[65]

The life of the building was short-lived, however. In 1819, it burned to the ground, a fate blamed by some on the sin of gambling, since the edifice was financed by a lottery. During the rebuilding process, the Presbyterians accepted Adam Empie's offer to occupy St. James "one-half of each Sabbath-day."[66]

In 1795, the Rev. Dr. Solomon Halling of Christ Church, New Bern, took on the rectorship of St. James Parish. Dr. Halling, a native of Copenhagen, was chief surgeon for the American Army in the southern colonies. He was stationed in Alexandria and was also ordained in Virginia by Bishop Meade. In Wilmington, Halling performed not only clerical work but also academic administration.

As the first principal of Wilmington Academy, Halling supervised and was chief fundraiser for the school founded on seed money bequeathed by James Innes. Col. Innes's will specified that, along with the colonel of the New Hanover County regiment, the rector and vestry of St. James were to be executors of his bequest.

James Innes was a hero of the War of Jenkins Ear and was commander-in-chief for American forces worldwide in the French and Indian War. George Washington served under Innes, as did Armand J. deRosset and Captain Thomas Wright.

Married to Sarah Moore Jones, widow of Frederick Jones, Jr., and a granddaughter of "King" Roger Moore, Dr. Halling was neither the first nor last rector of St. James who would marry into one of its most influential families.[67]

Dr. Halling remained at St. James until 1809 when he moved to Georgetown, S. C.[68]

For many months, St. James was "destitute for a Preacher." Volunteer efforts of erstwhile pew warmers were not enough to hold things together, and members began wandering away to other churches. At least temporarily, the Methodist church gained members from the Poisson, Brown, Noland, and McKenzie families. Finally, the faithful core had had enough. Parishioners and frequent visitors passed the proverbial hat to garner sufficient funds to employ a highly educated leader.

At least some sacrifice was involved because it was a time of serious financial depression. "Not since the revolution have the inhabitants of Wilmington and perhaps of America witnessed such distressing times as the present," wrote (the Rev. Mr.) Thomas Wright in 1812.

Some of St. James's most famous parishioners were hit hardest, but many made pledges that were paid over several years. A few members with ties to Trinity Church in New York were major contributors to the campaign. And Aaron Lazarus, a wealthy Jew who worshipped at St. James and would eventually purchase his own pew, pulled more than his own weight. The result was St. James's hiring of Wilmington's most accomplished rector.[69]

This image of Adam Empie was probably painted about the time of his second tenure as rector of St. James Church. James Lyons presented the portrait to St. James Church in Richmond in 1852. (Courtesy of St. James Church, Richmond. Published previously in *Not Hearers Only*, by Minor T. Weisiger, Donald R. Traser, and E. Randolph Trice.)

Adam Empie: "That Emphatic Preacher"

Dr. Adam Empie, memorialized both in and outside St. James, was a man who brought unwavering faith, powerful connections, and a surprise or two to Wilmington. His resume was impressive, but considering the physical challenges that he faced throughout life, his many accomplishments shine even more brightly.

Adam Empie was born in Schenectady, N.Y., "near the little falls," on September 5, 1785. His father, John Empie, was the grandson of Johannes Empgie, who emigrated from Worms, Germany, and quickly Anglicized his surname. The family of Adam Empie's mother, Anna Quackenboss Empie, came from Holland. The young couple sought a Lutheran church in Schenectady but finding none attended a Reformed Dutch church. Adam Empie stated that his parents were "poor" but described them as "strictly and devoutly pious."

Young Adam Empie attended the Dutch church but was schooled at a local Presbyterian church. However he never warmed to either and soon found that the Calvinism of the Presbyterian "catechism and confessions repelled" him. As a very young man, he turned to the "teachings and standards" of the Protestant Episcopal Church. In time, he became a powerful and elegantly outspoken advocate for the Low Church, even though he maintained treasured friendships with those who held tightly to other views. The Low Church was more consistent with the general Protestant church while the High Church bore more resemblance to the Roman Catholic faith.

Mr. Empie held various jobs while receiving his formal education at Union College in Schenectady, where he studied under legendary professors Eliphalet Nott and Benjamin Allen, who declared Empie "one of the best scholars that we ever had here." Adam Empie graduated with honors from Union College in 1807.[70]

For the next two years, Mr. Empie lived in Rhinebeck and Hempstead, N.Y., simultaneously studying for the ministry and teaching. In the course of his work, he made many helpful friends. He was instructed personally by the Rev. John Henry Hobart. Hobart, assistant rector of St. George's Church in Hempstead, was soon to be both bishop of New York and rector of Manhattan's Trinity Church, posts he would hold from 1816 until his death in 1830. Mr. Empie also tutored in the home of Thomas Tillotson, secretary of the State of New York, and taught in the Classical Academy of the Rev. Seth Hart. After Adam Empie was ordained deacon, in 1809, he was then admitted into the priesthood. The Rt. Rev. Dr. Benjamin Moore, father of Clement Clark Moore, a seminary professor and the author of "'Twas the Night Before Christmas", led his ordination service.[71]

The Rev. Mr. Empie's first assignment was St. George's Church in Hempstead, on Long

Island. He served as assistant to the rector, his old friend Seth Hart, and lived with the Hart family. The Rev. Hart took note of Mr. Empie's superior intellect, but said that "he is not of a robust constitution." Indeed, years of intense study and work had already taken their toll on the frail young man. His poor eyesight was compromised further by what he called the "midnight labors" of reading by dim candlelight, and his general weakness was exacerbated by long periods of sleep deprivation. From this time on, he suffered sporadically from debilitating headaches, as well as severe pain in his eyes, neck, shoulders, arms, and hands. He was diagnosed with "rheumatism."[72]

Despite his infirmities, his erudite and impassioned sermons coupled with the ability to ignite spiritual curiosity brought him much attention. By early 1810, Adam Empie was sought after by St. James. Adam Empie had already established ties to Trinity Church, on Wall Street, through his work and studies in New York. Judge Joshua Grainger Wright's brother, Col. Thomas Wright, was a Trinity communicant at one time and, through marriage, was related to William Willkings, a New Yorker who also kept a home in Wilmington, and whose family partnered with the Lippitts in a wholesale drug business.

William Willkings wrote the St. James vestry that Adam Empie "is a young man of a liberal education and whose manners and moral character will no doubt give general satisfaction." Perhaps Mr. Empie's ardent disdain for the institution of slavery accounted for the subdued wording. But the Rev. Mr. Empie had no way of knowing that a very Southern surprise awaited him in Wilmington; one that would "bring the situation home."[73]

The vestry of St. James offered Empie $1200 a year, suggested he take a side job at Innes Academy, and added a bonus: summer on Wrightsville Sound, probably on one of the expansive Wright tracts. "To this will be added the customary perquisite attached to the office of clergyman — during the sickly season as it is termed, should the town prove unhealthy we have a safe retreat on the sound…where you can retire with every reasonable prospect of health and comfort." However, despite the fact that virtually all the church's members abandoned their steamy town homes during summer, in good weather Mr. Empie was expected to mount his horse and ride to St. James "for the performance of Divine services once" on Sundays.

After months of discussion, Adam Empie took the job in 1811. His first sermon was in November and he recorded it in his notebooks as "being the first sermon the author ever preached to a congregation of which he was sole pastor; after having been for two years and a half assistant minister of St. George's Church, Hempstead, Long-Island."

After referring to the ecclesiastical vacancy that preceded his arrival as a congregation without its candlestick, he concluded his lengthy sermon with these words: "He has again sent you a guide, an instructor, a comforter, a friend. In the person of his ambassador, He again invites you to his house and to his table, and promises all you can desire, on earth and in Heaven. Oh! That we may all have a realizing sense of the goodness of God!"

His benediction was worthy of bronzing. “Great Shepherd of Israel, qualify me for the arduous duties that await me. Magnify thy strength in my weakness, and crown my ministration with abundant success. Water this congregation with the rich dews of Heaven, and make this people, a people with whom thou wilt delight to dwell — a people ‘zealous of good works,’ and maturing for Heavenly glory, and to thy name shall be the praise, through Christ Jesus.”[74]

Vestry records reveal that one of Empie’s first vestry meetings, held in “the Room of the Rev. Mr. A. Empie,” drew only four members: John Scott, John Willkings, William Giles, and James W. Walker. In fact, the whole church consisted of only 21 communicants, a fact documented by Empie himself. However, the new rector and his bold and studious sermons drew attention — and his successful efforts to repair and beautify the church lifted spirits. Soon new members and backslidden former members were filling the pews. And those who had somehow missed baptism were not allowed to ignore it.[75]

John Burgwin’s daughter Eliza Burgwin Clitherall was 26 years old and the mother of two children when Adam Empie first arrived in Wilmington. On December 21, 1810, being “convinc’d with Mr. Empie upon the subject,” she chose to be baptized.

“I was this day baptiz’d by the Rev. A. Empie, Minister of St. James’s, Wilmington. Oh may the solemn covenant, be duly weigh’d and estimated by me, and the Grace of God, be with me, assisting me in discharge of my duties.”

The following day Mrs. Clitherall was “admitted to the Lord’s Table” and reported that she “experience’d feelings not to be described.” Her sentiments were echoed in the general female membership of the church. And, in time, Empie’s presence and sermons brought more than just feeling. The women began, in 1820, ministering to the community in the name of the Ladies Working Society. Though their labor was not limited to stitchery, sewing circles made up of members of St. James provided money to help the poor and occasionally to augment the life of the church. They created handmade sweaters, baptismal gowns, scarves, and children’s clothing that can only be imagined for their detail and the time invested. Rather than donating the goods directly, the items were usually sold and the money used in projects to benefit the underprivileged. The St. James School was an outgrowth of their endeavors.[76]

Worthy projects propelled by scripture based admonishments gave the ladies of St. James a new link to the church — and particularly warm fellowship with one another. But in those days of fervent religion, their sewing labors never seemed to exceed their efforts to better understand the Scriptures. “Blessed is that happy house and blessed is that congregation where Martha still complaineth of Mary,” said Ann Hill, in 1821 — referring to the Biblical story contained in Luke 10:38-42.[77]

Many familiar names were already a part of St. James during the early days of Adam Empie’s ministry: Burgwin, Cowan, Winslow, deRosset, Wingate, Willkings, Reston, Scott, Poisson, London,

Lord, Jocelyn, Fleeming, Hostler, Giles, Hall, Meares, Harriss, Hill, Dudley, Hasell, Campbell, and Wright. Additionally, Aaron Lazarus contributed regularly, as did Philip Bassadier, a West Indian barber who apparently played the violin at services.[78]

Almost immediately, Empie went beyond his job description by pushing for the organization of a diocese, conducting his own unofficial census of N. C. Episcopalians, attempting to recruit erudite ministers for eastern North Carolina, and fighting to abolish the practice of creating vestries by public election. His letters during his early work at St. James indicate that he missed the stimulating society of highly educated men of the cloth, a scarcity in N.C. at that time. However, the local congregation delighted in his mental calisthenics and boasted of their bookish young rector.

Empie wasted no time getting the church building spruced up. James Marshall and Joseph Innes were hired to work on the interior. Also, Abijah Hanson, a talented church sexton, did significant new plaster work inside the church; crafted church furniture, including coped pews; and performed numerous alterations, such as raising the pulpit two feet in 1812.[79]

Also, the first vestry minutes to survive following the Revolution were recorded a few months after Empie arrived, on March 13, 1812.

John Davis was the doorkeeper of St. James, a job for which he received $1 a month and a seat in the "strangers' pew."[80]

It was during the early Empie years at St. James that the church received one of its most memorable gifts.

Gov. Benjamin Smith (1756-1826) gave communion silver to St. James following his administration in 1810-1811. His gift consists of one flagon, two chalices, one paten, and an altar spoon inscribed with the appropriate motto, "Cruce Christi Confido." In 1868, the flagon was recast with sterling silver to make it larger, and surmounted with rock crystal and a cross of solid gold. Gen. J. Johnston Pettigrew, C. S. A., paid for the improvements.[81]

Communion silver at St. James was given by the Hon. Benjamin Smith. (Courtesy of St. John's Lodge No 1, A. F. & A. M.)

Gov. Smith, a descendant of landgrave Thomas Smith of South Carolina, had been an aide-de-camp to General George Washington during the American Revolution. After the war, he received a gift of 20,000 acres of land in northwest Tennessee for his valiant service.

Smith was a charter trustee of the University of North Carolina who gave the school one of its grandest early gifts. On December 18, 1789, he donated the 20,000-acre tract of land in Tennessee. As a result, Smith enjoyed several "naming opportunities" at the fledgling school.

Gov. Smith's local residence was a large plantation known as Bellville. He lived there with his wife, Sarah, who was the daughter of Mary Rhett and William Dry III, the militia captain who helped salvage *Ecce Homo*. In 1796, the Smiths moved to their new home, Orton Plantation. Then, for an extra "five dollars and some cents," he enlarged the boundaries of his estate. He purchased Brunswick Town and the house and land that had been known at various times as Russellborough, Castle Dobbs, Castle Tryon, and Bellfont.[82]

Despite his comfortable position, both Smith's benevolence and an explosive temper got him in trouble. He lost much of his fortune when he loaned a large percentage of it to a friend, never to see it again. And he lost a good deal of favor for reportedly driving his brother away to South Carolina, and engaging in duels with many people including Maurice Moore, General Robert Howe, and Thomas Leonard. A bullet from Leonard's pistol lodged in Smith's body, but did not kill him. He lived on and eventually died a pauper with debts so large that his creditors were about to seize his very body, a practice sanctioned by ancient law.[83]

General Joseph Gardner Swift, a U. S. engineer who supervised the Cape Fear area, learned of his late friend's final woe. Smith's creditors had little chance against the first graduate of the U. S. Military Academy. Together with a small group of men who had stayed close to Smith, General Swift confiscated the body and buried it in an unmarked grave near Smithville, probably in a private cemetery. Both Smithville (Southport) and Smith Island (Bald Head) owe their names to the Benjamin Smith family.[84]

After some time, Swift decided to give Benjamin Smith a final honor. Smith had always wanted to be buried in the churchyard of St. Philip's, so General Swift made another secret trip to Smithville to exhume the body. There was confusion as to whether they had actually disinterred Smith or another person until a brave woman in the group thrust her hand into the body to probe for the bullet from the Leonard duel. She found it — and Benjamin Smith got his burial wish.

Church, Community, Family

It is probable that Adam Empie heard more than he ever wanted to about the tragedy of Samuel Jocelyn. For he taught young Episcopalians both on Sunday and at Innes Academy, where Mr. Empie did decide to teach. Innes Academy was located close to the site now occupied by Thalian Hall. The old academy was founded by Samuel Jocelyn, John deRosset, Nathaniel Hill, James W. Walker, and Joshua G. Wright. It contained a spacious theater — and acting skills were taught along with standard subjects. For this reason, many of Wilmington's privileged young men became the town's first amateur actors of note. The list included numerous members of St. James, including Dr. John Hill, James S. Green, William C. Lord, William Mercer Green, Robert H. Cowan, Dr. Thomas H. Wright, and Julius Walker.[85]

Under the leadership of Col. Archibald McNeill, many of them participated in presenting English dramas, including those by Shakespeare, for the benefit of the poor. Tickets sold for a dollar. In 1813, the Thalian Association made a contribution to St. James – a good indication that the parish budget was pinched. McNeill was a son-in-law of Sir James Wright, colonial governor of Georgia.

In 1813, Adam Empie conducted the funeral of N. C. Governor Samuel Ashe (1725-1813). Ashe was governor from 1795 until 1798. He also served as president of the board of trustees for the University of North Carolina and was a judge of the first supreme court of the state of N.C. The city of Asheville was named for Gov. Ashe.

One of the young men Empie became acquainted with was Thomas Henry Wright (1800-1861.) The two men would become lifelong friends. Wright's father, Judge Joshua Grainger Wright, died in 1811, leaving a widow and a house full of children. The close proximity of the Burgwin-Wright house to St. James and the fact that Empie often lodged during the summer either at or near the Wrights' soundfront home, Mount Lebanon, brought him in close contact with the entire family.

In 1814, the Rev. Mr. Empie's bond with the Wrights took on a permanent and legal nature. On March 24, 1814, when he was 28 years old, Adam Empie married the 15-year-old daughter of Susan Bradley and the late Joshua Grainger Wright, Ann Eliza. Though the bride's youth seems shocking today, it wasn't so unusual then. Nevertheless it must have been interesting news considering the occupation, strident sermons, and courtly manners of the groom, and the tender age of Miss Wright, a genuine Southern belle.

The newlyweds came from different latitudinal worlds. One of the first examples of their disparity came as a wedding gift to the bride: a slave. Eventually the groom found himself the owner of several slaves. He treated them well and then freed them. However, they were so fond of him and the conditions in which they lived that they refused to leave. According to one family member, the slaves "stayed right with the family until the good Lord freed them from this mortal coil."[86]

The Rev. Mr. Thomas Wright was a prize product of St. James Church — and the founder of Calvary Church in Memphis. (Reprinted from *The Great Book: Calvary Protestant Episcopal Church*, by Ellen Davies-Rodgers.)

The Wright family embraced Adam Empie, and the minister's influence on them was immense. Dr. Thomas Henry Wright would become one of the most effective laypersons Wilmington has ever known. His first cousin, the Rev. Mr. Thomas Wright (1785-1835), was so swayed by Adam Empie that he eventually left his profession as a Wilmington and New York businessman to go full-time into church work in 1820. "I hope to be a laborer in the Lord's vineyard though a feeble and unworthy one," he wrote from Wilmington on February 15, 1819. "We have reason to hope that our church in this State will rear her drooping head in a few years, and increase under the Divine blessing as she has done in other states."

Adam Empie officiated at the service at St. Paul's Church in Edenton when Thomas Wright and William Hooper (grandson of the signer of the Declaration of Independence) became deacons. The Rev. Mr. Wright served churches in Wadesboro and Salisbury, and preached frequently at Warrenton, where many of St. James's young people attended the Mordecai family's private school. A member of the Mordecai family, Rachel, married Wilmingtonian Aaron Lazarus, a steady contributor to St. James Church and a major financial force in the initial campaign to hire Adam Empie.

Then the dedicated missionary rode his horse all the way to Memphis, where he later founded Calvary Church on August 6, 1832. Today, Calvary still thrives, with 1300 members. The Rev. Mr. Thomas Wright also helped establish Immanuel Church in LaGrange, Tennessee — as well as churches in Randolph (St. Paul's), Brownsville, and Jackson. Thomas Wright and his wife, Mary Green, had twelve children, including a boy born in 1827 whom they named Ravenscroft.[87]

Thomas Wright encouraged his brother-in-law, an ordained priest named William Mercer Green, to take the same path to Tennessee. "I hope too that Wm. Green will follow me. He would be a great acquisition to the Church," wrote the Rev. Mr. Wright in December 1832. Thomas Wright died of cholera three years later. But his wish for Green to move to Tennessee would be granted in a big way when he became bishop in 1850. Green was at the impressionable age of thirteen when Adam Empie arrived at St. James. Surely Empie deserves a lot of credit for influencing William Mercer Green as well.

After learning of Thomas Wright's death, William Mercer Green wrote to Wright's widow. "My Dear Sister, when I first received Bishop Otey's letter informing me of your loss, I was strongly tempted to jump at once into the stage and go to see you with all speed. But our Convention is at hand....

"For what is our loss compared to the infinite gain of him we mourn?

"Your beloved companion has been called to experience the rewards of glory."

Calvary Church, Memphis – founded in 1832. (Reprinted from *The Great Book: Calvary Protestant Episcopal Church,* by Ellen Davies-Rodgers.)

The Rt. Rev. William Mercer Green. (Courtesy of Elizabeth Brown King)

Bishop Green (1798-1887)

Raised in St. James, William Mercer Green was the grandson of Dr. Samuel Green of Liverpool, who settled in the Cape Fear area about 1735. When Major John Swann and Sheriff deRosset called on Dr. Green for medical assistance after the skirmish in Brunswick with the Spanish, Dr. Green won accolades for his work with prisoners whose wounds ranged from burns to gunshots. Dr. Green, in addition to owning Greenfields (Greenfield Lake) and the Greenfield Garden Dairy, also owned Greenhall, later known as Shandy Hall, Pine Savannah (probably Pine Valley), a mill, and a good private library.

When Dr. Green died in 1771, his executors were Cornelius Harnett, George Moore, Alexander Lillington, and John Ashe. They fulfilled the conditions of his will, the first of which was plain and well-stated: "First of all, I desire to be interred in the church yard in Wilmington forty-eight hours after my decease in a grave adjoining to those of my sons without any pomp or expense except what common decency may require."[88]

His maternal grandfather, Richard Bradley, was a Quaker who married fellow Friend Elizabeth Sharpless of the famous New England family. William Mercer Green's father, William, and his mother, Mary Bradley Green, lived in Wilmington during the majority of the year and at Shandy Hall during the warmer months. When William was 12 years old, his sister, Mary Hostler Green, married Thomas Wright — the future rector who founded several churches in Tennessee.[89]

William Mercer Green graduated from the University of North Carolina in 1818. He was ordained in St. James on April 20, 1823, by Bishop Richard Channing Moore of Christ Church, Raleigh. He served in Williamsborough and Warrenton before becoming rector of St. Matthew's Church in Hillsborough, in 1825. Green did not stay long at St. Matthew's but sixteen years later, St. James and the Wilmington "cousinhood" would have another link with the church. The Rev. Dr. William Ashley Curtis served as rector of St. Matthew's from 1841 until about 1878. Dr. Curtis, who was also a famous botanist, was married to Mary Jane deRosset, sister of A. J. deRosset, Jr.

In 1827, the Rev. Mr. Green moved to Chapel Hill after being named professor of belles-lettres and Episcopal chaplain at his alma mater. The new position would have thrilled his grandfather Green who put great stock in quality education.

Green established a tiny Episcopal congregation in Chapel Hill, and, in 1842, obtained a plan for a building from none other than St. James architect Thomas U. Walter. The work went slowly and some of the brick was made in a kiln on the Greens' property. Bishop Ives dedicated Chapel of the Cross, in 1848. Ironically, St. James would share another architect with the Chapel Hill church. In 1921, Hobart Upjohn designed a major building that would make the original chapel an appendage.[90]

William Mercer Green received his Doctorate of Divinity degree in 1845 and was elected the first Episcopal Bishop of Tennessee, in 1849. He was a founder and the proposer of the name of the University of the South, in Sewanee, Tenn., and was named its first chancellor in 1867. He died, twenty years later, on February 13, 1887.[91]

Networks

In 1814, Ann Eliza and Adam Empie moved to West Point, N.Y. in the month of their wedding, and the groom started a new job as the first chaplain of the U. S. Military Academy. His position had been in the works since 1813, when General Joseph Gardner Swift contacted Bishop John Henry Hobart of New York and the Secretary of War to arrange it.

Swift, the first graduate of the U. S. Military Academy, supervised the institution from the conclusion of the War of 1812 until 1818. He had a network of powerful friends, including presidents Madison and Monroe. Gen. Swift visited Wilmington frequently after 1805 when he married a local woman, Louisa Walker (1788-1855), daughter of St. James communicant Captain James Walker. Swift and Adam Empie were fast friends, sharing not only their love of the Episcopal church but also their deep disapproval of slavery. Gen. Swift stated that, in addition to his duties as chaplain, Mr. Empie would serve as "professor of ethics and treasurer; a novel junction of functions."

The Empies lived with the Swift family in Brooklyn during Adam Empie's years as chaplain and they worshipped together at St. Ann's Church. Gen. Swift accompanied the Rev. Mr. Empie to his induction service at West Point on May 20, 1814. Swift commented that "the selection of an Episcopalian has been made because…the service of that church was deemed to be the most appropriate to the discipline of a military academy."

Adam Empie sought the help of the Rt. Rev. John Henry Hobart in finding a replacement, and most likely the bishop of New York *did* procure the rector who arrived in the fall of 1814: the Rev. M. Bethel Judd. He had served as rector of Christ Church in Hudson, N.Y., then a part of the Diocese of New York City, from 1802 until 1807. Judd then took a job as principal of St John's College in Annapolis, Md., but remained there for only a few years. Between 1812 and his arrival in Wilmington in 1814, Judd was rector of Trinity Church in Fairfield, N.Y., and lived briefly in Norwalk, Conn.

Mr. Judd, a scholar who most likely augmented his salary by teaching, was paid $1200 a year to shepherd the flock of St. James. During his time at St. James, the Rev. Mr. Judd received a visit from John Winslow of Fayetteville, formerly of Wilmington. Winslow was a director of the Bank of Cape Fear and the primary force in the Fayetteville bank branch. One of Winslow's sisters, Ann, was the second wife of High Sheriff Thomas Wright (1761-1798) of New Hanover County. Another sister, Catharine Isabelle, was married to Wilmingtonian Marshall Robert Willkings.

The Winslows' great-grandfather was the famous silversmith Edward Winslow. Their father was the Rev. Mr. Edward Winslow, a 1741 Harvard graduate who became a celebrated minister in Stratford, Conn., and Braintree (now Quincy), Mass. During the Revolution, he served as an Anglican rector in New York and as a Tory chaplain. He died in 1780 and was buried under the altar at St. George's Chapel in Manhattan. His widow, Jane Isabella Alleyne Winslow, was buried in the St. James Churchyard. Also, some of Rev. Winslow's maternal ancestors, the Savage family, subsequently moved to Wilmington. Edward Winslow, another relative, shipped an organ for the use of St. James from Boston to Wilmington in 1818.[92]

So when John Winslow came to pay the Rev. Mr. Judd a visit, he brought with him some good ecclesiastical baggage — and Bethel Judd listened. Winslow wanted a church established at Fayetteville and the young minister responded quickly. Judd moved to Fayetteville in January of 1817 and by April 7, Easter Monday, Fayetteville had an Episcopal church by the name of St. John's. St. James Church and St. John's Church, Fayetteville, would have strong connections over the next hundred years, most of them emanating from familial ties. Not only the Winslow family, but also the Huske, Mallett, Wright, Green, and Strange families in Fayetteville had close blood relatives or in-laws at St. James.

In 1818, Bethel Judd moved from Fayetteville back to his native New England where he served as rector of St. James Church in New London, Conn., until 1832. During his term there, in 1831, Trinity College in Hartford, Conn., conferred on him the degree of Doctor of Divinity. The school, founded for the purpose of educating Episcopal ministers, attracted several North Carolinians in the mid-1820s, including Joshua Grainger Wright (1809-1863) and Edward D. Winslow of Wilmington, and Paul Cameron of Fayetteville. Bethel Judd was probably one of the reasons.[93]

Judd eventually became rector of St. Peter's Parish in Cheshire, Conn., where he also served as principal of Cheshire Academy, the Episcopal Academy of Connecticut. The Rev. Dr. Judd lived until the age of 82 and died in Wilmington, Del.[94]

The bonds between Episcopalians in Wilmington and in Fayetteville remained strong for most of the 19th century. In 1851, a group of men and women from St. James took several steamers upriver to Fayetteville for the Diocesan Convention. The group included some young ladies who were members of the Green, Wright, Holmes, Walker, and Savage families of St. James — and all were related to John Winslow of Fayetteville. "Somebody is in danger in Fayetteville," wrote the editor of the *Wilmington Herald.* "Wilmington has always been noted for the beauty of its girls."[95]

Though Adam Empie's commission at West Point lasted until April 1817, the young couple and their second child, a son, negotiated an early move back to Wilmington. While he was away, the sexton, architect Joseph Jacobs, kept the record book of funerals, something usually done by the rector. In three years, 16 parishioners and "about 30 strangers" were buried in the churchyard. The group included a friend of a church member, a black, a sailor from afar, and some "Romanists."[96]

Indeed, the early church was open and kind to strangers, both living and dead. The church paid all burial costs and offered a burial place to "Mr. Horner, a poor stranger," in 1817. Adam Empie channeled discretionary funds toward a wide variety of pre-governmental welfare programs, including: a "Roman Catholic Priest in distress"; woodcutters who supplied the elderly with firewood during winter; shodding the shoeless; providing food for the hungry; and giving destitute sailors tiny monetary gifts that would sometimes travel to the far ends of the earth.

One young man who spent his formative years listening to the words of Adam Empie was the Rev. Augustus Foster Lyde (1813-1834). Lyde, through deep faith and voluminous correspondence, became the first Protestant Episcopal Church official to offer himself as a missionary to China. Though he died just as he was preparing to sail, he is still credited with the establishment of Episcopal missionary work in China. In 1959, the ladies of St. James commissioned a tablet in memory of the Rev. Mr. Lyde. The same year, the retired bishop of China, Andrew Yu-Yue Tsu, preached at St. James. He said he came to Wilmington because he "wanted to see the church that produced Augustus Foster Lyde."[97]

For a few months before Judd moved to Fayetteville, Bethel Judd and Adam Empie served St. James together. Empie was back at his beloved post at St. James in the company of an intellectual ecclesiastical soulmate — and his wife was happily reunited with her enormous Wilmington family.

Neither Empie nor Judd wasted any time launching a full-scale effort to organize a diocese. Both scholars had seen the value of church organization in New York. Adam Empie logged many hours of preparation during his first term as rector, corresponding and traveling in an effort to locate traces of the old Anglican congregations in North Carolina. He also requested that his friends "up north" send missionaries to the province. "If a sufficient number could be found it is greatly to be wished that the Church could be organized and accede to the ecclesiastical Union that obtains in the other Sections of the U. States."[98]

The Rt. Rev. Richard Channing Moore, Bishop of Virginia, officiated at confirmations soon after the Diocese of N.C. was formed. In April 1819 Bishop Moore confirmed 138 people at St. James.

In 1817 there were only three Protestant Episcopal rectors in North Carolina: Adam Empie, Bethel Judd, and Jehu Curtis Clay of Christ Church in New Bern. On April 24, all three were principals in the process of forming the Diocese of North Carolina. They met at Christ Church and were joined by John R. London and Marsden Campbell of St. James Church; John Stanly and John S. West of New Bern; John Winslow of Fayetteville; and Josiah Collins of Edenton.[99]

The three rectors, assisted by John London and John Stanly, drew up a constitution that was signed by all nine participants. Along with polite acknowledgments to the authority and the bylaws of the Protestant Episcopal Church, the constitution was submitted to the General Convention. Bethel Judd was named president of the new diocese and Adam Empie, secretary. In the absence of a bishop, Empie invited the Rt. Rev. Richard Channing Moore, Bishop of Virginia, to officiate at confirmations. Two years later he visited Fayetteville where he confirmed 48 people on April 17, 1819. A week later, he visited St. James where he confirmed 138 people. But that wasn't all. "To show how carefully this exemplary Rector cared for all classes of his people, we will add, there were at this time, [ten] slaves confirmed," wrote Clayton Giles, William Calder, and J. V. Grainger in a paper entitled "Dr. Empie's Services."[100]

By 1821, the diocese had great praise for the Rev. Thomas Wright who "labored zealously," visiting 11 counties and holding services in 12 towns in a four-month period. The Rev. William Mercer Green also won accolades for his efforts toward the "missionary cause." Wright's other brother-in-law, James Severin Green, would also become a passionate churchman, serving for many years as a lay reader alternately with Dr. Thomas Wright at Mount Lebanon Chapel.[101]

Though Empie was actually gone from St. James for less than three full years, apparently there was not much ongoing church maintenance. "The Episcopal church in recent years a total ruin," stated the *Cape Fear Recorder*, in 1819. "Completely dilapidated. (But) Episcopal church now renovated and galleries added AND BEAUTIFUL ORGAN." [102]

During the next ten years, Empie's second term as rector of St. James, church membership grew rapidly, necessitating the new side galleries. Adam Empie also created associations to educate the poor and to provide them with Bibles and other books. He added Sunday School and Bible classes to the church calendar. And he organized an effort to erect a parochial library.

Fortunately for Empie and other early rectors of St. James, most of the parishioners lived within about twenty blocks of the church. For not only did the rectors pay pastoral visits, but also most weddings and funerals still took place in people's homes. Following a home funeral, everyone would process or ride in carriages to St. James Graveyard. Also, according to historian J. G. Burr, "No church in the place could boast a bell of its own." Churches throughout the town held services at the same hour and the town bell tolled for all. By 1822, St. James had its own bell. Elizabeth Bishop was paid $40 a year to ring it. The bell and Ms. Bishop both lasted until at least 1839.[103]

Adam Empie also tried to provide music for the services. As was customary in St. James at the time, Empie advertised in distant newspapers for a musician to perform on the new organ, offering $50 to $60 a month. Two months later, in December 1818, he received an informal application from James L. Richardson, of Richmond: "I am, at present, engaged as Leader of a Band at the Circus." Richardson also offered the services of his wife, a dance instructor. It is not known if they were employed, but Empie kept Mr. Richardson's letter.

When it came to writing, Adam Empie was the master of St. James. His sermons were eloquent and carefully recorded. Though scholastically sound, they were also tender and indicative of the depth of his own religious experience. In 1813, he told his congregation, "If we acknowledged God in all our ways, and habitually paid Him the respect to which He is entitled, He would meet us wherever we went. He would be present with us wherever we were. Like the image of a beloved friend, He would constantly recur to our thoughts. We would frequently seek his presence and his smiles; and we would delight in holding communion with Him."[104]

Despite the tenderness in many of Empie's sermons, he sometimes interpreted current events in a sort of Sodom and Gomorrah mode. In 1819, when almost half the buildings in Wilmington burned during a windswept conflagration, Empie stood in the pulpit at St. James and declared that "it was a judgment for misconduct."

In Empie's eyes, the fire that burned about 250 houses and the new Presbyterian Church was reason for each member of St. James Church to search his heart. "See wherein you have offended," he implored the congregation. "Have you offered up an evening incense to the King of Heaven? Has the language of supplication, thanksgiving, and praise ascended daily to Jehovah from the lips of parents, children, servants? Have you loved the Lord Jesus Christ and endeavored through divine grace to testify that love by keeping his commandments?" His bold statements led the Rt. Rev. John Starke Ravenscroft, an admirer, to call him "that emphatic preacher."[105]

Everyone wasn't pleased, however. Empie's efforts had changed the routine of an estimated half of Wilmington's population. They attended church twice on Sundays, went to Bible study on Wednesdays, and conducted morning and evening family devotions at home. Ellen Mordecai observed the changes and, in 1818, declared that Adam Empie had rendered Wilmington "a dour and pious place."[106]

Wilmington native William Whitehead painted this image of the St. James churchyard. Samuel Jocelyn's tombstone has disappeared. The stone pictured is that of Mary Ann Robertson who died in 1837. (Courtesy of J. Robert Lane, Jr., photo by J. Robert Warren)

The Graveyard's Most Haunting Story

"In every folk tale there is at least a germ of truth."
– E. Lawrence Lee. *The Lower Cape Fear in Colonial Days.*

Not long before Adam Empie moved to town, one of St. James's greatest mysteries occurred. Two young Wilmingtonians, Samuel R. Jocelyn and Alexander Hostler, shared a remarkable number of interests and were practically inseparable. To some, their friendship seemed a peculiar example of brotherly love enduring all.

Both Jocelyn and Hostler shared a spirited fascination with the nature of the hereafter. Despite Biblical admonishments to the contrary, each promised the other that they would try to communicate, one world to the other, after the first to die departed. That time came early for 25-year-old Samuel Jocelyn, an accomplished horseman who took a nasty fall on a ride through the countryside. The fall did not kill him, but, one way or the other, he would be dead a few days later, in late March of the year 1810.

The body lay in state at Jocelyn's home for two days and, following the funeral, was taken to St. James Graveyard for burial. Two days later, Jocelyn's grief-stricken friend, Alexander Hostler, was in his room alone when he had the impression of Jocelyn's presence — and the message that his friend had been buried alive. "Open the coffin and you will see that I am not lying in the same position in which I was placed," were the words that have been passed down for almost 200 years.

Hostler had the same experience three times in three days before he shared the disquieting news with Louis Toomer. The two of them approached Jocelyn's grieving father requesting they be allowed to exhume the body. For privacy's sake, the disinterment happened at night, under the light of lanterns. After the shovels were set aside, they found Jocelyn was turned completely over, lying face down. The fact that one side of the coffin was loosened was interpreted as additional sign of a struggle.

According to historian Louis T. Moore, eighty years later the story was resurrected when Col. James G. Burr retold it at the Opera House (Thalian Hall). Col. Burr heard the story from his mother who, in turn, heard it from Hostler himself. Louis Toomer related a similar story to Catherine Kennedy (deRosset), a teacher of local renown. Mrs. Kennedy recorded the events in a document that was given eventually to Col. Burr. [107]

The story of Samuel Jocelyn's death is a permanent and famous part of the lore of St. James Graveyard, but it does invite questions. In the absence of sophisticated medical equipment, it *is* possible that Samuel Jocelyn was buried alive. But wouldn't the family have noticed that the body did or did not show typical signs of deterioration after two days of lying in state?

Could a rough interment, perhaps caused by a broken drop strap, account for the fact that Jocelyn was upside down and one side of the coffin was loosened? Could the active imagination of a young sensitive man in a fit of grief have accounted for his visions of his dead friend? Embalming was not common at the time. If Jocelyn were merely in a coma, did Hostler subconsciously note the fact that the athletic young man did not appear as "dead" as other bodies he had viewed. Was this the fuel of his "visions"?

Apparently Samuel Jocelyn's gravestone has not survived. As St. James's churchyard space gave way to church building space, many graves were moved. It is possible that Jocelyn was moved and reinterred at Honolulu, a summer property on Bradley Creek owned by the Reston family, who were related to Jocelyn. Honolulu, now known as the Bar Harbor subdivision, had its own family cemetery. When developers cleared the land, they disposed of all the headstones.[108]

It is also possible but not probable that Jocelyn's body was taken to Oakdale Cemetery, Wilmington's largest and most celebrated graveyard. It was established on December 27, 1852, and afforded a vast amount of space, most of it purchased from William A. Wright. The original board of directors included several members of St. James Church: Dr. Armand J. deRosset, Jr., president; Edward Kidder, James Cassidey, John A. Taylor, Henry Nutt, William A. Wright, and George R. French. The first burial at Oakdale was Dr. deRosset's six-year-old daughter, Annie, on February 5, 1855.[109]

Funerals were held at St. James for both white and black communicants. Today, church records of the causes of death read like a yellowed medical journal, with a few sensational notes. A disproportionate number of parishioners died of "bilious fever." But there were also those church members who succumbed to croup, nervous fever, dropsy, scarlet fever, and inflammation. Some died of accidental gunshots, seasickness, or worms. And a nameless small group gave way to suicide, or fatal cases of "intemperance." Some parishioners lived long, despite lack of sophisticated health care. "Old Mrs. Cowan died a few days ago (about 92) and was buried in St. James Church Yard," wrote Rod MacRae, on October 17, 1866.[110]

Though he was buried at Oakdale, the funeral of Charles Baldwin took place at St. James January 8, 1856. The name may not be familiar, but the legend sparked by his death has been known regionally for over a hundred years and has spurred thousands of trips to a sleepy spot in Brunswick County near "Rattlesnake Grade." In his paper, "Charles Baldwin, a likely Joe," historian James Burke espouses the credible theory that the Maco Light legend of Joe Baldwin is based on the true story of Charles's death. A conductor on the Wilmington and Manchester Rail Road, the former New Yorker lost his life in an accident that occurred on the rails near Maco, in Brunswick County. But Charles did not lose his head. He died hours after the collision as a result of trauma to the head, according to coroner J. C. Wood.

In the folklore version, Joe Baldwin was decapitated in a train wreck. "It was said that his body was retrieved but his head was never found," said James Burke. "The Maco Light, a strange electromagnetic phenomenon associated with the stretch of track where Baldwin was supposed to have been killed, was said to be the light from an otherworldly lantern held by the ghost of Baldwin as he searched for his missing head. The tale is very old. For generations, people would go out to the small community of Maco and wait in the dark to see the lights. After the tracks were taken up, the lights were no longer seen."[111]

St. James Churchyard, 2004. Lizzie Winston Broadfoot funded the largest beautification project of the 20th century — a project that turned an "unholy mess" into a clean space with relettered monuments. Mrs. Broadfoot also created a small garden near the churchyard entrance and gave a new fence in memory of her son, Winston. Inside the church, she did extensive repairs and beautification after the organ pipes were moved out of the chancel. (Photo by Elizabeth Futrelle)

Freemasonry

During Empie's tenure at St. James, Freemasonry was in its golden years in Wilmington. The earliest local organization, Solomon's Lodge, was established at "Masonborough Sound" in a neighborhood where property owners included members of the Moore, Grainger, and Wright families. Solomon's Lodge was ceremoniously dedicated by Thomas Thynne, the Viscount of Weymouth and Grand Master of the Grand Lodge of England in 1735, the same year he dedicated Charleston's famed Solomon Lodge. Wilmington's lodge existed until 1754.

In 1765, historic St. John's Lodge No. 1 was created. Many of the members also belonged to St. James. In 1804, the Rev. Mr. Solomon Halling, rector of St. James Church, officiated at the cornerstone ceremony at St. John's Lodge, at 114 Orange Street. St. James members by the name of MacRae, Brown, Harriss, Potts, Rankin, Peck, Burr, and Miller frequented the Orange Street lodge.[112]

Adam Empie himself was a strong advocate and teacher of Masonic truths. Although belief in the deity of Jesus Christ is not a prerequisite for becoming a Mason, to Empie, Christianity and freemasonry were complementary. "If we wish to be bright and consistent Masons, we must follow St. John Baptist's example," said Empie, June 24, 1824, in a speech delivered in Wilmington to a gathering of Masonic societies.

"We must strive to be holy ourselves and to make others so also. We must let our light shine. We must endeavor to spread the truth, and bring all around to embrace and practice it. For the Masonic spirit of universal benevolence is one which, if carried out into its natural consequences, will lead us to act in direct coincidence with those precepts of the Saviour…."

And Adam Empie even linked the weaknesses of some Masons and Christians. "For as many, who profess a belief in the Christian religion, know little about it, care little about it, and live not according to its precepts, precisely so it is in Masonry.

"Many Masonic books contain trifling, indecorous, and bacchanalian songs — many bad men belong to their societies; and they, in some places, hold meetings merely for dissipation. As Christianity is not accountable for the shocking crimes that have, sometimes, been committed by persons who called themselves Christians, so Masonry itself is not to be blamed for the misconduct of some of its members. These abuses spring from the badness of the human heart and character; not from the badness of Masonry or the Christian religion."[113]

Among many other members of St. James who were Masons, Cornelius Harnett and Governor Benjamin Smith achieved great distinction among their fraternal brethren. Judge Joshua Grainger Wright, a 32nd-degree Mason, was a part of the group that approved the Masonic symbol embedded in the original plans for the campus of the University of North Carolina. Archpatriot

Harnett served as master of St. John's Lodge and deputy provincial grand master of America. He has been given credit for establishing both North Carolina's second lodge, in Halifax, and the state of Virginia's first lodge in Norfolk.

Governor Smith was grand master of Masons of North Carolina from 1808 until 1811. According to local tradition, when George Washington visited Wilmington in 1791, he presented Benjamin Smith with a Masonic apron. Also, John Winslow of Fayetteville was Grand Representative to the Grand Lodge of the U. S., in 1851.[114]

Some of Wilmington's most notable visitors of the mid-19th century were Masons: Henry Clay, John Calhoun, and Daniel Webster. Thomas U. Walter, the architect of the 1839-1840 St. James building also was a Mason. It is tempting to think that the new building erected for St. John's Lodge, in 1841, could also have been designed by Walter.

The cornerstone ceremony occurred on December 27, 1841, with the Rev. Paul Repiton serving as chaplain. Located at 125 Market Street, the handsome building boasted graceful Gothic windows. Inexplicably, the façade of the old lodge has since been altered. Whether or not Walter designed it, his "team" at St. James did the work. John Norris was a Mason. So were the Wood brothers and J. H. Dahl, who were all members of St. John's Lodge #1.[115]

The gothic windows of St. John's Lodge (far right) look out on this Market Street parade day scene, about 1910. Only three Gothic Revival buildings were erected in 19th-century Wilmington: St. James Church, St. Thomas Catholic Church, and St. John's Lodge #1 at 125 Market Street. (Photo reprinted from *Do You Remember When?* by Henry Bacon McKoy.)

The Empies Move to Williamsburg

Adam Empie continued to enjoy a close relationship with Bishop Ravenscroft, who spoke of his friend and the Parish of St. James at the Diocesan Convention of 1827. "The personal attachment of the members to their pastor, their attainments in Christian knowledge and experience, their active exertions to communicate religious instruction by means of their Sunday School and catechismal classes, with the number of orderly and respectable colored communicants, denote such an earnest and zealous engagement for the promotion of the redeemer's Kingdom as was highly gratifying and refreshing to my spirit, and speaks a language not to be mistaken as to the diligence and faithfulness of him who is entrusted with their spiritual interest."[116]

Despite Ravenscroft's praise, there was some grumbling in the congregation about the rector's outspoken stance on slavery. Indeed, throughout Empie's ministry, his popularity went up and down like a crenellated parapet. In 1827, the Empies moved to Williamsburg where he served as rector of Bruton Parish Church, and, for nine years, as president of The College of William and Mary, and "professor of belles lettres, logic and ethics." He was credited with many improvements at the college, but perhaps a friendship that developed there had more ramifications. Adam Empie had long decried the lack of quality technical education in America. His William and Mary protégé, a chemistry professor named William Barton Rogers, left Virginia at Empie's bidding to lead a fund-raising campaign in Boston for the creation of a technical school. The Massachusetts Institute of Technology was the result.

It was during Empie's time in Williamsburg, in 1830, that he received an honorary doctorate of divinity from the University of North Carolina. Though he deserved it, this honor was probably made easier by the fact that his father-in-law had served as attorney for the University, and all his brothers-in-law were Carolina men.

While at Bruton Parish, Adam Empie's ideas on slavery met with great resistance. Some of his parishioners protested bitterly when he invited slaves to be a part of the worship service and appealed to the government for help in curbing Empie's actions. Doggedly, Dr. Empie appealed to the Virginia State Legislature and his actions were upheld. However, his views greatly strained relations.

Adam Empie decided to make a move. General Swift, William Lord, Thomas Wright, A. J. deRosset, William Wright, Joseph Hill, and James McRee all wrote glowing recommendations for their friend, recommending he be named president of the University of South Carolina, but the appointment went to someone else. Instead, in 1836, Empie moved to Raleigh, where he taught for one year at Episcopal High School. That job ended when he discovered that the school, in his words, "was a speculation upon borrowed capital, and verging to its ruin." After Empie's departure, wealthy businessman Duncan Cameron purchased the struggling institution. It still survives: St. Mary's School.[117]

Dr. Empie's last parish was in Richmond where he helped organize, in1837, St. James Church, named after his beloved post in Wilmington. He created a "Classical School for young men ten years of age or older" that met in the Richmond church. One of the classes he taught was "elocution," something he described as the "act of speaking so as to convey the sense, gratify the ear, and impress the mind...."

Though his students were usually privileged, Empie never lost sight of the disenfranchised. He encouraged the creation of slave galleries in the existing white churches in Richmond. He also founded a slave mission, on Broad Street, and taught Bible lessons there. His work during this period was rewarded when he was named "A Maker of Richmond" in the 1940s. Today, Richmond's St. James Church boasts over 2,000 members, and Adam Empie's favorite Bible verse still graces the entrance and altar: "Be ye doers of the word and not hearers only."

Years later, Edward V. Valentine of Richmond remembered the physical suffering of Empie, the man who was his rector, teacher, and friend. "The Doctor was highly esteemed by his flock, but unfortunately was a sufferer from pulmonary trouble, and I imagine rheumatism also," he said. The very proper Dr. Empie was in such pain in Richmond that he purchased and wore a magnetic curative of dubious value called "Dr. Christie's Galvanized Ring."[118]

Valentine also remembered the original features of the church that was built under Empie's leadership. "Behind the pulpit were stained glass windows with Moses and Aaron represented full length. It was either Moses or Aaron who reminded me of good old Dr. Empie."[119]

In 1864, Civil War general, J. E. B. Stuart was buried from St. James Church in Richmond. The rector, Dr. Joshua Peterkin, sang "Rock of Ages" with him as the general lay dying.

Adam Empie served in Richmond from 1837 until 1853, but he kept business ties to Wilmington. In addition to church work, Adam Empie and his brother-in-law, Dr. Thomas H. Wright, shared an interest in local business affairs. Though Dr. Wright obtained a medical degree from the College of Physicians and Surgeons at Columbia University in 1823, he soon found he enjoyed the world of business more than medicine. He served as president of the Bank of Cape Fear, an establishment in which Adam Empie held stock. Empie had real estate investments in Wilmington that Dr. Wright maintained, including a house, a cottage, several lots, and a wharf. Empie also banked royalties from a book of his sermons, one thousand of which were printed by a New York publisher.[120]

And even in his absence Empie continued to influence St. James Church. He sometimes was asked to provide names from his list of contacts to St. James for various jobs. It was Adam Empie who suggested Thomas Atkinson as a ministerial candidate in 1843. And Empie also stands in the shadows of the 1839 building campaign.[121]

Adam Empie, in addition to his network of powerful connections, arrived in Richmond in 1837, the same year construction began on the Greek Revival-style First Baptist Church building — designed by Thomas U. Walter. The 1837 church, located at 12th and Broad streets, is currently owned by the Medical College of Va. Empie's church was located just 15 blocks away.[122]

Empie had stayed close to the family of Bishop John Henry Hobart, a powerful proponent of the High Church. The Rt. Rev. Hobart's son-in-law, Levi Silliman Ives, was consecrated as Bishop of N. C. in 1831. Ives immediately began waging a steady campaign for Gothic Revival architecture in church construction, a style that reflected the ideals of those in favor of the High Church. Gothic Revival style had begun to bud in North Carolina as early as 1817. Twenty-two years later, it would make its way to the southeast corner of Third and Market.[123]

Bishop Ravenscroft

"The chaste mind, like a polished plane may admit foul thoughts without receiving their tincture."
–Lawrence Sterne, quoted by Bishop Ravenscroft[124]

After Adam Empie left Wilmington in 1827, John Starke Ravenscroft considered taking his place at St. James Church. Though he initially accepted the position, for reasons not known Ravenscroft never took the job. Nevertheless, he was a presence at Third and Market. The year Empie moved to Williamsburg, Bishop Ravenscroft confirmed eleven whites and ten "Africans" at the altar of St. James.

Brilliant, but blunt, Ravenscroft moved the antebellum masses with the directness of his sermons – and the physicality of his being. Though lacking in "the graces of oratory," his august appearance and demeanor caused young confirmation candidates to tremble. J. G. Burr, himself confirmed by Ravenscroft, shared his memories of the bishop in his 1874 history, *Sketch of St. James Parish.*

"He would attract notice in any crowd…from his commanding appearance and the dignity of his manner – a dignity that repelled all attempts at familiarity, but at the same time was natural and unaffected. Over six feet in height, with a frame of Herculean proportions, indicating great powers of endurance, he towered among men like Saul among his brethren, and, as he walked the streets, the groups that gathered on the sidewalks would turn again to gaze upon that noble specimen of vigorous manhood."

"The bishop spoke the accent of Northern England, where he was raised, with an amazing voice. "His voice was of wonderful power, deep toned and sonorous, and when under the influence of strong emotion or excited by his subject, it rolled forth like peals of thunder."[125]

Ravenscroft's interesting peculiarities extended to requesting that most every song be sung to the same few tunes. In announcing a hymn he would inform the choir that he wished the words sung to a certain tune. "The tune 'China,' for instance, which was a great favorite with him," said J. G. Burr. "He would announce thus: 'Sing the 75th hymn to the tune of 'Chany,' as he invariably pronounced it, and no other tune but 'Chany' was sung – it mattered not whether the tune was appropriate to the words or the reverse…."

The deRosset family had such strong affection for Ravenscroft that they hung his portrait on the wall of their library. The A. J. deRosset, Jr., residence on the northeast corner of Second and Dock streets is now the City Club.[126]

were sold for the benefit of the church. With the proceeds, they funded a charity school, purchased a tract of land (1835) from John Swann to expand the church property, built "Society Hall" (1834), and performed innumerable charitable deeds. In 1843, they hired brothers J. C. and R. B. Wood to build the stone walls that line the northern and western sides of the church, and to create an iron railing and coping. In 1845, they hired the Woods again to make improvements to the front entrance, including work on the steps, and pavement. Also, the ladies made a generous contribution toward the construction of St. John's Church. From 1822, the year the first women's group was established, until 1843, the society raised $4,500 — a staggering amount in those days.[131]

The Ladies Working Society continued throughout the 1940s. Participants include Allie Fechtig, Mary Strange, Lula Sprunt, Helen Farmer, Frances Penton, Jane Rhett, Julia Harriss, Mrs. Ochs, and Margaret MacRae. (Courtesy of UNCW)

They had style and knew something about marketing. The following advertisement ran in the Wilmington *Chronicle*, December 15, 1847. "The Ladies of the Episcopal Church design holding a fair for the sale of articles of their own manufacture, at Society Hall, on evenings of Wed. and Thurs., Dec. 22 and 23d. Various kinds of refreshments will also be offered."

This was the same period at which the diocese was becoming acquainted with a new bishop. Episcopalians across the state had mourned the death of Bishop Ravenscroft, who died March 5, 1830. He was a beloved man whose visitations caused great joy wherever he went. His successor never created an equal core of affection among the people but managed to create his own good mark on the diocese, for a time. Levi Silliman Ives was nominated bishop on May 21, 1831, and elected by an almost unanimous vote. Only Chief Justice Thomas Ruffin withheld his vote, presenting a blank sheet of paper until he could learn more about the candidate. Eventually Ruffin fell into step and reported that Ives's "selection seems almost to have been providential; for few of us knew of the gentleman pointed out."[132]

Levi Ives had an interesting background of English ancestors who settled in the Massachusetts Bay Colony, and Presbyterian parentage. But as a young man, he chose the Episcopal way and studied under legendary teacher Bishop John Henry Hobart, at General Theological Seminary in New York City in 1819. He was ordained a priest in 1823 by Bishop William White of Pennsylvania. He served churches in Batavia, N.Y.; Philadelphia and Lancaster, Pa; and Christ Church and St. Luke's in New York City before moving to North Carolina.

The Rev. Mr. Thomas Wright, son of New Hanover County High Sheriff Thomas Wright, traveled to New York to inform Levi Silliman Ives of his nomination as bishop. He recorded his experience in a letter to his wife, Mary Green Wright. "Mr. Anderson and I have dined with Mr. Ives and the professors of the [General] Theological Seminary. He is very learned, but very modest, or rather diffident and not morose, as I had been told. He is also very charitable and several of his few relations live with him and are supported by him.

"Mrs. Ives is plain in person however I am told intelligent and amicable."[133]

"Mr. Anderson" was Walker Anderson, a nephew of planter and esteemed churchman Duncan Cameron, and a faithful member of St. Matthew's Church in Hillsborough.

Bishop Ives was ordained September 22, 1831. Like Empie and Judd, he arrived with a good education and a big city network. But Ives had even more ties to the heart of the national church, for his "plain" wife was Rebecca Hobart, daughter of the Rt. Rev. John Henry Hobart, who was considered "the most outstanding leader in the Protestant Episcopal Church." He founded Hobart College and General Theological Seminary. Hobart's advocacy of the High Church tradition was a posture that many blamed for Rebecca and Levi Silliman Ives's conversion to Roman Catholicism in 1852.[134]

Rt. Rev. Levi Silliman Ives (Courtesy of The Episcopal Church in North Carolina, 1701-1959)

In May and June of 1832, the Rev. Thomas Wright accompanied the Rt. Rev. Levi Silliman Ives on his visitations across the state. Later that year, Bishop Ives visited Wilmington, St. Philip's Church, and Orton Plantation, then the home of Dr. Frederick Hill and currently the property of Mr. and Mrs. Laurence Gray Sprunt. He led services at St. James for three days. "My intercourse with the congregation of St. James was most gratifying," he wrote.[135]

During the final months of Mr. Cairns's term as rector, Sunday night services were established for blacks at St. James. Attendance averaged about 300, double the membership of the church. But as far back as September 1832, the congregation became critical of Mr. Cairns. He was panned for his "abrupt manner" and said to become "impatient if not petulant under advice." And he irked parishioners because of "the want of practical religious conversation during his visits."[136]

Mr. Cairns left to go to St. Paul's Church in Edenton. In 1839, he moved to Georgia. After Mr. Cairns's departure, the Rev. Mr. John Burke, principal of the Academy, occupied the pulpit for a few months. Burke became rector later at Christ Church, New Bern, from 1835 until 1837.

In late 1833, a native son ascended the pulpit of St. James. The Rev. Mr. Thomas Frederick Davis, son of Thomas F. Davis, abandoned a successful law career for the ministry and was ordained by Bishop Ives in St. James Church. Davis was noted as a pulpit orator who was "remarkable for the clear elucidation of his subjects, his powers of analysis and argument and for the fervent piety that breathed in every word." Davis was elected Bishop of the Diocese of South Carolina in 1853.[137]

In 1834, the men organized their own society: The Bible, Tract, Prayer Book, and Missionary Society. The Rev. Mr. Davis, Dr. A. J. deRosset, William C. Lord, and James S. Green served as officers for the group.

While Davis was rector, Mount Lebanon Chapel, "a very neat and commodious chapel," was built. Davis left Wilmington in the spring of 1836 for health reasons and moved to Salisbury. Here he served at St. Luke's Church until transferring to South Carolina where, on October 17, 1853, he became bishop. The Rt. Rev. Davis died in 1871.

Mount Lebanon Chapel, about 1949. (Photo by Gilliam Horton. Courtesy of Josephine Corbett Horton.)

Mount Lebanon Chapel

The story of Mount Lebanon Chapel really begins on New Year's Day, 1800, when Judge Joshua Grainger Wright purchased 320 acres of land for 110 pounds. Col. Thomas Wright, Judge Wright's brother, handled the estate sale in his official capacity as High Sheriff of New Hanover County. The brothers were great-grandsons of Wilmington cofounder Joshua Grainger and sons of wealthy privateer and Wrightsboro planter Captain Thomas Wright (1714-1771), by his second wife, Ann Grainger. The older brother, Col. Thomas Wright, attended Trinity Church in New York from about 1788 until 1792. One of his children is buried in the Trinity churchyard. Trinity Church, located on Wall Street, was the site of George Washington's thanksgiving service on the day of his inauguration, in 1789. Washington continued to worship at Trinity for the next two years.[138]

Col. Wright was responsible for the relocation of portions of three related families to Wilmington from New York and New England: Scott, Winslow and Willkings. He also had the "saddle of honor" when George Washington rode into Wilmington on April 24, 1791. The younger brother, Joshua G. Wright, was a respected attorney and Speaker of the N. C. General Assembly. His wife, Susan Bradley Wright, was the daughter of Richard and Elizabeth Sharpless Bradley, devout Quakers who had made sure their daughter had more than a passing knowledge of the Bible. Going against the social trend of the day, they may have been less than pleased that their daughter was marrying a member of St. James Church, but at least they could console themselves that the groom's maternal side, the Joshua Grainger family, had also been Quakers.

Joshua Wright and Susan Bradley had been neighbors in what they simply called Wilmington and what is now known as the Historic District. Joshua Grainger Wright lived close to St. James Church, on the southwest corner of Third and Market streets. Joshua's father, Captain Thomas Wright, had leased the elegant home and put it under a verbal offer-to-purchase contract with owner John Burgwin. In 1799, the son would make good on the offer when he bought the house for 3500 Spanish milled dollars.

Though slightly different versions of the naming of Mount Lebanon exist among Wright family papers, the one remembered by Judge Wright's granddaughter, Ann Eliza Meares, might be closest to the truth. Shortly after he purchased the property, Susan and Joshua Wright were riding horses on their newly acquired soundfront estate. There were cedar trees all around them, a wood considered soft in America but prime building material in the Middle East. Susan Bradley was familiar with Old Testament history in which the mammoth cedars from Mount Lebanon were floated down the water toward Jerusalem for the construction of Solomon's temple.

So, according to the "cherished tradition," with a gentle touch to her pony, she rode forward to an eminence near which stood large cedar trees and said, "We will build here and call our home

Mount Lebanon." It is interesting that she chose not to incorporate the name "Wright," leaving it to others to name waterfront locales after her husband's family.

Place names change, not only through new ownership but by being altered with use. The name Susan Bradley chose, Mount Lebanon, has been "dismounted" on and off for at least 204 years. Her own husband used "Lebanon, near Wilmington" as his return address, but their son, Dr. Thomas Henry Wright, preferred "Mount Lebanon."

After the Herbert Latimer family purchased the eastern portion of Dr. Wright's tract, in 1886, they called it Lebanon. Pembroke Jones, after purchasing a large portion of Mount Lebanon, referred to the land as "the old Wright farm." Before the name Wright took hold, the Sound was also known as New Topsail, Summer Ville, and Governor's Point. And the entire neighborhood, all the way to Rogersville Road, was called simply "Wrightsville," from the early 1800s. It is a tradition that continues today among some older natives.

On a prominence at Mount Lebanon, "immediately on the Sound," Susan Bradley and Joshua Wright built a two-story frame house, with a full basement. Mount Lebanon House had six fireplaces, though seldom were they necessary. Insurance documents state that each story measured 40' by 20'. The dimensions seem small for such a large family: the Wrights had thirteen children, eight of whom survived childhood. But there was little more room in their town house: The Burgwin-Wright house measured about 50' by 25' before the 19th-century addition. However, both houses were augmented by outbuildings. The 1600-square-foot house at Mount Lebanon had an attached storage room, a detached kitchen 60' east of the house and a lumber room.

The six-pointed Star of David, the ancient symbol of Israel, was carved into the house's chimney, and was also part of a stained glass design in the house. Although the Star of David was also adopted as a symbol of Freemasonry, when used by Christians, it is usually a reminder of Jesus' earthly ancestry through the lineage of King David, and of our adoption into the "chosen" through the new covenant. Even if the house didn't survive, the Star of David still appears at Mount Lebanon. Stained glass windows moved from Fairntosh Plantation, in Durham County, to Mount Lebanon Chapel in 1974 include the symbol.

The Sound provided a change of scenery, a breezy place to escape some of the staggering heat of Wilmington summers, and what was thought to be natural medicine. Space, breeze, and salt baths were considered therapeutic, and many seasonal Sound residents did not return to town until the first frost.

In 1810, when William Willkings first tried to entice the Rev. Adam Empie to accept the rectorship of St. James, he wrote him, offering $1200 a year salary. "To this will be added the customary perquisity attached to the office of a clergyman – during the sickly season as it is termed, should the town prove unhealthy, we have a safe retreat on the sound, being about 8 or 9 miles away from Wilmington on the seashore where you can retire with every reasonable prospect of health and comfort. And on Sundays, in fair weather, you can easily ride to town for the performance of divine services...."[139]

After 1821, Dr. Thomas Henry Wright, the eldest surviving son, took possession of his late father's homes. At either location, it was a busy place with the presence of his mother, Susan; his wife, Mary Allan; and Dr. Wright's eight children who survived infancy. Despite happy confusion at home and a number of jobs, Dr. Wright spent so much time on church work that he is still remembered as St. James's most dedicated layperson.

Dr. Wright was influenced not only by Adam Empie, but also by his mother who, long before the days of government assistance, was a sort of one-woman faith-based charity. Needy people often begged for food at her home on the Sound, in summer, and at the Burgwin-Wright House the remainder of the year.

Though possible to travel to Wilmington for Sunday morning services, it was difficult. The road taken, now known as Wrightsville Avenue, was a mere bumpy dirt path in the 1830s. Planking and shelling would come later. The time span of the nine-mile journey was dependent upon weather, the horses' health and mood, and the buggy or carriage's condition. Typically, it could take as little as one frenzied hour or as much as three tiring hours.

Dr. Thomas Henry Wright (1800-1861) (Photo of Dr. Wright's portrait courtesy of the Lower Cape Fear Historical Society and the Wright family)

Some Wrightsville Sound families, like the William and Thomas Wrights, and the Gileses, served at different times as hosts of house or "front porch" worship services. The Restons who lived at Honolulu, a tract now known as Bar Harbor, and the Bradleys, who had purchased a 65-acre portion of the Wright property in 1808 for an in-law price of five shillings, also participated. Sunday morning offerings were collected at these services from at least 1821, and the take was respectable. All proceeds were turned over to St. James Parish.

The Giles property, now home to Katherine Rhett and Judge James Fox, is on the north side of Bradley Creek. Descendant Harriet Bellamy Jewett described the orthodox rules of the Sabbath. "No work of any kind was allowed to be done by anyone, including the servants, on the Sabbath, and all cooking for Sunday had to be done on Saturday."[140]

In 1835, Dr. Thomas Henry Wright, who then owned 57 acres of Mount Lebanon, decided to create a dedicated house of worship for the summer neighborhood. He chose a spot in the middle of a grove of moss-laden trees. In his own words, he "presented" a 6.5-acre tract, with water access, to "St. James Church for the purpose of creating an Episcopal house of worship on Wrightsville Sound." The waterfront parcel allowed easy access for Sound neighbors who traveled by water for services. Dr. Wright requested it be named Mount Lebanon for his "country seat of which this tract forms a part."

Though other individuals contributed to the construction, it was Dr. Wright who was the primary financier of the project. It called for a vernacular rural chapel with smooth plaster walls, wooden pegs, wide-board heart pine floors, a cedar shake roof, and a chapel bell. Architect Richard Upjohn would eventually publish a book entitled "Upjohn's Rural Architecture" that would feature buildings that "could be built by any hammer and saw carpenter." Though about 20 chapels would be built across N. C. from his plans, Lebanon Chapel does not conform to them. To date, the architect, if there was one, is unknown. [141]

Dr. Wright's Durham County friend, Duncan Cameron, possibly obtained a plan for the chapel he built at Fairntosh Plantation from William Nichols, the state architect. Nichols mentioned the project to Cameron as early as 1825, though Salem Chapel would not be dedicated by Bishop Ravenscroft until October 1827. The completion date gave Dr. Wright plenty of time to see it before he started work on Lebanon in 1835. William Mercer Green, Wright's first cousin, was the official rector of Salem Chapel from 1827 until at least 1843, a job that paid $100 a year. Green probably served as such until he was elected Bishop of Mississippi, in 1850. He held services once a month at Salem throughout his rectorship at St. Matthew's in Hillsborough and after he joined the faculty at U.N.C. Green was also called upon from time to time to provide spiritually meditative moments for Duncan Cameron, a brilliant businessman whose mind, at times, raced so feverishly that one of his physicians prescribed "cold applications to the head."[142]

Architect Nichols favored Greek Revival styles and both Salem Chapel at Cameron's Fairntosh Plantation and the original design for Mount Lebanon Chapel fit the bill. Each building was situated within a grove of oak trees, though the area surrounding Lebanon has changed a lot since 1835. Wright and Cameron shared strong interests in diocesan business, state banking, railroads, and the University of North Carolina. Wright's father, Joshua Grainger Wright, was a trustee of the university and worked alongside Cameron's father-in-law, Richard Bennehan, to shape the young school.[143]

Lebanon was erected by area craftsmen. The contractor, Hillary Bryant, lived nearby — roughly in what is now the neighborhood of Turtle Hall and Shinn Creek Estates. Bryant must have worked fast, for construction began in spring 1835, and just a few months later, during summer, the first service was held at Mount Lebanon. It was the tricentennial of the printing of Coverdale's Bible, a fact noted by Dr. Wright in the chapel's new Bible. Officiating was the Rev. Cameron Farquhar MacRae, a descendant of Alexander MacRae of Wilmington and the son-in-law of the Wrights' old friend, John Fanning Burgwin.[144]

At the Diocesan Convention of May 4-9, 1836, it was announced that "a neat village church has been erected at Wrightsville, within eight miles of Wilmington." Dr. Wright as well as T. R. Davis, Jr., Richard Price, William Giles, and Frederick C. Hill were delegates.[145]

Clean line pine benches surrounded Mount Lebanon Chapel, and a little bridge spanned a nearby creek. After 1835, the creek was called "Church Creek." It was dammed up in 1902 when Sarah Green Jones created the garden at Airlie.

By 1836, regular services were being held in the chapel, led alternately by Dr. Wright and James S. Green, a relative who also served as a lay reader at St. James Church. In June of that year, the new rector of St. James Church, the Rev. Dr. Robert B. Drane, administered the first Holy Communion at the chapel and performed the first baptism in the chapel. The baby was the fifth of Dr. Wright's children: James Allan Wright. Like many rectors before him, Dr. Drane probably enjoyed lodging at the Wrightsville Sound home of either Thomas or William Wright during the summer.

The architectural style of Mount Lebanon Chapel is classified as Greco-Gothic and the National Register of Historic Places considers it a "robust example." The Greek portion speaks of the building's original symmetrical simplicity. Gothic overtones were added in 1912 in preparation for the wedding of Sadie Jones and architect John Russell Pope. Mr. Pope could have designed the changes, but Henry Walters, with his love for art, was probably looking over his shoulder.

Early on a dewy summer morning, with all the leaded windows flung open, the surrounding creation seems to become part of the building and usually as much a worship aid as a vaulted ceiling. Prior to the closing of Deep Inlet, due east of Lebanon, participants in the service could hear ocean waves breaking in the distance. Refreshing salty breezes, shimmering green leaves and the songs of birds remind the habitues as well as visitors to Mount Lebanon Chapel of the beauty of God's creation.

During summer, the chapel had plenty of people in it – and in those days, they were usually the same people. "The usual migration to the Sea-Coast is going on," wrote the editor of the *Herald.* "The neat little Church at Wrightsville, lifting its modest front among the tall Oaks, will be filled with the customary worshippers."[146]

The Lebanon churchyard was born of necessity. The bodies of the Armstrongs, father and son, were the first to be buried in Mount Lebanon Graveyard. Both lived near the chapel and were victims of an electrical storm, in 1841. The elevation of the land made it a natural choice. According to Dr. Wright, "The bodies of the deceased were deposited on the hill south of the church."[147]

From 1841 until about 1890, most of those buried in the cemetery were members of St. James Church who had property on Wrightsville Sound. Usually a bell echoed throughout the soundfront community tolling the news of an impending funeral. Because of the large number of Giles family members who were interred there, the graveyard at Mount Lebanon was sometimes called "Giles Cemetery." The name persisted throughout the Corbett family's ownership (1948 through 1999) of the surrounding acreage. However, during the height of the Sarah and Pembroke Jones era at Airlie, eight members of the Giles family were all disinterred on one day: January 26, 1910 — and reburied at Oakdale. At least one of the bodies, that of Richard Giles, had been resting near the chapel since 1843. They were Almeria Giles, William B. Giles, William B. Giles, Jr., Major John R. Giles, Christine Giles, James Giles, Annabella Giles, and Richard Bradley Giles.

At one time, Mount Lebanon Graveyard boasted many handwrought iron enclosures. Today only three remain. One is the Hill plot. Another is the Wright-Bradley plot, recently restored by Eleanor Wright Beane. And the last one is an ironwork fence so small it looks almost like a crib. Luciana Poisson Pickrell, who lived at 315 South Front Street, explained the mystery of the little plot on May 4th, 1974.

"As a child," she explained to the Rev. Mr. Herbert Aman, "I lived at the Latimer home (the old Mount Lebanon house) on the Point every summer and I used to go over to Lebanon Chapel often. My great-grandmother Cutlar would go with us to put flowers on her sister-in-law's grave - Jane Fleeming, wife of Daniel Fleeming.

"It's the little iron fence back of the church - just inside the gate. There used to be a small marker, but a tree grew up in the middle of the fence and took the fence right up from the ground. I suppose the marker was in the tree. Mr. (Waddell) Corbett had the tree removed.

"I thought this might be of interest to you as the fence looks so lonely."[148]

Jane and Daniel Fleeming were both members of St. James Church. The Fleemings were merchants who specialized in, among other things, importing and selling fine wines. Jane Fleeming was a benefactor of St. Paul's Church during its early years.

Rev. Robert Brent Drane, D.D. (Courtesy of New Hanover County Public Library.)

Introducing Dr. Robert Brent Drane

The Rev. Dr. Robert Brent Drane officially took charge of St. James Church in July 1836 and would lead the church through many tough years. A native of Prince George County, Maryland, Robert B. Drane received his education at Harvard University, graduating in 1825. He was ordained by the Rt. Rev. Philander Chase in Washington, then became rector of St. John's Church in Hagerstown, Md., in 1828. After he came to St. James in 1836, he shepherded the congregation for 25 years, with the exception of several months. In 1851, he married "a fair widow of Tarboro," Catharine Caroline Parker Hargrave.[149]

Dr. Drane, a leader in the campaign to build the 1839-1840 building, was almost immediately lost to St. James when Christ Church in Raleigh attempted to lure him away. He declined, but then in 1847, he received another call — this one from a church in Annapolis, Md. But Robert Brent Drane had become deeply fond of Wilmington and the network of interesting people who filled his church on Sundays. He decided to stay, a decision that probably shortened his life.

Dr. Drane invested much time and effort in the new building. Though consecrated, it was not complete and would not be fully used until 1860. Many services were still held in Society Hall. About 1850, when talk was constant about the need for a new church, Dr. Drane suggested the new church be named "St. John's," because James and John, two of Jesus' disciples, were brothers and he wanted brotherly love to exist between the two congregations. He remained involved in the drive to build St. John's Church, at Third and Red Cross streets, to such an extent that he gave not only leadership, but also a generous financial contribution.[150]

His regular church duties involved travel since it was still a long way to anywhere outside downtown Wilmington. During the summer, most Sundays, Dr. Drane continued to hold services at St. James for the small crowd that lingered in town. But he augmented his salary by traveling to Wrightsville and Smithville. He spent two Sundays conducting services at Mount Lebanon and two Sundays leading the congregation at "Old St. Philip's." His work in Smithville spawned new church life.

By 1843, Brunswick County had a new church building. First called Chapel of the Cross, the small building served Fort Johnston. In 1851, the name was changed to "Old Saint Philip's." The church would become a favorite project for Bishop Atkinson. According to St. Philip's historian Charles Pollock, "Three major factors caused the new church to do well in the 1850s — the Military, the upriver plantations and Wilmington, especially the clergy and Ladies of Saint James.

"The ladies of St. James played a significant role in the life and financial well being of the church. Several times the records indicate the ladies of St. James helped St. Philips by retiring small debts, helping to furnish the church after the war, and by holding fund raisers to assist in providing for a rectory."[151]

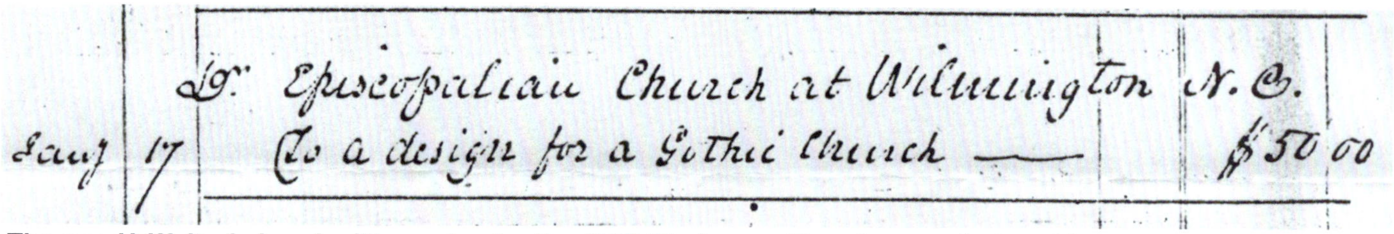
Dr. Episcopalian Church at Wilmington N. C.
Jany 17 To a design for a Gothic Church —— $50 00

Thomas U. Walter's handwritten entry for the 1838 St. James Church commission. (Courtesy of the Athenaeum of Philadelphia)

For the most part, this Easter photo shows the features of the chancel as they looked from 1840 until about 1892. (Courtesy of UNCW)

The 1839 Building

"Many and vast have been the changes in the parish since the corner stone of the church was laid. (But) that church still lifts its turrets to the skies, still firmly stands, the visible emblem of the "the Church of the living God, the pillar and ground of the truth."

— Col. James G. Burr, 1874 *(One Hundredth Anniversary Commemorating the Building of St. James Church, Wilmington, N. C. April 30th and May 1st, 1939.)*

By 1838, the term Gothic Revival was an everyday term among local Episcopalians. Though the tedium of church politics attached itself to the style, the spiritual aspects of its design delight. A Gothic church is a soaring worship aid: a vertical concrete reminder of the unseen realities of infinity. Gothic arches were designed to rise evenly toward the heavens, then soar to a point that pins the viewer's attention upward. In Gothic architecture, even rooflines carry a message. Horizontal lines stretch only so far before breaking upward, falling back, and then returning skyward again — thus forming a crenellated parapet, or battlement.

The walls of Gothic churches are full of processed light because the solid structure is heavily perforated to make way for spacious windows of translucent glass. Light becomes a verb within a stained glass window, bringing to life the darkest hues — and beautifying what is mundane. When studied, even the smallest detail of some stained glass windows can revisit the mind, bringing delight. Many windows include scenes from Scripture, thus adding instruction to mere beauty.

Though the spiritual ramifications should have attracted virtually everyone, the "High Church" connotations of Gothic architecture probably made some parishioners wince. Those of a more Roman persuasion saw Gothic architecture as a symbol of the unbroken line of apostolic succession from St. Peter. St. James Church still had too many members who were steeped in the "Low Church" training of Adam Empie not to question that such a move would bring the congregation dangerously close to the shadow of the Pope. Disagreement was to be expected.

Meanwhile, talk of a fresh new building of any style skewered disgruntlement some held with the old church. The Rev. Dr. Robert B. Drane described it as being "partly in the street, decayed," and decried it for "the inconvenience of its internal arrangements." The church was growing, both in membership and activity – and the building was staying the same size.[152]

On October 30, 1837, the vestry decided it was time to solicit funds for the "erection of a better place for Episcopal worship than the temple in which we have hitherto assembled." After little more than two weeks, enough money had been pledged to take action. Although the resulting church would be enormously handsome, there were those who wished passionately for something even greater — perhaps in keeping with the new English Gothic Revival churches.

"For our own part," wrote an anonymous church leader in November 1837, "we would have advocated a different situation, and a grand building — the most costly that the means of the congregation and its friends could possibly erect. Still we cheerfully acquiesce in the decision that has been made, and think it far better that we should lay our offerings upon the humblest altar with a feeling of perfect love in God, than to burn incense in a temple more glorious than St. Peter's, with emotions of bitterness and malevolence flowing in our hearts."[153]

A rare front view of St. James Church. (Courtesy of Cape Fear Museum)

During the construction process Bishop Ives proclaimed that St. James was "making a praiseworthy effort to erect a neat and commodious Gothic church edifice in place of the inconvenient and much decayed building in which they have hitherto worshipped."[154]

Meanwhile the Wilmington newspaper, *Peoples' Press*, carried the news that construction was beginning on New York's Trinity Church. Whereas St. James is repeatedly described as a neat Gothic building, Trinity was said to be "purely and severely Gothic." The new church campus in New York would include a monument to Bishop John Henry Hobart.[155]

In 1838, right in the middle of its own building campaign, St. James participated in another church's project. Paul Repiton, the chaplain of St. John's Lodge #1, founded the Orange Street Baptist Church, a house of worship for "laboring classes who were too poor to pay a minister." Repiton, who earned his undergraduate degree from Richmond College and would receive a D.D. from the College of William and Mary, was the son of Joseph Repiton, a Williamsburg resident who printed one of Adam Empie's books. Repiton was orphaned at the age of eight and he spent the rest of his youth in Norfolk where he was a member of a Baptist congregation that would eventually employ Thomas U. Walter to design a new building.[156]

A year after moving to Wilmington, Paul Repiton married Sarah Cowan, a member of St. James Church. Sarah had a special link to George Washington. He spent a night at her grandfather's inn, the "Sage Ordinary," when he passed through Onslow County in 1791.[157]

Repiton served the Baptist church with no remuneration. The rest of the church budget came mostly from members of St. James, particularly the Cowans and their closest relatives. The Orange Street Baptist Church was burned during the Civil War. The congregation sold the vacant lot and gave the proceeds to First Baptist Church, a congregation that was in the midst of a construction project at 421 Market Street (1859-1870.) The donation was given "to be used for the pulpit and baptistry as a memorial of the Orange Street church."[158]

The Rev. Mr. Paul Repiton could already have known architect Thomas U. Walter through their shared interest in the Baptist denomination and Freemasonry. Walter first examined the site of

St. James's new church when he visited Wilmington in November 1837. While in town, he designed a portico to the "Anderson House." The Mitchell-Anderson House still exists on the southeastern corner of Front and Orange streets. It was owned at the time by Alexander Anderson (1785-1844), the son of James Anderson who worked for George Washington as supervisor of Mount Vernon. Young Alexander was a favorite of Gen. Washington and they sometimes rode horses together at the farm. The Mitchell-Anderson House is located only yards away from the site where Washington was entertained with a "grand ball and illumination," during his stay in Wilmington.[159]

It's interesting that at the time of Walter's first known visit to Wilmington, there were two people living in the town who had strong ties to St. James and links to George Washington. Also, Gen. Washington, Repiton, Anderson, and Walter were all dedicated Masons.

Thomas Walter, who gained fame for designing the U. S. Capitol dome, began his career in Philadelphia as an apprentice bricklayer, under the supervision of his father, Joseph Saunders Walter. Thomas's mother was named Deborah Wood — and it is tempting to try to draw genealogical links between her and the Wood brothers who constructed the church building.

As a bricklayer, the younger Walter worked on the Second Bank of the U. S. in Philadelphia for six years. The bank building was designed by William Strickland, an architect who, in turn, learned much about graceful design from Benjamin H. Latrobe. According to Walter authority James Moore Goode, Walter then attended the Franklin Institute where he studied under John Haviland and learned architecture as well as the art of watercolor.[160]

Walter had acclaimed government and church buildings in his portfolio: a church in New York and one in Philadelphia; and Moyamensing, a Gothic style prison in Philadelphia. And one of his greatest designs was already taking on concrete form: Girard College (1838-1848), an orphanage endowed by Philadelphia merchant Stephen Girard. The Girard commission came with a bonus: the trustees sent Walter on a tour of England, Ireland, France, Italy, and Switzerland where he studied "Roman buildings, many Gothic cathedrals, but mostly neoclassical public buildings built between 1750 and 1838." Because Stephen Girard left instructions in his will for the roof of the orphanage to be marble, Walter made a special study of buildings with heavy roofs and domes.[161]

What Walter learned would be channeled into his design for the U. S. Capitol dome when he won the commission in 1851 to make additions to the Capitol. According to Goode, the project involved the "construction of a pair of massive marble wings, and later, an enormous iron dome. It was notable in many ways in American architectural history, especially as the largest construction project for a single building ever attempted in the country to that time."[162]

If Dr. Empie, Alexander Anderson, or Paul Repiton was not the only Wilmington link to Thomas U. Walter, there were many other possibilities. Bishop Ives, General Swift, and Adam Empie had more than enough ties to Philadelphia to know of Walter's work. Bishop Ives had served as rector of Trinity Church in Philadelphia and most certainly knew of Thomas U. Walter. Gen. Joseph

Gardner Swift was a relative of the Nantucket Coffins. The Coffins were related to the Wood family — and Thomas U. Walter's mother's maiden name was Wood. In addition, Walter used granite from quarries in Massachusetts for the Philadelphia County Prison at Moyamensing — and the quarry, for a time, was under Swift's supervision. To further complicate the possibilities, Gen. Swift served on the vestry of Trinity Church in Geneva, N.Y., an edifice that predated the 1839 St. James building – and looks a lot like it.[163]

Though many communicants, particularly William C. Lord, contributed to the project, it seems that Dr. Wright played some leading role in the process. Dr. Robert B. Drane eulogized Wright in 1861, saying, "It is no exaggeration to say that but for his wise counsels, his munificence, his untiring energy and perseverance, coming in aid of your own," the 1839-1840 St. James building and the original St. John's Church would not have been built.[164]

Strong ties to New York's Trinity Church could have held sway in a vote for style. And some members of St. James had already toured Gothic Revival churches in Europe. Along with the deRossets and Gileses, the Wrights were great travelers. "....I received a very polite and affectionate letter opus today from Dr. Wright," wrote William Giles, "proposing to visit England, Ireland, Scotland and Italy to see everything that was to be seen from the Queen to the Pope - strange as it may sound, if your health was good I would not hesitate a moment as such an opportunity will never present itself again. Of all the people with whom I am acquainted there is none to be compared to the Dr. as a travelling companion."[165]

These drawings by John Henry Hopkins predate St. James's 1839 building by three years. Hopkins said, "The Church is the house of God. It is the place where his people assemble to transact the concerns of eternity." (Images previously published in *Essay on Gothic Architecture*, by John Henry Hopkins.)

On January 17, 1838, Thomas U. Walter wrote up a new account: "Episcopalian Church at Wilmington, N. C. - a design for a Gothic Church: $50.00." In May, Walter added a plan for a reading desk and chancel railing. The chancel railing was probably carved wood, but was changed to a brass — then to the carved railing that exists today. Thomas U. Walter's church projects were money in the bank, but also labors of a higher love. According to James Moore Goode, Walter "was a devout Baptist and I am sure relished church designs in the 1840s and 1850s before the Civil War disrupted his profession."[166]

The 1839 St. James building is similar to churches built earlier in England. Both St Luke Church (1820-1824) in Chelsea (designed by James Savage), and St. Peter Church (1823-1828) in Brighton, Sussex (designed by Sir Charles Barry, architect of the houses of Parliament), are reminiscent of St. James. Perhaps in Mr. Walter's 1838 tour of England he visited both churches. But whether he did or not, he surely was familiar with the first significant American work published on the subject: *Essay on Gothic Architecture, with Various Plans and Drawings for Churches*, by Bishop John Henry Hopkins. The slender volume was broadly distributed and contained a design more similar to St. James than the churches in Brighton or Sussex.[167]

John Henry Hopkins saw church design as a prayer made with bricks and mortar. (Br. Robert Lentz, artist)

It is interesting that Bishop Hopkins traces Gothic architecture back not only to the European churches, but to a much earlier building program: Israel's Temple of Jerusalem that was envisioned by King David and built by King Solomon almost a millennium before the birth of Jesus. Hopkins draws parallels to the proportions of height and width, window openings, and decorative designs. He even connects the Gothic arch to the ancient Eastern precedents found in the pinnacle and the minaret. There's little doubt that Hopkins would have taken delight in the scenic illustration Wilmington offers to his observation: The Temple of Israel with the points of its gleaming onion domes pointing skyward — and St. James Church, with its expansive collection of arches that aim towards heaven.

Bishop Hopkins also gave a boost to the finances and efforts of church construction by shaming those who could not think the aspects of ecclesiastical architecture were important. If parishioners simply tithed there would be plenty of funding for fine buildings. And discussions concerning church architecture were just part of keeping the faith. Citing God's detailed instructions to Moses concerning the tabernacle, and the Hebrews inspired efforts to build and document the great Temple, Hopkins concluded, "Most unscriptural, therefore, would be the censure ... which would seek to dissuade the clergy from applying themselves to the art of erecting the earthly houses of God in a fitting and an appropriate manner. It is a symbol of the heavenly temple where the redeemed should one day be privileged to worship with celestial joy."

In January 1839, the vestry announced "immediate measures to erect a new church." "Artificers and labourers" had been engaged by the building committee, a group that consisted of C. Robeson, John Walker, E. deRosset, P. K. Dickinson, J. T. Miller, and W. A. Williams, William C. Lord, and Thomas H. Wright. Churchwardens were Dr. Armand J. deRosset and William Campbell Lord. Lord, a lay reader at St. James Church, was the father-in-law of Dr. Armand J. deRosset, Jr. The vestry immediately made arrangements with the Ladies' Working Society to use Society Hall for services during the construction period.[168]

Although the original plan was to build on the same spot as the old church, foresight and artistic placement prevailed. Dr. Armand J. deRosset, who lived in a three-story home that used to sit on the northwest corner of Third and Market streets, owned the prize building lot adjacent to the old church. He agreed to sell it to St. James Church for $1,000. The purchase price could not begin to pay for the man-hours of service rendered by the deRosset family. Dr. Armand deRosset, a physician who studied under the famous doctor Benjamin Rush, served for many years as senior warden. Then his son, Dr. Armand deRosset, Jr., took his place. After this time, the benevolent dynasty of serving an extended term as senior warden would pass to Clayton Giles. Subsequent longtime senior wardens were Thomas Davis Meares, John Victor Grainger, George B. Elliott, Robert Strange, and Peter Browne Ruffin — each following the other.[169]

The Ladies' Working Society and Juvenile Sewing Society came up with the majority of the purchase price for the deRosset lot. The estimated cost of the entire imposing building was $15,500. A total of $11,000 was recouped from advances for pew rents. However, the church would also have to get a loan to complete the building, since the cost of construction eventually crept up to $20,000.[170]

The vestry comprised only seven members during the construction period: Dr. A. J. deRosset, William C. Lord, Dr. A. J. deRosset, Jr., William A. Williams, James T. Miller, and Dr. Thomas H. Wright. All the men were described as "prominent alike in Church and State, whose character shed a lustre upon this community."

The last service was held in the old church March 24, 1839. In his sermon, Dr. Robert Brent Drane recounted the history of St. James. It was so beautifully done that Dr. Thomas Henry Wright requested Dr. Drane write it out and make it available to anyone who was interested. "We can place it in our archives," wrote Dr. Wright. "Historical Notices," by Robert Brent Drane, D. D. (1843) was the result. It was reprinted in 1939 when St. James celebrated the centennial of the Thomas U. Walter building.[171]

Newspaper editor and St. James parishioner Asa A. Brown fancied that affectionate preservationist sentiments such as the following were "passing through the minds of many of the congregation."

"Will not fond love avert the fearful doom,
Sounds there no warning voice from yonder tomb -
Farewell old Church, we bid thee then farewell,
Yet do the parting words with sorrow swell
Our hearts and eyes, and e'en we linger still,
The cord that binds us here cannot be broke at will."[172]

The next day, workmen began taking down the building to use brick and other materials in the new church. The ambitious project was underway. The activity at Third and Market would be the most exciting thing to happen in Wilmington for months. The smell of new wood, the sounds of saws and hammers — and the softer sounds of lathes and trowels would fill the air and make good conversation around dinner tables and in the taverns down by the river.

The cornerstone of the new church was laid on April 3, 1839, a sunny day that dawned "auspiciously upon the scene." Bishop Ives was unavailable so the Rev. Robert Brent Drane officiated at the 10 o'clock service. Despite beastly descriptions of the old building and actions to build a new one "with a degree of unanimity rarely equalled in undertakings of this kind," the destruction of the old church was protested by some of the older members of the congregation.

"It was one of the landmarks of the town," wrote church historian J. G. Burr in 1874. "It withstood the storms of the Revolution, and, though battered by the elements, and gray with the mosses of age, was a connecting link between the present and the past — an object venerable from its antiquity and hallowed by the tenderest associations.

Some who stood and watched the dismembering of their beloved old church cried when they saw "the dismantled roof, its crumbling walls (and) listened to the wild winds sweeping through its deserted courts, and syllabling, the names of other days."[173]

A large number of things were deposited in the cornerstone, including a scroll on which was written various historical notes on the church and the diocese, as well as the following items:

"A Bible and Prayer Book, Journal of Convention for Diocese of North Carolina, 1838,

"Bishop Ives's Charge to the Clergy of the Diocese;

"Journals of General Convention, 1838;

"A Churchman's Almanac;

"Sword's Almanac;

"The Banner of Cross, Philadelphia;

"The Churchman, New York;

"The Episcopal Recorder, Philadelphia;

"The Spirit of Missions;

"Journal of Religious Education;

"Children's Sunday School Magazine;

"Wilmington Advertiser,

"Wilmington Weekly Chronicle;

"Charter and Plates of Bank of Cape Fear;

"Charter of Wilmington and Raleigh Rail Road;

"American Coins."

It seems only natural that they included the Bank of Cape Fear and the Wilmington and

Raleigh Rail Road. From the date of its charter in 1804 until its demise in 1861, the Bank of Cape Fear was controlled by men who were associated with St. James Church. Presidents of the bank included Joshua G. Wright, Thomas H. Wright, and William A. Wright, John London, Richard Bradley, and George Hooper. John Hogg, John Fanning Burgwin, Joshua Potts, Henry R. Savage, and Col. James G. Burr also held powerful positions in the Bank of Cape Fear.[174]

The Wilmington and Raleigh Rail Road, one of the bank's biggest customers, was also dominated by members of St. James. In 1848, the board of directors of the Wilmington and Raleigh included Platt K. Dickinson, Dr. Thomas H. Wright, and Robert Cowan. Frederick J. Hill, William B. Meares, William A. Williams, Oscar Parsley, Alexander MacRae, and William C. Lord were also on various committees when church construction began.[175]

Drane saluted the Gothic Revival style of the new building in strong words that were repeated many times. His words leave no doubt as to which side he was on during the architectural style debates within the church. "The style of the building is peculiarly adapted to sacred uses. The experience of the ages has proved it is better calculated than any other to fill men with awe and reverence, to repress the tumult of unreflected gaiety, and to render the mind sedate and solemn."[176]

A ceremony for another important Walter building took place just 16 days before the service at St. James. The cornerstone for Hibernian Society Hall in Charleston was laid on March 18, 1839, and it was completed January 20, 1840, just two months ahead of St. James. Walter probably made the 1837 trip to the south just to garner commissions. The Philadelphia market for architectural work dried up during a depression that occurred that year. Walter suffered additional strain when ten personal loans he made went bad. By 1841, he had lost virtually all of his money and most of his prized possessions — but none of his sterling reputation as an architect of quality work. [177]

Walter's original plan called for the brick from the old church to be used in the new building. The brick was cleaned and reused, but not according to plan. According to Elizabeth F. McKoy, "the architect intended to leave a clear demarcation to show where the old brick gave out and the work went on with the new; but he was out of town a while and the work went on without following his plan."[178]

Since the original building and graveyard jutted out into Market Street, after its removal, "traffic" reclaimed the building site and the final resting place of some of Wilmington's earliest leaders, including John Ancrum. Various paving materials eventually covered the area, but all did not go smoothly. On at least one occasion, the road collapsed. "A cave-in occurred at the intersection of Fourth and Market yesterday," stated the *Morning Star*, on May 25, 1878, "leaving a hole in the space between the rails of the street car track about 10 feet deep and 2 or 3 feet across. A venerable citizen suggests that a vault may have been located at the spot where the earth gave way."[179]

John S. Norris served as supervising architect of the Walter building, a job for which he received $5 a day. Christopher H. Dahl was the lead carpenter. The two men worked as a team. Both came to Wilmington from New York. Mr. Dahl, a native of Shelbourne, Nova Scotia, had already logged in 25 years as a carpenter in New York before he arrived. He would die soon after the church was completed, while working on the deRosset House on the northeast corner of Second and Dock streets.

In July 1841, Eliza Ann Lord deRosset wrote, "Poor old Mr. Dahl. The head workman and superintendent of Armand's building was taken off yesterday with a bilious fever. He has left a large family whom he intended to bring on next year. He is more regretted, I suppose, than any other man of that class in town – and that being a stranger somewhat, it has excited a great deal of sympathy."[180]

Mr. Dahl, who died at age 49, was buried in St. James Graveyard. After his death, his son, John Dahl (sometime written as Dall), worked with John S. Norris. The Norris-Dahl team, active in the Wilmington building movement from 1839 until 1846, was at the center of a flurry of construction that included not only St. James Church, but the United States Custom House and the new façade of the Bank of Cape Fear. Apparently John S. Norris either designed or altered houses for A. J. deRosset, Jr., Thomas H. Wright, John Wooster, and P. K. Dickinson.[181]

Platt Dickinson, John Wooster, Thomas H. Wright, W. B. Giles, and Robert Brent Drane signed a testimonial to John S. Norris before he moved his business to Savannah. "The taste and durability displayed in the buildings, public and private, which have been erected in this place under your superintendence have given general satisfaction and they have been built, we believe, at a cost having a due regard to the interests of your employers."[182]

Norris left Wilmington for Savannah where he worked in the years leading up to the Civil War. His most famous houses there were the Mercer House, made famous by the John Berendt book, *Midnight in the Garden of Good and Evil*; the Andrew Low House; and the Gothic style Green-Meldrim House. But Norris's influence continued to shape Wilmington after his departure. His "understudy," local builder Benjamin Gardiner, contracted the 1847-1848 Market House, and the 1847 John A. Taylor House — a study in marble located at 409 Market Street.[183]

John Coffin Wood served as principal mason of St. James. His brother, Robert Barclay Wood, was the "builder." Robert had lived in Wilmington briefly in 1833 when he assisted his uncle, Phineas Fanning, with his newspaper, *The People's Press*. Fanning may have come to Wilmington because of a connection with Gen. Joseph Gardner Swift since they were both related to the Coffins of Nantucket. Fanning was a member of St. James and presumably was the agent by which the church obtained the talented Wood brothers in 1838.[184]

St. James would be the Wilmington debut of a grand career for the Wood brothers. "These gentlemen erected many of the handsomest brick edifices in the city," wrote W. B. McKoy. "Among other buildings put up by this firm may be mentioned the entire block on the north side of Market Street, from Col. Hedrick's store to the corner of Second Street; the building at Exchange Corner and others to the west of it; Granite Row on South Front Street; the Anderson House, now a part of Orton

House; the Post Office; the City Hall and Opera House; the Front Street Methodist Episcopal Church, the Central Carolina Railroad office building and many others."[185]

After the Great Fire of 1841, the Wood brothers were joined by master carpenters "Mr. Haines and Mr. Ferguson," also from Nantucket. Together, they "built up the town with brick houses of a far better sort than had been known here," wrote Robert's son, Dr. Thomas Fanning Wood.[186]

The pew floor plan for St. James was based roughly on another building Walter designed: Church of the Epiphany in Philadelphia. At St. James, the actual pews were a gift to the church from Dr. Thomas Henry Wright. The church then sold the pews for different prices, depending on location. Downstairs, front and center pews tended to cost $500. A good pew in the rear could cost $200, and a few pews in the gallery went for a bargain price of $75. Printed forms were distributed that left the option open: "Subscription for a Pew valued at _____ in the Church Edifice, to be erected under the direction of the Vestry of St. James Church."[187]

On March 16, 1840, the vestry declared that no changes could be made to the new building's paint, construction, or furnishings without consent of the vestry. Apparently this included the new crimson-colored pew cushions. Although parishioners supplied their own cushions, architect Thomas U. Walter was known to request that they all be the same color. As late as 1880, church members also brought their own rugs for their pews, creating a patchwork effect throughout the church.[188]

The consecration of the new building occurred on March 29, 1840, only roughly a year after construction began. Indeed, the church was not entirely finished and would not be for several years. The exterior was still lacking stucco, but the brick must have been beautiful considering the compliments it earned. For a city of just 3500 people, the raising of such a church was a masterful achievement.[189]

Clergymen from the diocese were in attendance — as well as virtually every member of the church who had the physical strength to attend. Ives proudly declared St. James Church, "a model of Church Architecture" and stated that the building's "appropriateness of style, beauty of proportion, and elegance of finish" was unsurpassed by any Church edifice in our country.

Bishop Ives was assisted by the Rev. Dr. R. B. Drane and several other clergymen, including the Rev. Mr. William H. Spear of St. Michael's Church in Charleston. During the three-day event, Edwin Geer was ordained. He would serve as rector of St. Peter's Church in Washington, N.C., and as a post chaplain in Wilmington during the Civil War. Vestrymen present included A. J. deRosset, A. J. deRosset, Jr., W. B. Giles, W. C. Lord, William A. Williams, and Thomas H. Wright. [190]

Then proudly, the bishop proclaimed: "I, Levi Sillman Ives, by divine permission...have on this 29th day of March, in the year of our Lord one thousand eight hundred and forty...consecrated and set apart to the service of the Almighty God, a building by the style and title of St. James Church in the town of Wilmington; Separating it henceforth from all unhallowness, ordinary and common used, and dedicating it to the service of God."[191]

Adam Empie had added his own note of endorsement and praise on March 9, 1840, when he wrote, "I rejoice to hear that God has thus far crowned your efforts with success and that your church is ready for worship." However, he was probably not altogether pleased with the style which would have been a little too "High Church" for his tastes. Besides, Empie happened to be in the midst of building campaigns at St. James in Richmond — and the style wasn't Gothic. Low Church advocates like Empie probably smiled to themselves when, in 1847-1848, Wilmington's St. Thomas Catholic Church began to rise from the ground, looking for all the world very much like St. James Church.[192]

When the building was at a reasonable state of completion, bronze chandeliers, a reading desk, and the deRosset pulpit were put in place. All were gifts of the "ladies of the congregation," led at the time by "Mrs. Caroline Holmes, Mrs. E. H. Lord, Mrs. E. A. Wright, Mrs. E. J. deRosset, and Miss M. M. deRosset." The ladies paid a firm in Philadelphia $320 for the whole group of chandeliers. The lights were in place by December 2, 1840, eight months after the church building was dedicated. The women also contributed two chairs for the chancel for which they paid $55. In addition, they gave a whopping $592 for other church furnishings. A new organ had been delivered long before the building was ready. It arrived from New York in sixteen boxes in October 1839.[193]

The tower bell and clock were installed about August 1840. Both were gifts of Platt K. Dickinson, a wealthy lumber merchant. Dickinson paid George Handel Holbrook of East Medway, Mass., $622.52 for the bell and clock. The Holbrook firm was already an old one, being the third bell foundry in the U. S. The founding member of the family had been an apprentice of Paul Revere. George H. Holbrook created over 10,000 church bells in his career, as well as bells for cities and colleges. George J. Read escorted the St. James bell and clock from Medway to Wilmington, and installed them in the tower. Dickinson paid Read $132.10.[194]

The bell came with a warranty, but that didn't help when it was "broken in ringing" about December 1842. The new one was installed in 1843. It weighed 1540 pounds and proved to be "of excellent sound."[195]

In 1834, Platt Dickinson spearheaded Wilmington's first railroad, the Wilmington and Weldon. The line was completed the same year the clock and bell were installed. They are gifts that seem almost symbolic of the old railroad: time and bells. Dickinson also gave so much financial support to St. James that he was rewarded with a free lot "for family vaults" in the churchyard. Platt Dickinson and his wife, wife, Alice, raised Alice's nephew Pembroke Jones as their own child after Jones's mother died in 1859.[196]

The Rev. Dr. Robert Brent Drane chose the marble baptismal font. However, again it was the distaff membership of the church that footed the bill. The money was "placed in his hands by the little girls of his charge."[197]

Dr. Drane resigned in January 1843 to serve as president of Shelby College, an Episcopal school of brief promise in Shelbyville, Ky. Dr. Drane would return to Wilmington a year later, but the church was left temporarily in the lurch. Many ministers were called but declined.

Finally, the Rev. Mr. Richard Hooker Wilmer (1816-1900) accepted a call. Though he served for only a short time, he was a distinguished rector with a rich background. A Virginian who graduated from Yale in 1836, Wilmer received his D. D. in 1850 from the College of William and Mary, and his LL.D. from Oxford in 1867. He served parishes in N. C. and Virginia until 1864 when he was consecrated Bishop of Alabama by the Protestant Episcopal Church of the Confederate States of America.

The Rt. Rev. Richard Wilmer. (Richard H. Wilmer, *The Recent Past From a Southern Standpoint: Reminiscences of a Grandfather*)

Richard Wilmer, whose family was acquainted with Robert E. Lee, is credited with the words of the Prayer for the Officers and Crews of the Confederate States Navy. As a result of the Civil War, Bishop Wilmer garnered much publicity for an act reminiscent of an event at St. James: He asked his clergyman to omit the prayer "for the president and all in authority." General George H. Thomas disciplined Wilmer by relieving Wilmer of his position — but President Johnson reversed Thomas's action.

Interestly, Richard Wilmer's brother, George, was his assistant at St. James. Their interest in the church was only natural. The brothers were great-nephews of James J. Wilmer, the clergyman who proposed the name, "Protestant Episcopal Church" to a meeting of the "Church of England in the Colonies," in 1783.[198]

Richard and George Wilmer were sons of the Rev. Dr. William H. Wilmer, a distinguished churchman who published a periodical, the *Washington Theological Repertory*, and served as a founder of Virginia Protestant Episcopal Seminary. Also, like Adam Empie, William Wilmer was president of the College of William and Mary, and rector of Bruton Parish Church.

Perhaps one reason a beautiful new church would have trouble getting and keeping a rector could be finances. One Sunday in April of 1845, vestrymen distributed a form marked by the words, "...to be read after leaving the church." Noting financial concerns as an embarrassment, the vestry

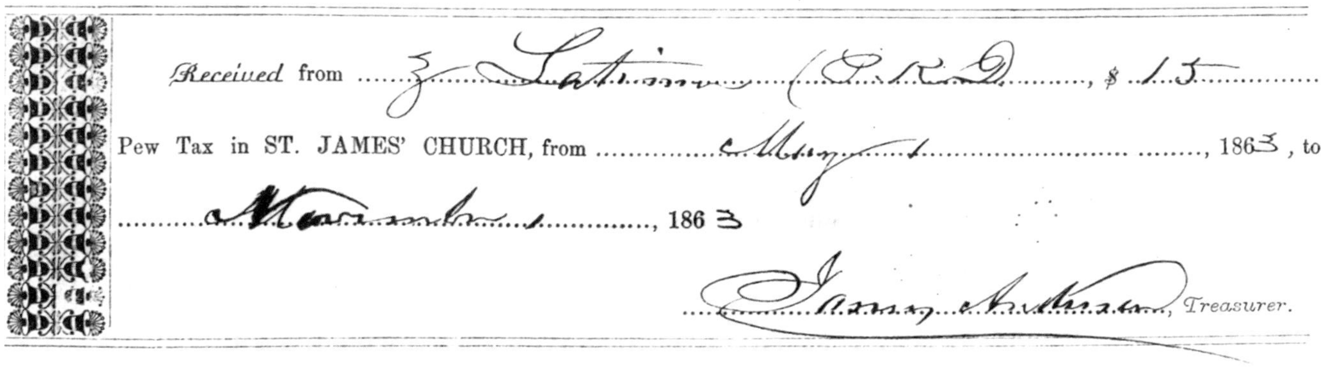
Received from ....Z. Latimer (P. R. D.)........., $ 15..........
Pew Tax in ST. JAMES' CHURCH, from ....May 1.................., 1863, to
........November 1.........., 1863
..........................., Treasurer.

Pew taxes, a throwback to Merry Old England, bolstered the church budget. (UNCW)

appealed for donations.

"In order that the Edifice in which you now worship might be completed, the Vestry were authorized to borrow the money…." Interest on the loan, insurance on the church and rectory, taxes, the sexton's salary, the organist's fee, repairs, and lights and fuel amounted to a whopping $450 a year. However, pew rents and taxes afforded only enough money to pay the rector. The finishing work on the church was not completed either. The vestrymen pointed out that if the members did not give more generously, the "rectory, — the home of your pastor" would have to be sold. The communication closed with the words "By order of the Vestry."[199]

Apparently the church members came through, for soon the Wood brothers began improvements to the front entrance of the church. They built or rebuilt steps and paved the walkways. About the same time, the church realized more capital when 16-foot squares of land were offered for sale as gravesites. The new part of the churchyard, now sometimes called "The City of the Dead," was created on land left vacant after the old church was dismantled." Speed was imperative in buying and using them. "As it is probable that interment in the grave yard may in a short time be prohibited, persons wishing to purchase had best make early application," read the advertisement in the *Peoples' Press*.[200]

The following year, there was unexpected work to do. One of the side finials blew off the roof of the new building during October, usually a windy month for Wilmington. It landed on the iron fence that surrounded the church, and destroyed one of the "panels."[201]

The fence panels were distinguished-looking wrought iron units, about four feet across. Within each rectangle, there were about three diagonals of iron crisscrossed by three other diagonals. It was a handsome fence that ran down the Market and Third street sides of the church.[202]

The finial was repaired in a timely manner. The first known photograph of Wilmington, taken in 1847 or early 1848, features them all intact. The photo, the first known landscape image of North Carolina, was possibly taken by famous daguerreotypist John Plumbe, Jr. The next known

This daguerreotype, taken from an upstairs room at St. John's Lodge (125 Market Street), is the first known image of Wilmington, and the first landscape photo taken in North Carolina. Pictured here about 1848, the new St. James building still has all its finials. (Courtesy of the Lower Cape Fear Historical Society and Amon Carter Museum)

image of St. James, an engraving done for *Ballou's Pictorial Drawing Room Companion* in 1855, indicates that only the westernmose two side finials had survived — and those attached to the tower. An unnamed hurricane may have been the culprit.

Apparently the 427-pipe organ was not as well-received as the building and was probably bought used. A new organ was needed. In March 1848, the following announcement appeared in *The Wilmington Commercial.* "Advertisement! The organ, at present in use at St. James Church, Wilmington, is well suited for the purpose of a small Church or Musical Society, and will be sold low; apply to S. Jewett, J. Gammell, or W. A. Burr."[203]

Mr. and Mrs. Armand J. deRosset spent the month of July, 1846, on "the Sound" as guests of Dr. and Mrs. Thomas H. Wright. That month at Mount Lebanon must have been like Episcopal camp: Four adults, 8 Wright children and 10 deRosset children. In fact, writing of her brother's family, Eliza deRosset said, "They have a monstrous family." The youngest deRosset was Annie, 3 months old, who would live only to the age of nine and would be the first person buried in Oakdale Cemetery, in 1855. The two men both grew up across the street from the church. The deRossets lived directly across the street from the Burgwin-Wright House. Their shared summer vacation indicates that they were truly good neighbors.[204]

Although he lived most of his middle years in the house he built at 23 South Second Street, Armand J. deRosset, Jr., was born and died in the deRosset House on the northwest corner of Third and Market streets. Dr. Wright lived his entire life in the Burgwin-Wright House and at Mount Lebanon. Both were doctors who abandoned medicine to pursue lucrative business interests. Both were directors of the Wilmington and Weldon Railroad. Armand deRosset had the honor of traveling to England in 1849 to sell local bonds and choose iron rails that would replace the railroad's wooden ones. And the two of them were arguably the strongest St. James laymen of the 19th century.

According to Mary Ellen Gadski, a noted historian and an authority on the deRosset family, "Much of the deRossets' social life revolved around their activities in the Episcopal Church. During his lifetime, Armand J. deRosset, Jr., held every ecclesiastical position that could be held by a layman: vestryman (for 62 years), warden, deputy to Diocesan and General Conventions, treasurer of the Diocese, Chairman of the Committee of Canons, and a delegate to all Diocesan Conventions from 1855-1897 (plus 5 scattered years)."[205]

Armand J. deRosset, Jr., was also a trustee of the General Theological Seminary in New York — an honor shared by at least one other St. James communicant: Walker Taylor III. DeRosset's wife, Eliza Jane Lord deRosset, was active in all the women's activities at St. James and was the chief organizer of charity bazaars that were held every December. The deRossets "almost always attended the yearly Diocesan conventions together as the highlight of their social season," wrote Ms. Gadski. "When the convention was hosted in Wilmington, such as it was in 1854, their houses were filled with out-of-town guests for weeks at a time."[206]

On January 22, 1847, Phineas W. Fanning and J. Ballard announced that the "Burying Ground" was in for some changes – and a little defining. Open spaces were to be graded and unmarked graves were begging identification. "Notice is given to all persons having friends buried therein…to come forward immediately and make arrangements…concerning bodies that may have been deposited in the ground. Otherwise, after the grading is made, particular graves cannot be designated, and it will be impossible to lay off the ground with any reference to the promiscuous manner in which it has heretofore been occupied."[207]

On May 14, 1848, sixteen days after it left New York, a new church organ steamed up the Cape Fear River aboard the schooner *Tioga.* However, much assembly was required: It arrived in 20 cases. Parishioners must have marveled at the quality of the instrument crafted by George Jardine of New York. An organ maker since 1839, Jardine eventually created instruments for St. Patrick's Cathedral; Most Holy Trinity, in Augusta, Ga.; St. George's in New York City; and many other churches, as well as private residences.[208]

But church organs were the last things on the minds of some parishioners. Gold glittered far brighter. In 1849, a significant number of Wilmingtonians moved to California during the great "gold rush." St. James lost some of its most adventuresome members, including Richard Savage, John Walker, Jr., Henry Savage, P. C. Calder, and several members of the Ware family. Henry Bradley would also move to San Francisco where he would become a renowned photographer.

By 1850, St. James Church had already outgrown its new building. Though too small for its needs, it was too aesthetically pleasing to alter. In early March of that year, Magdalene deRosset lay dying of appendicitis. Unmarried and only 33 years old, she requested that her father, Dr. Armand deRosset (Sr.), give her portion of his estate toward the purchase of a building lot for a new church congregation.

Fund-raising campaigns followed and many older members of the church gave liberally. In all, St. James supplied $15,000 in building funds. Most of the older folks remained at Third and Market. However, a large group of younger generation members of St. James left to create the new congregation. On November 21, 1853, Bishop Atkinson, Dr. Drane, and wardens Dr. Thomas H. Wright and Dr. A. J. deRosset helped lead the way when members processed from St. James to the laying of the cornerstone for the new church at Third and

Wilmington artist Claude Howell created this image of St. John's Church. (Louise Wells Cameron Art Museum)

Red Cross streets. The event was filled with "prayer and praise."

But St. James's support of St. John's didn't end with the ground-breaking ceremony. Youth groups held fundraising events, and even the younger children helped create a reason for giving. "The street tonight has been perfectly illuminated by skyrockets and Roman candles," wrote Eliza Gibbs to Mrs. William B. Giles, on December 27, 1853. "The children had a fair Friday and Saturday night for the benefit of the new church and though the weather was very bad, they made about five hundred dollars."[209]

Additionally, the women of the church kept their needles clicking for the cause. "The Ladies of the St. James Sewing Society are vigorously continuing preparations for the Fair to be held on the 22nd, 23rd, 24th, December," announced a local newspaper. "The proceeds will be applied to the completion of St. John's Church. Contributions of money, fancy articles and refreshments from friends in town or country may be left at Dr. Drane's, or Mrs. W. C. Lord's, or made through any member of the congregation."[210]

The surviving Cedrus Deodara tree in the churchyard was one of two given to Elizabeth Cassidey in 1850. The wedding gifts arrived on sailing ships from Maine. Miss Cassidey, who married J. T. Munds, is said to have planted the trees herself. (Virginia Bellamy Ruffin notebooks, Lower Cape Fear Historical Society.)

By the time of the Diocesan Convention of 1853, St. James had 241 white and 25 black communicants. Dr. Thomas Wright, James Severin Green, Joshua Grainger Wright, and Asa. A. Brown served as delegates. Again, it was a family affair. The first three were grandsons of Elizabeth Sharpless and Richard Bradley, and Asa A. Brown was married to the Bradleys' great-granddaughter.

The Cedrus Deodara tree, or Cedar of Lebanon, just south of the church, was a wedding gift to Elizabeth Cassidey who married the Rev. James Theus Munds in 1850. Miss Cassidey was the daughter of Sophia and James Cassidey who moved from

Wilmington artist Claude Howell drew this image of St. James in 1932. (Courtesy of the Cape Fear Museum)

Anything but Civil

"I have been driven many times to my
knees by the overwhelming conviction
that I had nowhere else to go."
– Abraham Lincoln

The Civil War began April 12, 1861. It would bring death, despair, and ravaged bank accounts to most families of St. James Church. For those at home, the sadness was most bitter and intense when sons of the church lost their lives. They were bright-faced young men the congregation had watched through boyhood, seen confirmed at the altar — and observed as they came and went to college and for their Grand Excursions abroad. Some gave their lives, and others bore ill effects of their wounds for the rest of their days.

Inner conflicts must have made fighting even more difficult for many of the St. James boys, for Adam Empie's anti-slavery stance had echoed through their homes, causing some masters to free their slaves. Additionally, St. James had strong New York-New England ties as a result of family connections, church business, and commerce. And the tenderness that is evidenced in correspondence from those days testifies to a warm bond between whites and the blacks who worked for them. A letter from young James Allan Wright to his brother, Tommie, is representative of the interest shown in the blacks who worked in their households. Corresponding from Dublin, Ireland, in 1855, he said "....write to me and tell me all about the boat races — the news at the Sound — Clayton (Giles), Johnnie Bradley, and Willie Gus (Wright); and the servants."[217]

But just because a war was raging did not mean that other tragedies stopped. Five months after the war began, Robert Drane mourned the loss of parishioner, church neighbor, and friend Dr. Thomas Henry Wright.

Dr. Drane, defying his own self-imposed ban on eulogies, praised Wright in such glowing terms that he apologized during the funeral service. "I know the force of the language I am using. It is an occasion, to me, far too solemn and painful." Drane said that not only St. James, but St. John's would probably not have been built if it had not been for Wright's efforts. He was a graceful force in leadership, spirituality, and finance. There were many occasions in which his weekly offering to St. James rivaled the sum total of all the other contributions for the day. Wright served as vestryman, warden, and "chief financial agent"; a representative to diocesan and general conventions; and as a member of the Board of Missions. [218]

Dr. Wright even served as a public relations man for St. James by contributing anonymously many news items to the *Wilmington Daily Herald.* He died on September 21, 1861, after five years of nursing his wife, Mary Allan, who was blinded and horribly disfigured in an accident that occurred January 18, 1857: a rare day of snow and ice. All the while Dr. Wright battled what seemed symptomatically to be rheumatoid arthritis, a painful and, in those days, fatal illness. Dr. Wright's own physician and pharmacist, Dr. William B. Giles, did what he could for his patient, but the prevalent local drugs of the day — camphor, paregoric and laudanum, could do little to heal.

When Dr. Wright died, family friend, Mount Lebanon neighbor, and Confederate soldier

> *"A father in our Israel has fallen.*
> *We behold his earthly tabernacle*
> *before us in ruins.*
> *The pure, heaven-born spirit,*
> *which so lately inhabited it,*
> *has gone to Him who gave it."*
>
> *— from Dr. Drane's eulogy for Thomas H. Wright, 1861.*

John Reston Giles wrote to Mrs. Wright from Thunderbolt Battery, near Savannah. "From my earliest childhood, I had learned to love the Doctor, and in my mind he has ever been associated with all that is good and right. How I used to love to see him in the little pulpit at the Sound!

"How I loved to hear him reading the beautiful service of our church; for there was always so much fervor and so much warmth in his manner - and then too, his deep piety and Christian spirit were so apparent and so beautifully displayed that I had always regarded him as one of the finest of earth - This feeling too had grown with my growth, and you cannot realize how I used to miss him whenever his place was vacant - really, his presence used to have such an effect, and add so much to the devotions of the whole congregation."[219]

John Giles would become yet another Civil War casualty, dying July 8, 1863, from wounds he received at Gettysburg. He was buried in Mount Lebanon Graveyard.

Dr. Wright's son, James Allan Wright, wrote, "My heart is full of gratitude when I remember how immeasurably kind and generous he was to me and full of sorrow when I reflect that his kindness can never more be manifested to me. I remember now when last at home how he would surpress the cry of pain to talk pleasantly to me about my campaign and my company and I feel like crying when I remember his last token of respect and affection for me - how, sick as he was, he dressed himself to be down at breakfast with me (this an unusual thing for him) and to say what doubtless he feared would be his last goodbye and which it proved to be.

"I was writing to Tommie the other day and was telling him that among the memories of our fine Father none came to me with more love or more freshness than his teachings during my

Robert Drane Williams, the son of Sarah and W. A. Williams, was baptized October 8, 1838. His was the first baptism in the new St. James church building. (Courtesy of Robert M. Williams, Jr.)

childhood. Ungrateful indeed must we be if any of his children can ever forget the fond solicitude with which he watched our studies and implanted within us a knowledge of what was right. And in late years too it seemed to me as if he was a part of my life; so thoroughly attached is he in my memory to everything I love at home.."[220]

Nine months later, the eloquent writer of that tribute was also dead. James Allan Wright, that first baby baptized at Mount Lebanon Chapel, would be one of the first to die — in 1862, at the Battle of Mechanicsville, Va. Historian James Sprunt said that Capt. Wright "was the most brilliant young man of Wilmington — and of the state."[221]

Robert Drane Williams, the first baby baptized in the 1839 St. James church building, was also a Civil War-era casualty. According to his great-nephew, Robert M. Williams, Jr., he was a Confederate naval officer who died of yellow fever while on duty in Bermuda. Other casualties included William Wooster, John F. S. VanBokkelen, and Thomas Charles Wright.

But the Rev. Dr. Drane persevered, despite the horrors of war and the growing local terror: the 1862 yellow fever epidemic. The mosquito-borne disease struck about 1600 residents of Wilmington and proved fatal for around 600. The town shrunk to a population of 4,000 from deaths and mass evacuation. All businesses in Wilmington closed and citizens stayed at home, parting their draperies just long enough to see if the sound of horses' hooves signaled another makeshift hearse rolling toward Oakdale Cemetery[222] Virtually every family in town suffered at least one loss to the epidemic. Death by yellow fever is a painful and particularly nasty demise. A graphic description of the visual effects of the disease and the smells it produced would be enough to make many people feel ill. "The atmosphere was impregnated with the poison from pestilential vapors and noxious gases," wrote James G. Burr, "and the gentle breeze that cooled the heated frame brought death in its embrace."[223]

But Dr. Robert Brent Drane did not break stride. According to eyewitness James G. Burr, Dr. Drane "never for a moment wavered, but stood manfully at his post, and, undismayed by the horrors around him…could be seen at all hours visiting the sick, supplying them with such necessaries as could be obtained, administering the consolations of religion, and closing the eyes of many who had looked their last upon this earth."[224]

Even in the face of "death in the hovel and death in the hall," Dr. Drane "moved calmly forward on his errands of mercy, ministering to all without distinction of creed, bringing relief to the wearied body, and comforting the departing spirit with words of consolation and of hope." While St. James parishioner Marie Louise DuBrutz Reston recuperated from a near death experience with the fever, her two-day old son died. On October 11, 1862, Dr. Drane and William Reston took the tiny body to Oakdale Cemetery and buried it. The rector was probably already suffering from yellow fever, for three days later he was dead.[225]

"Fell with his harness on," was how they said it at St. James. What members of the church who were still alive, and still in town, were devastated.[226]

The Rt. Rev. Thomas Atkinson, D. D., wore two vestments briefly when he became rector of St. James about two months after Dr. Drane's death. Even with a skeletal congregation, there was much to do. The Rev. Mr. Cameron MacRae, who was in Wilmington intermittently in 1862, assisted with some ecclesiastical duties, including funerals. Bishop Atkinson subsequently turned over the keys to St. James Church to his new assistant, the Rev. Alfred Watson, on March 2, 1863. It was Watson, who spoke to the Diocesan Convention two months later, recommending that the clergy not shy away from speaking of the war in their pulpits. Without knowing it, he also painted his own picture of the Civil War that would last for at least 141 years.

"And how shall the Church now guide her children aright," he asked, "if she looks not around her at the actual horizon; if she perceives not the circle of lurid flame that engirdles her; if she sees not the heavens black and still gathering blackness; if she feels not the earth as it rocks to the tread of armies and the roll of artillery; if she sees not the burning homes and trampled harvests of her children; or her widows and helpless infants and aged women, driven forth at one moment with a view to swell the supposed ravages of famine, and at another compelled by the invaders to remain as a breastwork for themselves; if she hears not the groans of the wounded and dying or the moans of the widow and fatherless, as, not one by one, but in great sheaves, the dread mower reaps down on the red field of battle, husband and father and brother and son? How shall God's Church teach faithfully the lessons of the hour, if she fails to see that War is in the land—or, seeing it, thinks it beneath her dignity to take notice of it in her pulpits?"[227]

In December 1864, Watson became rector and Bishop Atkinson resigned his post at St. James. But the bishop kept a large presence at St. James, often officiating at holiday morning services, while Watson took would take over the evening services.

Alfred Augustin Watson was born in Brooklyn, N. Y., in 1818. Like Bishop Atkinson, his first path of study led him to a law degree. But after graduating from New York University, and passing the bar, he moved to North Carolina where he worked as a tutor. Perhaps contact with Bishop Ives led him to a different vocation, for Watson soon entered the school where Ives had strong connections: General Theological Seminary in New York. In 1844, Alfred Watson was ordained deacon at St. Ann's in Brooklyn, the same church that the Swift and Empie families attended when they were living together thirty years earlier.[228]

When Alfred Watson returned to North Carolina, he served briefly at Plymouth before being ordained for the priesthood by Bishop Ives, in 1845. Watson supplemented his income by tutoring children who lived on plantations from Plymouth to New Bern, where in 1858 he was made rector of Christ Church. When the Civil War began, he enlisted as chaplain of the 2nd N.C. Infantry. In addition to services that were expected, he surprised the troops with his uncanny abilities as a scout. He resigned as chaplain in 1862. In 1868, Watson received an honorary doctorate from the University of North Carolina.

But in December 1864, Watson inherited a spotty congregation. Hordes of Wilmingtonians had fled the city. Members of the church who left town usually did not travel too far from Wilmington. Some members of the Wright, Murchison, and deRosset families were in Fayetteville. The Calders, Restons, and Gileses were in Hillsborough. Mr. and Mrs. Adam Empie, Jr., were in High Point. Other popular cities during the war were Pittsboro and Chapel Hill.

But for those who stayed, there were almost carnival-like amusements and distractions. The town filled with a wide variety of people from afar who mingled in the streets with a few of Wilmington's gentlemen who had been exempted from service. Almost everyone was trying to make money off the situation. Some of the newcomers were thieves and lifelong drifters. A few were murderers and bodies turned up with regularity.

But some of the visitors were well-heeled Europeans grabbing up chances for quick profit. The Burgwin-Wright House was occupied by employees of a British import company known as Alexander Collie and Co. Described as good-looking, young, blond, blue-eyed men, the Collie agents gave the communicants at St. James a lot to talk about. Cockfights, parties that lasted through the night, and activities that would make the Ladies' Working Society shudder filled the grand old house and spilled out under the old crabapple tree on the front lawn.[229]

Blockade runners continued to glide through the black waters when the moon was obscured. Europeans wanted cotton and Southerners needed almost everything. Of those who

Florie Maffitt Wright (1842 –1883), baptized aboard the frigate *Macedonian*, was the daughter of famed Civil War captain John Newland Maffitt, and the wife of Joshua G. Wright. She accompanied her father to Nassau on the *Gordon* in 1862, then ran the blockade again when she returned home aboard the *Nassau*. During fire from Yankee guns she sat on deck enjoying the excitement until the captain advised her to "go to her cabin." Florie Maffitt Wright, who died at the age of 41, was an aunt of Bishop Robert Strange who commissioned this portrait. (Courtesy of Agnes Rankin Beane.)

ran the blockade, Gabrielle deRosset, Florie Maffitt (Mrs. Joshua Grainger Wright), Capt. John Newland Maffitt, James Sprunt, and Capt. John Pembroke Jones are some of the names that were then or are now associated with St. James Church.[230]

The black market affected most locals adversely because they were offered the most ragged European and Oriental goods for the highest prices. Finer merchandise — teas, oranges, bananas, silks, fine wines, brandies, and preserved foods — were often scooped up by speculators who resold them at a profit. And the best products made their way directly to the Confederate administration in Richmond.

Sometimes civilians would wake in the night to the sound of cannons in the distance, and would know that a blockade runner had been spotted. Many vessels slithered through, but shipwrecks did occur, and when they did, the "demoralized men got intoxicated and stayed so for a week or two afterward." The Chaplain had his hands full.[231]

It was amazing that Fort Fisher, the gateway to Wilmington, stayed open as long as it did. But at Christmas 1864, all that changed. Union forces under General Benjamin Butler and the naval task force commander, Rear Admiral David Dixon Porter, attacked Fort Fisher. The naval bombardment was the largest of the Civil War, continuing relentlessly for two days. On Christmas Eve, at 1:40 a.m., anyone who was still in Wilmington felt the earth heave, the walls shake, and the bubble glass in their windows rattle, if not break; Benjamin Butler's powder ship had exploded. The ship contained 215 tons of ammunition and the wind was blowing in the direction of Wilmington. The sound of it was terrifying. One couple attempted to say the Lord's Prayer but found they had forgotten the words.[232]

The next day was Christmas Sunday. The shaken but faithful members of St. James gathered in the church to pray for God's help. But in the midst of their entreaty the big guns sounded, "boom, boom, boom."

During the bombardment, the deafening reverberations terrified civilian residents of Wrightsville Sound, where the regiment of Walter Gwynn MacRae was stationed. "We packed our trunks [at Honolulu, on Bradley Creek] and moved back to town," wrote Marie Louise Reston, who soon found her house occupied by Yankee officers and whose apartment at the bank [where her husband worked] was commandeered by Gen. Braxton Bragg.

That night, about 9 o'clock, Braxton Bragg sent his wife upstate on a special train. It was a "keynote of alarm." Word got around fast, and all who could, left Wilmington. But on Monday, the Union fleet sailed away. Confederate General W.H.C. Whiting recommended that Bragg beef up the Fort Fisher forces by bringing in forces from Virginia. Bragg, who stayed in a position of authority by the indulgence of President Jefferson Davis, refused. His lack of action verified a Richmond official's comment when he heard Bragg was being sent to Wilmington: "Goodbye Wilmington!"[233]

On January 13, 1865, Porter's armada renewed the attack on Fort Fisher. Outnumbered five to one, the Confederates were bombarded into submission and forced to surrender two days later.

According to Chris E. Fonvielle, Ph.D., a nationally recognized authority on the Civil War, and a cradle roll member of St. James Church, "In anticipation of the Federal capture of Wilmington, the Reverend Watson had obtained permission from the diocese bishop to refrain from offering prayers for Confederate leaders. So as not to offend St. James largely pro-Confederate congregation, the bishop directed Watson to so modify the liturgy as to avoid expressing allegiance to the United States. Prayers were only to be said for 'those in rightful authority,' or 'those in civil authority.'"[234]

"This I felt I had no canonical right to do," said Watson at the Diocesan Convention in 1866. "For this reason, and because I would, by its use, have made myself a party to the infringement of the liberty of the Church to direct her own worship, I refused compliance. The key of the church were then seized by military orders, emanating, I believe, from Major General [John M.] Schofield."[235]

Once again, Wilmington was occupied by the enemy, this time beginning on Ash Wednesday 1865. It was a painful blow not forgotten by any and never forgiven by some. "The Yankees turned the congregation out of St. James Chuch, Wilmington, N. C. and used it for a Hospital," wrote J. R. London.

His grandmother, Mrs. Eliza Hill Lord, said it differently: " The Heathen have entered our Land. They have spoiled our heritage, they have closed the Doors of our Prophets...."[236]

The Burgwin-Wright House and St. James Church were commandeered by Union General Joseph R. Hawley after Watson refrained from praying specifically for the president of the United States. The church occupation seemed particularly hateful. There were other large spaces available, and other hospitals around town, including the Seaman's Friend Society at Front and Dock streets. According to Alfred Watson, the beds moved into the church "were, indeed, never much more than half filled."

Church member J. G. Burr wrote, "General Hawley was born in N. C., we have understood, in Robeson County. His parents removed to Connecticut when he was an infant. While in command of the post of Wilmington, during the occupancy of the Federal troops, he boastingly remarked that he had returned to his native State to enforce correct principles. This wanton desecration of the Temple of God was, certainly, an apt illustration of his idea of 'correct principles.'"[237]

During the Union occupation of St. James, the congregation worshipped at "St. Paul's Chapel," a church housed on the northeast corner of Fourth and Orange streets. The Rt. Rev. Thomas Atkinson established St. Paul's in 1858 as a church of free pews and accommodations for blacks. The property was purchased from the Methodists and construction of the chapel was underwritten by Jane Cutlar Fleeming — sometimes spelled Fleming. The little church of "mixed congregation" was received into the Diocese of N. C. in 1859. Among others, Zebulon Latimer was a force in setting the church in motion. Bishop Atkinson conducted services there whenever time allowed.

The choir at St. Paul's was open only to blacks and they were taught everything possible without breaking the law. Since it was illegal before emancipation to teach minorities to read, the leaders of St. Paul's taught the catechism, Psalms, and hymns orally. War and yellow fever took its toll on St. Paul's and, except for occasional weddings, its doors closed from about 1862 until 1865.[238]

In 1865, St. Paul's had many uses. Not only did it serve as a temporary church home for members of St. James, but it was also a school for blacks. Between 200 and 300 black children attended the school that was funded by the Protestant Episcopal Church's new Freedmen's Commission. After St. James was again usable, St. Paul's reverted to a "colored congregation." Both St. James and St. John's Episcopal congregations supported the church. About 1869, St. Mark's Episcopal Church emerged from St. Paul's as, at the time, an exclusively black church. It was a joint project of St. James, St. Paul's and St. John's churches. In 1872, St. Paul's was re-established as a white church. In 1914, the congregation of St. Paul's chose to move to the new suburbs, a change recommended by the Rt. Rev. Robert Strange. With additions and alterations, St. Paul's Church remains on the northeast corner of Sixteenth and Market streets.[239]

The U. S. Army failed to tidy up when they vacated St. James Church. Alfred Watson expressed his feelings in a beautifully penned letter to the nation's capitol.

Wilmington, April 12, 1865
"To his excellency
Abraham Lincoln
President of the United States

Sir:

"When the forces of the United States arrived at that place they found...many persons...remained (80 families left in church) who had made up their minds to submit to the power of the United States.
"When Yankees entered, the church was closed by military authority, till Friday April 7, when it was seized for a hospital, entered by a crowd of soldiers and its internal arrangements removed. At the time of doing this there were and still are upon the same street and within 3 blocks, two other unfinished and unoccupied churches.

"The Temple of our Fathers where the present generation has been baptized, married, and received to the Communion, and whence the dead...have been buried – the principal church of the Diocese, has with every circumstance of irreverence, been torn to pieces with pickaxes and hammers....

"As the house of the most high God, it was scarcely a suitable object of political or military vengeance. As the sanctuary around which so many of the associations of the people cluster, its desecration and destruction were scarcely consistent with the spirit of conciliation or paternal government......" – Alfred Watson.[240]

But Lincoln would never see Watson's correspondence, for on that *very* same night, the President went to a play at Ford's Theater.

Watson also wrote to Edwin Stanton, the Secretary of War, requesting money to repair the building. But the funds did not come through and the congregation of St. James was forced to foot the bill. The church reopened triumphantly the second Sunday in Advent, 1865.[241]

Bishop Thomas Atkinson was the voice of divine diplomacy when Civil War sentiments threatened to permanently divide the National Church. (Reprinted from *Pictorial and Historical New Hanover County and Wilmington, N.C.,* by William Lord deRosset.)

Bishop Thomas Atkinson, in addition to the fact that he founded many churches and performed meritorious service in regard to looking after the needs of the newly freed slaves, also earned a place in national church history. According to Lockert Mason, M.D., author of "Separation and Reunion of the Episcopal Church, 1861-1865: The Role of Bishop Thomas Atkinson of the Diocese of N.C.," "Bishop Atkinson, more than any other person, kept the Protestant Episcopal Church together after the Civil War. There was no permanent split like there was with some other denominations."[242]

Bishop Lay was also a force for reconciliation. Richard Wilmer, former rector of St. James, and the Bishop of Alabama during the conference, also added that the absence of bishops Elliott and Davis " meant a great deal. There is no divine sanction in the legislative union of dioceses; and their absence meant, 'Let us wait, and see what it will be best to do.'"[243]

After the Civil War's end, the old church key was returned to Alfred Watson and would be used until at least 1940. A piece of the original 1839 key had been broken off, not unlike the condition of the congregation. Members of St. James Church struggled to adjust to heartbreak and losses. The death of sons in battle and family members to disease formed the most painful wounds of the heart, but economic losses pinched the pocket and sometimes required major changes in lifestyle. The collapse of the Bank of Cape Fear eroded many fortunes within the parish. "I felt as if I had been asleep and woke up in another century," said Phila Calder after she returned to Wilmington.[244]

In 1866, the Rev. Alfred Watson led the first Easter tower service at St. James. The ascension became a tradition and continues unbroken to the present day. The children climbed the stairs inside the 65' tower at daybreak and sang Easter carols. In later years, they sang "Waken Children of the King" by Annie Jones Hart, a beloved local schoolteacher who sang in the St. James choir. At 7:30 am, the Litany was said. Nida Brown, Anna Grant, and Maria Walker were three of the children who participated that first year. "That was part of the parish's expression of joy in having the use of their church again," wrote Maria Walker, about 1935.[245]

The children were also present for the 11 am morning prayer service and the 4 pm children's service. New communicants were confirmed during the evening service, making it a very long but inspirational day for the youngsters. Often, musicians who weren't members of St. James were invited to add their particular expertise. In 1901, Simeon A. (Happy) Schloss and James E. Wilson played cornets as they accompanied the children up the tower. Schloss (1865-1913), a relative of the Bear and Nathan families of Wrightsville Beach, owned theaters across the state. And music director Scotty Robertson would play the accordion, much to the delight of the children.[246]

In 2004, Jean McKoy Graham remembered the Easter traditions of her childhood, in the 1920s. "Mother always gave me oatmeal for breakfast on Easter morning. She said we had to have a substantial breakfast or we might get dizzy in the tower."

"We paraded by age. Silver crosses were awarded for perfect attendance on Easter afternoon."

Another postwar tradition was the St. James Home, a benevolent effort of the women of St. James. In 1861, the first seeds were sown for the project. Eliza Ann London Wright was the young widow of William Henry Wright, a tutorial student of Adam Empie, then a graduate of the College of William and Mary and the U. S. Military Academy. Eliza Wright died in 1861 at the age of 44. She left directions in her will that $1,000 be paid to St. James Church "upon the condition that they shall apply the same in the establishment of a church orphan asylum for that parish." Perhaps having lost two of her three children gave her an extra dose of love for all children.[247]

Then a subsequent will added to the fund. Mrs. Wright's mother, Sarah Elizabeth Lord London, left $500 to the same fund that would receive her daughter's gift. Mrs. London died in December 1865. Platt Ketchum Dickinson, Mrs. London's son-in-law and the businessman who spearheaded the creation of Wilmington's first railroad, had urged the church to make use of Eliza London Wright's gift in 1863. By the time Mrs. London's will was probated, in 1866, the fund contained at least $1500, a small fortune during Reconstruction.[248]

In 1866, the new arm of the Ladies' Working Society, the St. James Ladies Society for Parochial Work, included the following members: "Mrs. William Lord, Miss Lizzy deRosset, Mrs. P. K. Dickinson, Miss Empie Miller, Mrs. Alex McRae, Mrs. Dr. Thomas, Mrs. Graham Davis, Miss Eliza Walker, Mrs. Wm Wright, Mrs. Burr, Miss Annie Hotchkiss, Mrs. William Lippitt, Mrs. Jos. Lippitt, Miss Mary Lord, Mrs. William deRosset, Mrs. Armand deRosset, Miss Athalia Keith, Miss Mary Walker, Mrs. Mary Hill, Miss deRosset, Mrs. Gaston Meares, Miss Eliza Whitehead, Mrs. A. A. Watson, Mrs. deRosset, Mrs. Watson, Mrs. Meares, Miss Burr, Mrs. Wm Wright, Jo Lippitt, and J. Hill."

Though not members of the new ladies' group, Mrs. George Davis and her daughter-in-law, Mrs. Junius Davis, visited with the group and contributed to the cause. Mrs. Davis's husband, George Davis (1820-1896), is memorialized in the statue that sits on Market Street just north of the church.

He was an elegant writer, sought-after speaker, and a lawyer of distinction. He also served as an Attorney General of the Confederacy. The statue was sponsored by the United Daughters of the Confederacy but was due almost entirely to the efforts and generosity of James Sprunt and Gabrielle deRosset Waddell.

In 1868, the Ladies' Working Society had another great victory when they raised $1300 for the St. James Home during a winter festival. To put that kind of money in perspective, two months later, Mr. A.H. Van Bokkelen paid for the south side porch that leads from the St. James vesting room to the south lawn. It cost $100.[249]

On October 3, 1868, the Ladies' Working Society made another generous gift, but this time the recipient was the church. Representatives E. J. deRosset, Frances H. Watson, Alice H. Dickinson, and Eliza Lord "sold" Society Hall to the wardens and vestry of St. James for $1.00.[250]

Large churches require great maintenance and sometimes a faulty feature simply slips between the proverbial cracks. The church tower seemed to be municipal property at times. The city fire alarm was attached to the bell in the latter half of the 19th century — and the church clock, so prominent and handsome, once served as the town clock. But the bell and clock's care and repair has always been the responsibility of the church — and one of the easiest things to put off until "another time."

In 1869, during one of the clock's many long pauses, a local newspaper reporter sounded off. "Every time that we happen to pass St. James Church, our eyes involuntarily turn to the city clock, whose silent machinery, deathlike face, and immovable hands always excite our pity — pity that the poor old clock, which might be so industrious, cheerful, and happy is never permitted to do a particle of work, but is kept in about the same condition that the man would be in if suffering under the effects of a powerful drug — always in a *perfect stupor*, when a few hundred dollars judicially spent in doctoring it, would impart new life and vigor to its frame, and, like Magiell's pills, 'send the life blood bounding through its veins.' "[251]

Problems with the clock seem to be eternal. Brad Cantwell took care of the tower clock for about ten years or more, in the late 20th century. Local jeweler Albert Rhodes was called in for special challenges, but Mr. Cantwell changed the clock twice a year for Daylight Savings Time. "For Fall Back he could just turn the clock off, go eat lunch at the Cape Fear Club and come back to turn it on an hour later," remembered his wife, Nancy, in 2004. "But 'Spring Forward' involved a lot of math and me standing across the street shouting out the time. Spring Forward was a little stressful."[252]

The Rev. Johannes Adam Simon Oertel (1823-1909), who had charge of St. James for two months in late 1874, was one of the church's most interesting rectors. Born in 1823, he was a native of Furth, Germany (Bavaria). Oertel studied engraving in Nuremberg and painting in Munich. About 1848, he moved to New Jersey, where he worked as an art teacher, bank note engraver, and portraitist, all the while nurturing a deepening interest in the Protestant Episcopal Church.

Between 1857 and 1858 Oertel designed the ceiling in the chamber of the House of

Representatives in the Capitol. It is an interesting coincidence that at the same time, Thomas U. Walter, in addition to designing desks, designed 262 chairs for the House of Representatives chamber. When the South seceded in 1861, many of the chairs were redistributed. Photographers Matthew Brady and Alexander Gardiner received Walter's chairs. Subsequently, Abraham Lincoln was photographed in one of them.

Johannes Adam Oertel painted this portrait of Mariah Nida Brown McKoy as an angel. Nida Brown was a participant in the first Tower Service. (Courtesy of Jean McKoy Graham. Photo by John Bankson.)

Oertel's work there brought him into close contact with St. James architect Thomas U. Walter. Oertel and Walter, both members of the Washington Art Association, stood together professionally during some of the controversies that developed during the construction of the U. S. Capitol. Oertel became an Episcopal priest in 1871. In 1876, the Ladies' Memorial Association of N. C. commissioned him to paint the flag of the state as part of the centennial celebration. A year later, Oertel's painting, "The Prophet Elijah at Mount Horeb," won high marks from *The Union*, a publication located in the nation's capital.[253]

Johannes Oertel covered a lot of ground. His work is located in the National Cathedral in D.C. and the University of the South in Tennessee. He designed the Church of the Good Shepherd in Raleigh, and the reredos for the Church of the Incarnation in Washington, D. C. He created chancel paintings for St. Mary's Church in Abingdon, Md., and became best known for another religious work, "Rock of Ages."[254]

On June 6, 1875, St. James Church finally received a deed to the 6 1/2-acre Mount Lebanon Chapel tract. Although it was reported that the deed was lost or mislaid, the 1875 transaction includes the words, "The late Thomas H. Wright, being the owner of the tract of land which the parcel of land…is a part, agreed and determined to grant and appropriate the parcel of land referred to…for the use of the congregation which might thereafter desire to worship as members of the Protestant Episcopal Church, and whereas the late Thomas Henry Wright departed this life without having made the necessary conveyance of the same…."[255]

Dr. Wright's eldest son, Dr. Adam Empie Wright, also failed to deed the property to St. James. He inherited both the Burgwin-Wright House and Mount Lebanon but got little pleasure from either. Ill, financially insolvent, and suffering from Civil War wounds, the young surgeon, schooled at the New York University of Medicine, sold the town house in 1869 for $5,000 and lived his last painful years at Mount Lebanon. The guardian of his children, Marion Potter, fulfilled the original intent. "Marion Potter desires in full to carry into effect the praiseworthy puposes" of Dr. Wright.[256]

The chapel continued to be used regularly until about 1902. They were pleasant years at

Wrightsville. The Sound population had grown and the increased popularity of boat racing had added a new charm and camaraderie. One of the chapel-goers remembered it fondly. "Some of the memories of the old chapel parishioners are the sights of friends in a small boat poling across the marshes from the banks or up the Bradley's Creek bringing the families to worship. Horses and buggies came over the corduroy shell-topped roads — and the little chapel was filled."[257]

In 1871, St. James called in a genuine authority when they hired architect Henry Dudley to orchestrate repairs and improvements. An English architect who moved to New York after designing many churches in his homeland, Dudley is recognized as one of the leaders of the Ecclesiastical Movement, in which ancient Gothic architecture was molded and reinterpreted for the creation of buildings and edification of worshippers.

Henry Dudley, partnering with Frank Wills, designed a number of important buildings in the U. S. Dudley's work includes St. James Church, Bronx (1864); Grace Episcopal, Amherst (1865); St. Andrew's Church, Meriden, Conn. (1866); Church of the Resurrection, Richmond (1874); Church of the Nativity, Huntsville, Ala. (1859); and St. Paul's Church, in Syracuse, N. Y. (1884).

Dudley's 1871 improvements included repairing the church ceiling and roof. The ceiling had to be removed in March because it had been declared "unsafe." Even a small piece of ceiling could do significant damage after it fell 26' to a pew below. During March and early April, the congregation met for services at St. John's Church.[258]

After the plaster ceiling was replaced with an oak hammer-beam roof, workmen oiled and varnished the ceiling and tracery. Back on the ground floor, they also added seats on hinges for young children. The little seats were attached to the front of pews around the chancel.[259]

Henry Dudley also recommended expansion of the building. However, for budgetary reasons, the vestry tabled his recommendation It would not be considered again for fourteen years. In 1885, Dudley made revised proposals to add the south transept, organ chambers, and a choir room. The church's entire music program got a boost from the Rev. William H. Lewis, rector from 1885-1887. He was a lover of the arts who preached the spiritual benefits of song.[260,261]

In 1870 and 1871, James B. Purcell was assistant rector at St. James. Much about Purcell is a mystery, but it is known that he wore many hats – and was associated with a Wilmington hotel known as the Purcell House.[262]

One of the building's features came from some friends of the congregation a block away. "The inscription over the doors," explained Allan T. Strange in 2003, "was meant for the Temple of Israel. It was delivered to and installed in St. James by mistake. Back when they caught the mistake, members of St. James offered to have it removed and placed at the Temple of Israel. But they said to consider it a gift from them. I think we've redone it and we treasure it.

"St James and the Temple of Israel have always had a good relationship. We respect one another. The bond goes back a long way."[263]

In 1871, Wilmington earned a new title, one that stuck for a long time. Thomas M. Haddock, editor of *Haddock's Wilmington Directory* wrote, "Wilmington could, with propriety, be called 'The City of Churches.' We do not think it at all extravagant to say that some of the most imposing church architecture to be found in the entire South may be seen in this city. These churches are filled every Sabbath with orderly and devout worshippers, and the stranger visiting the city is struck with the remarkable quiet and calm which has now become characteristic of a Sunday in Wilmington. It is seldom that any disturbance whatever occurs to interrupt the peaceful monotony which broods over us, relieved only by church going, a stroll to the cemeteries, or an exchange of social pleasures."

On March 30, 1875, Easter morning, worshippers were greeted with a brilliant new sight. A solid brass lectern had just arrived from Europe and was used for the first time that spring morning. Bishop Atkinson conducted the morning services and confirmed 14 persons. Alfred Watson officiated at the evening where gas illumination made the brass lectern dance with light.[264]

A reporter from the Charleston *News and Courier* visited St. James in 1886. "The windows are very handsome, but the gems of the church adornment are a lectern and reading desk of richly fashioned and highly burnished brass."[265]

He described the church itself as an "ancient edifice ... surmounted by what can only be described as a bob-tailed tower, if the term is not too irreverent, and has just been enlarged by the addition of a wing, which if it were extended farther north would give the church a cruciform shape.

"....The organ and choir are placed in the chancel, the east wall of which is adorned with the *Ecce Homo* picture. The choir consists of about 20 acolytes, who wear surplice and soutane, from which it will be seen that St. James is 'High Church.' The Baptistry is situated to the left of the chancel and contains a rich marble font."[266]

John D. Bellamy's wife passed down one of the most famous quotes about St. James. During the 1930s, remembering the days when blacks sat in the balconies, she recalled one black woman shouting during a church service. An usher rushed to her side and urged her to be silent. According to Mrs. Bellamy the woman replied, "I've got religion." The usher's "well-remembered answer" to her was, "Don't you know that St. James Church is no place to have religion?"[267]

The St. James Home

"Sir, we would see Jesus." — John 12:21 (Text used by Mortimer Glover to describe the efforts of those who ministered through the St. James Home and Church of the Good Shepherd.)

In 1867, one more gift helped make the St. James Home a reality. Dr. and Mrs. Armand J. deRosset, Jr., "sold" St. James Church a block of property between Eighth and Ninth, and Orange and Ann streets for a dollar. Listed as Wilmington city lot number 133, the land came with at least one building. The property was deeded to "aid in establishing a home for indigent widows and orphans," a group that, "due to the capricious and indiscriminate ravages of war," included a few of Wilmington's elite citizens.[268]

Dr. deRosset also provided funds that would help maintain a residence on the property. The following year St. James Church began operation of the St. James Home. The building sat on a parcel of land that fronted 130 ' on Ninth Street and 230' on Orange Street. In 1871 the church enlarged

The Drs. deRosset, father and son, were both benefactors of St. James. Armand John deRosset, M.D., (1767-1859), a Princeton graduate, was physician for the Seamen's Hospital for 25 years. He rode horseback to make house calls until he was 90 years old. Dr. deRosset owned the property where the church now stands. His residence sat across the street diagonally. (Courtesy of UNCW)

Armand John deRosset, Jr., M.D., (1807-1897) was a physician at the U. S. Marine Hospital (Mount Tirzia) before becoming a successful businessman. Dr. deRosset built the house now know as the City Club at 23 South Second Street. He served on the St. James vestry for almost 60 years. (Courtesy of UNCW)

the St. James Home and erected a chapel. A school was also added to the main building.[269]

In 1873, a widow from Louisburg, N.C., known as "Mrs. Lawrence," began work at the St. James Home and School.

By 1879, the St. James Home campus was the chief venue for volunteer work for the women of St. James Church. But the effort had grown to a size that required administrative help. Part of the growth stemmed from a blue-collar population boom in Dry Pond, a working-class neighborhood that begins five blocks south of St. James Church. The establishment in 1875 of the Wilmington Cotton Mills brought many new people to live in factory houses . Lots of them had been struggling since the Civil War to put food on the table and clothes on their backs. A large factory with towering smokestacks, the complex was located on the Cape Fear River just north of Dawson Street. Though several members of the MacRae family founded it, Donald MacRae (1825-1892) became the dominant force in 1878. After his death, his sons, Hugh and Donald, Jr., both M. I. T. graduates, operated the mills, in addition to other business endeavors. The residence of Donald MacRae, Jr., at 25 South Third Street, is now the St. James Church parish house.[270]

For most of the years that volunteers and teachers ran St. James School, legendary educator Amy Morris Bradley was also teaching in Wilmington. But there was need for more than just Tileston School. Many of the Dry Pond neighborhood children held jobs, so St. James School arranged class times to conform to their schedules. The school also provided less classical training and more lessons in basic hygiene and manners.[271]

Because of the mission's rapid growth, Bishop Atkinson sought the assistance from Bishop Henry Codman Potter of New York in employing Episcopal nuns to lend a hand. Sisters of the Good Shepherd was an order headquartered in New York City. The initial meeting of the group was held in 1869 at a service in Brooklyn's St. Ann's Church, the same place that had been a church home to the Empies and Swifts from 1814 to 1817.[272]

Apparently, Mrs. Lawrence then left Wilmington to prepare for sisterhood in New York. A few months into her period of "probation," or training, Bishop Potter transferred two women to St. James to work under the supervision of Alfred Watson. One was already a nun, and the other was Mrs. Lawrence, known by that time as "Sister Cecelia." It is unclear what happened to the anonymous nun – or the other two who would join them later, but Sister Cecelia made a very beautiful name for herself through thirteen years of selfless good deeds. Bishop Atkinson officiated at St. James Church when she was fully received into the Order of the Good Shepherd in 1880.[273]

According to the 1879 records of the Diocese of New York, "One of these [nuns] has had charge of a parish school, now numbering 55 pupils, a sewing school for the same, and a weekly night class for those boys and girls who work in a factory all day. The other has the charge of St. James' Home, and gives her whole time to "house to house" visits among the poor whites, and 'cottage readings' in their own houses and in the school room.

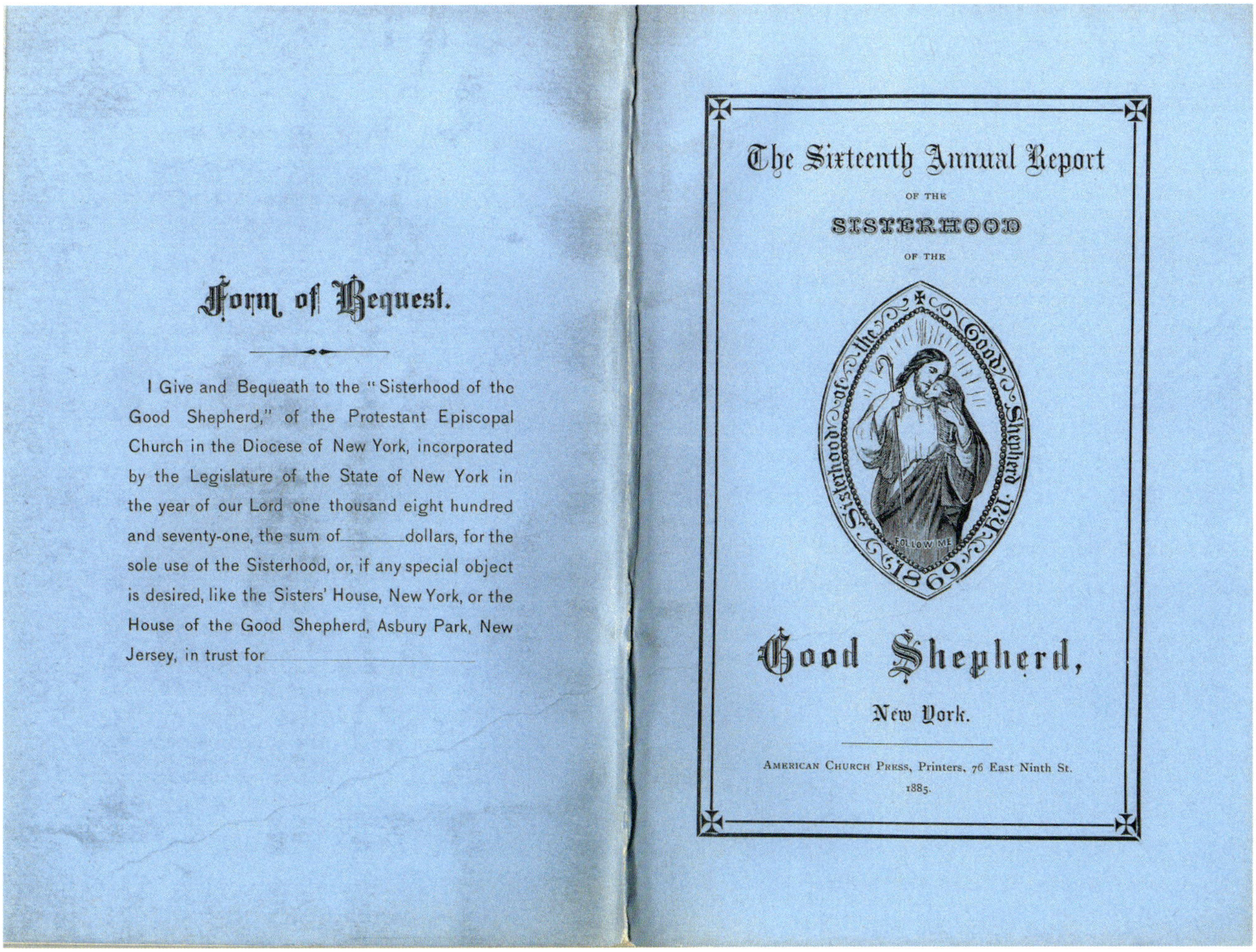

Form of Bequest.

I Give and Bequeath to the "Sisterhood of the Good Shepherd," of the Protestant Episcopal Church in the Diocese of New York, incorporated by the Legislature of the State of New York in the year of our Lord one thousand eight hundred and seventy-one, the sum of________dollars, for the sole use of the Sisterhood, or, if any special object is desired, like the Sisters' House, New York, or the House of the Good Shepherd, Asbury Park, New Jersey, in trust for______________

The Sixteenth Annual Report

OF THE

SISTERHOOD

OF THE

Good Shepherd,

New York.

American Church Press, Printers, 76 East Ninth St.
1885.

The nuns of the Good Shepherd and many members of St. James Church gave selflessly to the St. James Home and school. Sister Cecelia sent home to New York reports that were published in the annals of the Sisterhood of the Good Shepherd. (Courtesy of Wade H. Kempton, archivist of the Diocese of New York)

"Recently they have taken into the 'Home' two men, obliged to leave the Hospital, and having no home of their own where they could be nursed."[274]

The "cottage readings" were very popular. One elderly woman who had once attended the St. James Church Sunday School walked two miles just to hear the readings. The "house to house" visits were credited with for most of the increase in attendance.

The nuns also conducted cooking classes and established an early daycare center for infants. They also arranged outings for the "poor women and children" – field trips that opened wider the small world of their charges. Several times they took river excursions aboard the *Passport,* Captain John Harper's steamer. Members of St. James paid their passage and it was reported that even the women were refreshed by the trip and the infants basked in the river breeze. Individual parishioners

Members of St. James Church made sure that the women and children associated with the St. James Home got a trip on the *Passport.* The steamer belonged to John Harper, the debonair captain who eventually owned the *Wilmington*, the *Southport*, and the train at Carolina Beach known as the *Shoofly.* (Courtesy of Lower Cape Fear Historical Society)

also gave valuable services to the ministry. Dr. George Thomas provided free medical care. Anonymous angels, possibly Kate Walker Whiting and Kate deRosset Meares, provided carriages whenever the nuns were called to minister anywhere out of walking distance.[275]

The St. James School's enrollment would soon grow to its limit of 130 pupils. The institution would eventually serve to educate thousands of students who had few other options during Reconstruction. In addition to academic and trade school programs, the pupils were schooled to be fine young Episcopalians. The annual baptism often exceeded that of St. James Church. In 1885 alone, 35 children and 15 adults were baptized — and in 1885, Bishop Watson confirmed 19 new communicants.[276]

Eventually, Sister Cecelia not only managed the St. James Home and school, but led worship services, started a Sunday School program, and acted as a family counselor. Her work inspired others to donate to the St. James Home. A $500 bequest from the estate of Mrs. James Dawson, who also left pews 29 and 75 to the vestry, helped make the construction of a chapel possible. Funds were also provided for a new "day nursery," in 1887.[277]

By 1892, the mission campus was becoming cramped. The day school had an enrollment of 100 pupils and the Sunday School comprised 140 members. Word was sent to the Diocese of New York that "the work has outgrown present accommodations, and is in great need of a Mission Church."[278]

That same year, perhaps because of illness, Sister Cecelia announced she was leaving the school and moving to New York. In June 1892, the St. James School was closed by order of the vestry: a group that included Dr. A. J. deRosset, Clayton Giles, Col. John W. Atkinson, Col. W. L. deRosset, Hon. A. M. Waddell, Dr. George G. Thomas, William Calder, W. A. Williams, T. D. Meares, J. Hal Boatwright, H. A. Burr, and Joshua G. Wright. The vestry and Alfred Watson gave Sister Cecelia a large farewell party at the Bishop's House at 510 Orange Street.[279]

The St. James Church vestry made plans to build a separate chapel for the St. James Home and situate it in a central location for the regular worshippers. Funds were collected in 1892 and chapel and hall were constructed at Sixth and Queen streets. The new mission was named "Chapel of the Good Shepherd in honor of the Sisterhood under which Sister Cecelia labored here so long and faithfully."[280]

On January 21, 1894, Sister Cecelia died in New York City, at Hospital of the Good Shepherd. She was only 58 years old. Her body was brought back to Wilmington and buried at Oakdale Cemetery in a plot purchased just the day before by Katherine Walker Whiting, the wife of General W. H. C. Whiting. The Rt. Rev. Alfred A. Watson, assisted by the local Episcopal ministers, conducted the funeral service at St. James. The Rev. Mr. Robert Strange led the graveside service. Seven of her former students, Alexander Leslie, John Hughes, William Spooner, George Herbert, Richard Spooner, Tilghman Howard, and William Harker, served as pallbearers. The vestries of St. James and Church of the Good Shepherd served in an honorary capacity.[281]

Kate Walker Whiting, the widow of Gen. W.H.C. Whiting, provided a final resting place for Sister Cecelia at Oakdale Cemetery. (Courtesy of Cape Fear Museum)

There were probably few if any dry eyes in the group assembled there. It was reported that "the grave was covered with flowers and floral emblems of offerings of affection. It was touching to see the humble members of her own Bible class coming forward with their simple tokens of love for her who had been indeed a mother to them."[282]

Because of Sister Cecelia's devotion and unsought fame, Robert Strange issued a statement to the local press: "While we deeply grieve and mourn, we rejoice in the belief that she has been one of the choice vessels of the grace of our Heavenly Father and one of the lights of the world in her generation."[283]

The nun's work echoed years later in the words of an unnamed woman who lived in a modest dwelling on the Sound. "The happiest time in my life was when my oldest boy went to the Parish School. When I was done with my work and had tidied up so that I could sit down, he would repeat to me the hymns and Bible verses he had learned in school. The sisters were among my best friends."[284]

The Rev. John B. Gibble, an assistant minister at St. James, supervised the Good Shepherd Mission. The first service occurred on November 6, 1892, and the centerpiece was the historic altar from St. James Church, given to Good Shepherd while the mother church was making room for the new Silas McBee altar. St. James also gave the "old St. James reredos and altar," and a baptismal font to Church of the Good Shepherd. The Rev. Mr. Robert Strange officiated and the Rev. Mr. Gibble delivered the sermon.[285]

"St. James has established a Mission plant on corner 6th and Queen," reported the *Morning Star*, on November 3, 1892. "It is a neat church seating 200 people, a hall about 25 feet-square and a small dwelling house of four rooms. It already has over 50 communicants. Services will be held morning and night every Sunday, and Sunday school in the afternoon. In the hall will be a day school, night school, meetings of the Girl's Friendly Society, Knights of Temperance and monthly social gatherings of the congregations."[286]

In addition to the Rev. John Gibble, who called himself "the bishop of Dry Pond," other faithful helpers at Church of the Good Shepherd included J H. Boatwright, Emma Maffitt, Mary Bridgers, Robert Jewett, Susie Price, Carrie Price, and the Rev. Thomas P. Noe.[287]

In 1895, Mary Lily Kenan, a member of First Presbyterian Church, joined in with "Miss Gibson, Emerson Mitchell, U. M. Robinson, C. H. Robinson, Jr., Mrs. Westbrook, Miss Sadie Williams, Miss Bridgers, and Miss Lola Martin," to present a musical in the Parish House for benefit of the mission.[288]

The improvements didn't last long. The St. James Home buildings burned on April 4, 1896. The church collected almost $4,000 in insurance.

Many of the women (pictured here in 1949) gave generously to subsequent phases of St. James's mission involvement and the endowment fund. They are (seated, left to right), Mrs. J. K. Wise, Mrs. Thomas H. Wright, Mrs. J. V. Grainger, Mrs. Marsden Bellamy, Mrs. George F. James, Mrs. Theodore G. Empie, Mrs. Fred Dick and Mrs. Graham Kenan. (Standing) Mrs. Richard Gwathmey, Mrs. J. Laurence Sprunt, Miss Jennie Murchison, Mrs. A. Sidney Williams and Mrs. W. R. Marvin. (Courtesy of Thomas S. Kenan III, and New Hanover County Public Library)

A Church of Bishops

Bishop Thomas Atkinson died in 1881 and was buried beneath the chancel of St. James. By that time, the diocese he led had grown to a cumbersome size. In 1883 the Diocese of East Carolina was created and St. James rector Alfred Watson was elected its first bishop. He was consecrated at St. James on April 17, 1884. The Rt. Rev. William Mercer Green, age 85, officiated at the ceremony.[289]

According to parishioner Katie Grainger, "The consecration of Rev. Alfred Augustine Watson to the Bishopric of East Carolina began a new era in the church in N. C. It was the new order of 3 Dioceses. I remember well, though a very young girl, just where I sat, and how crowded our beloved Parish was - every seat taken, and in the long galleries. Bishop Layman preached the sermon. His text was 'His Bishoprie let another take.'

Among the many guests at St. James that day was Caroline Belestierre, who would later marry Rudyard Kipling.[290]

In December 1887, the Rev. Robert Strange took leave of his post at Church of the Good Shepherd in Raleigh and, as rector, ascended the narrow winding stairs to the pulpit of St. James. Mrs. Strange occupied Pew 83, reserved "for use of the rector." The corner of Third and Market streets was a spiritual home to Robert Strange. His father, grandfather and great-grandfather had been vestrymen there.

Born in 1857, Robert Strange attended Jewett's School, then Cape Fear Military Academy in Wilmington, where school officials rated him "excellent" in Latin, grammar, geography, history, and elocution. Other students who attended the academy at that time included Pembroke Jones, John D. Bellamy, Thomas Atkinson, Samuel Bear, William H. Sprunt, Charles Bruce Wright, William Reston, J. W. Murchison, F. A. deRosset, Robert Cantwell, and J. B. Harriss. Most of the boys would stay close throughout their lives.

Strange prepared for college at Horner and Graves Military Academy in Hillsborough then attended the University of North Carolina, from which he graduated in June 1879. He continued his studies at the University of the South at Sewanee before graduating from the Berkeley Divinity School at Middleton, Conn., in 1883.

Robert Strange was ordained a deacon by Bishop Watson at St. James Church, April 23, 1884. Between deacon and priest, he was in Lawrenceville, Virginia, assisting Pattie Hicks Buford, a famous champion of the disenfranchised, in her mission work among the blacks of Virginia. Mrs. Buford built a hospital, orphanage, home for the aged, and a school for blacks.

In 1886, Robert Strange married Mrs. Buford's daughter, Elizabeth Stone Buford. He said of his mother-in-law's loving endeavors, "It is a work which stands alone, as far as I know, in the southern states. For the amount of money expended, it relieved more human pain and distress than any other institution in the United States. To her, the question was never who are they, but 'what is their need?'"[291]

Friendships forged in his childhood would form the grid of some of Robert Strange's most high-profile ecclesiastical work. When he helped officiate at the wedding ceremony of Sarah Wharton Green and his cousin and old schoolmate, Pembroke Jones, in 1884, it was easily one of the grandest social occasions of the year. A thousand guests attended the reception at Tokay Plantation outside Fayetteville — and a large percentage of the guests were members of St. James Church. Sarah Green Jones's Fayetteville family members were lifelong friends of the Stranges. Her younger sister, Mable Ellery Green, married George Blow Elliott who would have a long tenure as a St. James senior warden. Elliott, president and general counsel of the Atlantic Coast Line Railroad, was one more link in the Jones-Walters circle.[292]

George Blow Elliott, president of the Atlantic Coast Line Rail Road, served as a vestryman for almost four decades. (Reprinted from *The Cape Fear Club*.)

Robert Strange was also closely aligned with the Kenan family of Wilmington. The friendship predated Strange's generation and included Civil War connections. The Kenans probably made it possible for Strange to receive an honorary doctorate of divinity from the University of North Carolina, in 1895. At the time, he was the youngest man ever to receive a similar honor from UNC.

In 1904, after he became a bishop, Strange lived in the William Rand Kenan house at 110 Nun Street. Throughout Robert Strange's rectorship at St. James, members of the Kenan family who usually worshipped at First Presbyterian Church popped up frequently at St. James. During that period, Strange's close friends, Mr. and Mrs. Pembroke Jones and Henry Walters, introduced Mary Lily Kenan to her future husband, Standard Oil cofounder Henry Flagler, at Airlie.

Robert Strange's connections to the congregation must have caused some interesting moments during his rectorship. He was part of Wilmington's famous "cousinhood"— and so were a great many members of St. James Church. A partial list of families related to Robert Strange includes deRosset, Brown, Bradley, Jones, Wright, London, Lord, Dickinson, Bridgers, Green, Hill, Holmes, Wooster, Giles, Miller, Swift, and Boatwright. His maternal grandfather was Dr. Thomas Henry Wright. His paternal grandfather, U. S. Senator Robert Strange, was a Fayetteville judge and the author of the first novel written by a North Carolinian: *Euneguski, the Cherokee Chief.*

The 1901 wedding party of Ann Nessfield Green Cotchett and Bradley Wootten was heavy with members of St. James Church. (Front Row) – Mary Wootten, Mellie Cotchett, Anita deRosset White, Elizabeth Cotchett, Lucy Wootten, Della Clark, Marie Peschau Steadman. (Back Row) - Unidentified, May Houston, Swift Boatwright, Ed Wootten, Clayton Giles, unidentified, George Crow, Marsden Bellamy, James Cotchett, Leonora Cantwell, Fred Bolles. (Courtesy of Elizabeth Brown King)

To add some twists to the general genealogical maze at St. James Church, many of the children were given the same names, either to honor an ancestor - or just as a matter of convention. Meta Davis Rountree, daughter of George Davis whose statue stands at Third and Market streets, recalled as an elderly woman the confluence of monikers. "When I was a girl, Bishop Watson's wife, whom we called Aunt Fanny, used to invite the young girls to supper at the rectory. The rectory was then that old-fashioned house on Market Street next to the YMCA. One time she'd ask all the Marys, another, all the Alices, or Annies or Betsys. I was Meta and there was no other Meta so I went with the Marys."[293]

One of the first things the Rev. Mr. Strange did at St. James was to found the Sanctuary Guild, a group made up of young unmarried women. Rowe Wiggins was its first president. The Sanctuary Guild gave many parties at the church and elsewhere for the benefit of St. James. The fact

The old rectory property at 311 Market Street (on right) was acquired in 1830 and sold in 1919 to Dr. and Mrs. John B. Cranmer. The Cranmers gave the Children's Chapel in memory of their daughter Alice, who died in 1951. Alice, or Sister Alice Madeline, was an Episcopal nun in the Order of St. John the Baptist, an organization based in New Jersey. (Photo by Louis T. Moore. Courtesy of New Hanover County Public Library)

that the hostesses were some of Wilmington's most eligible young women did not hurt attendance.

No matter what powerful social connections he had, Robert Strange followed his spiritual heart when times got tough. During Wilmington's tragic race riot of 1898, Strange put his life on the line for his convictions. He was about 5' 6" tall and weighed 135 pounds, but he stood tall as a giant during the town's most embarrassing moments. When violence broke out, Strange transported black editor Alexander Manly in his own carriage to the train station to keep him from harm. His act of bravery, both physical and social, ranks with that of James Sprunt, who wrapped himself in an American flag before standing between rampaging rioters and the blacks who had sought refuge inside his warehouse.[294]

Strange also gave his time generously to worthy efforts outside the church. He spoke several times a year at area schools and worked hard to establish playgrounds. He also held services and served sometimes as chaplain for the Seaman's Friend Society located on the northwest corner of Front and Dock streets. The bethel was a four-story building that served as a bustling haven for sailors. Robert Strange and James Sprunt were "workers together" to promote "the welfare of the toilers of the sea."[295]

The Seaman's Friend Society followed an earlier effort. The Wilmington Marine Hospital, or Mount Tirzah, as it came to be known, was organized in 1835 by a group that included St. James members: Gov. Edward B. Dudley, Henry Savage, Samuel Potter, and Dr. Thomas H. Wright. Located on a 150-acre tract of riverfront land near Greenfield Lake, the hospital functioned for twenty years. Not long after the Seamen's Friend Society on South Front Street was operational, the Civil War began. Like St. James, the building was also used as a military hospital. But the seamen's bethel was used by Confederates early in the war, then Union soldiers.[296]

Robert Strange stayed at St. James until 1900 when he moved to St. Paul's Church in Richmond. At that time, the Rev. Mr. Horsfield of Cambridge, N. Y., was appointed acting rector for one year. In 1902, Robert Strange experienced a near fatal case of food poisoning while vacationing at Sweet Springs, W. Va. During one of the meals, like many other guests, he drank milk that was contaminated. Suddenly, the diners who were "strolling on the lawns" began to drop "on all sides. It looked for a moment as if a battery of artillery had suddenly opened with grape and canister on the gay gathering." Strange's recuperation took months.[297]

On November 1, 1904, a Tuesday, the Rev. Robert Strange was consecrated as bishop coadjutor in a service at St. James Church. Seats were so precious that tickets were issued. "The usual seating capacity of St. James Church is about 675, but by placing extra chairs in the aisles and baptistry, accommodation has been provided for 829," reported the *Wilmington Messenger.*

Robert Strange, who became bishop in 1905, had an aura of greatness all along. The local press said he was "one of the ablest divines of this diocese," and "a man of charming dignity." (Courtesy of UNCW)

Seven bishops, many rectors, and numerous dignitaries were invited to the 11 am consecration. Visiting bishops included Ellison Capers of South Carolina, Alfred Magill Randolph of Southern Virginia, Junius Horner of Asheville, and Robert Atkinson Gibson of Virginia. Local hosts for the visitors included James Sprunt, E. C. Holt, George Thomas, and the Giles family. All gathered that evening in the Wilmington Light Infantry building at 411 Market Street (the John A. Taylor House) for a "glittering reception."

Missing from the service and festivities was the Rt. Rev. Alfred A. Watson. "Owing to his continued enfeebled condition Bishop Watson, of East Carolina, was persuaded to remain away from the consecration services, his friends being apprehensive lest the excitement of the occasion would be too much for his weakened constitution." Bishop Watson died almost six months later, on Good Friday, April 21, 1905. In 1906, the church dedicated a handsome memorial tablet to Alfred Augustin

On June 28, 1890, the Rt. Rev. A. A. Watson married Mary Catherine Lord, a granddaughter of William C. Lord, at St. James Church. The Rev. Robert Strange performed the ceremony, after which Bishop and Mrs. Watson left by train for New York to embark on a tour of Europe. The bishop was 72. The bride was 45. (Courtesy of UNCW)

Watson. Made by Tiffany, the plaque is framed by black marble and features a Bishop's mitre, crook, and key. It reads, in part, "First Bishop of East Carolina, From its organization, April 1884."[298]

Just nine years after Alfred Watson's death, Bishop Strange died, on August 23, 1914. His death was tolled from the church bell tower and the remaining members of the O.A.N. club served as bodyguards when his body lay in state at the church. Bishop Strange had organized the club of men when they were little more than boys. They met in a two-story building that once sat in the churchyard. On August 25, 1900, the O.A.N. building was dismantled and the timber was reused in "an old ladies' home at 6th and Queen."[299]

Church decorations in the 19th century required the efforts of many people. Banners, like this one used on Easter, were common on major holidays. (Gift to St. James from Swift Miller Boatwright, 1919. Courtesy of UNCW.)

Hearts and Flowers

St. James has gone through many phases of floral decoration, from the heartwarming efforts of the sexton in the old building to the sophisticated floral designs of today. For the most part, in the old days, the materials were local and church members did the work. Sometimes St. James was hung with festoons of Spanish moss, an intruiging thought for locals who know that tiny urchins that lurk therein. Nevertheless, it must have provided plenty of visual delight when the lamps of St. James were lighted at night. At other times, "large and fine palmetto trees" were brought in by steamer from Bald Head Island to grace the church.[300]

On Easter Sunday 1875, a *Star News* reporter attended the morning service and recorded the decor in detail. "The decorations were profuse and very handsome. In the rear of the pulpit was the inscription in beautiful lettering, 'The last Enemy that shall be destroyed is Death.' Over this inscription was a large cross, set in a mound of flowers, with a large and magnificent calla lily rising

The St. James Lenten Choir, about 1891. Robert Strange stands unidentified on the back row. (Courtesy of UNCW.)

from the base, and above the cross was a crown composed of evergreens and beautiful flowers. Each corner of the chancel railing and the Baptismal font were also handsomely decorated, while other portions of the building were rich in floral adornments, festoons, and wreaths of evergreens."

However the Christmas season brought the most dramatic decorations to St. James. One newspaper reporter noted " three magnificent arches of evergreens that span the interior of the building." Most of the decorations were made by the young people of St. James. Victorian times and the absence of automobiles made dating a very different thing back then. Girls and their "beaux" used to gather evergreens and then sit together as couples inside the church while they made garlands.[301]

"The boys would tear small twigs from the branches of holly and cedar," recalled Mary D. Davis, remembering the 1890s. "The girls would tie them into small bunches and hand them to the boys to fasten onto a long strand of rope. When done the garlands were round and a foot or more thick. When finished these were wrapped around the pillars supporting the balconies and looped in festoons."[302]

On Christmas Day 1897, the *Star News* reported that the St. James Choir "was composed of 14 boys, 11 ladies and 6 gentlemen: Ed Bailey, Rob Calder, Willie Gore, Fred Hamme, Charlie Morriss, Norwood Orrell, Lewis Orrell, Harry Poezolt, Alban Pleasants, Howard St. Johns, Joe Smith, Willie Smith, Harry West, Charlie Yopp, Mrs. W. L. Latta, Misses Fair W. Payne, Lola Martin, Carrie Myers, Annie Lee, Annie B. deRosset, Mattie Horne, Cammie Lord, Ada Cooper, Belle Anderson,

Elizabeth Waddell, Messrs, C. H. Cooper, J.V.B. Metts, Eugene Beery, Thomas deRosset, Robert Rankin, A. S. Holden." E. H. Munson directed the music and played the organ.

In 1902, the "ancient churchyard" was restored again. The church hired Wilmington architect H. E. Bonitz to do the work, but Col. W. L. deRosset, Capt. T. D. Meares, and Major W. F. Robertson were the official supervisors of the project. Workmen laid brick for a parapet fence, then added coping purchased from Portner Brownstone. They made repairs to vaults and tombs, relettered a number of tombstones, and filled in a pit near the Parish House that had been agape for several years. When the project was complete, the artistry of the 18th-century stonecutters was again apparent. Surely reading inscriptions such as that of William Millor who died in 1788 relieved the monotony of the restoration work: "He was an honest and inoffensive man."

During the 1902 restoration, the top of one of the most ancient vaults gave way. Exposed were the remains and uniform of what was described as "a pre-Revolutionary soldier," in uniform — complete with cartridge, steel box, and brass buttons.[303]

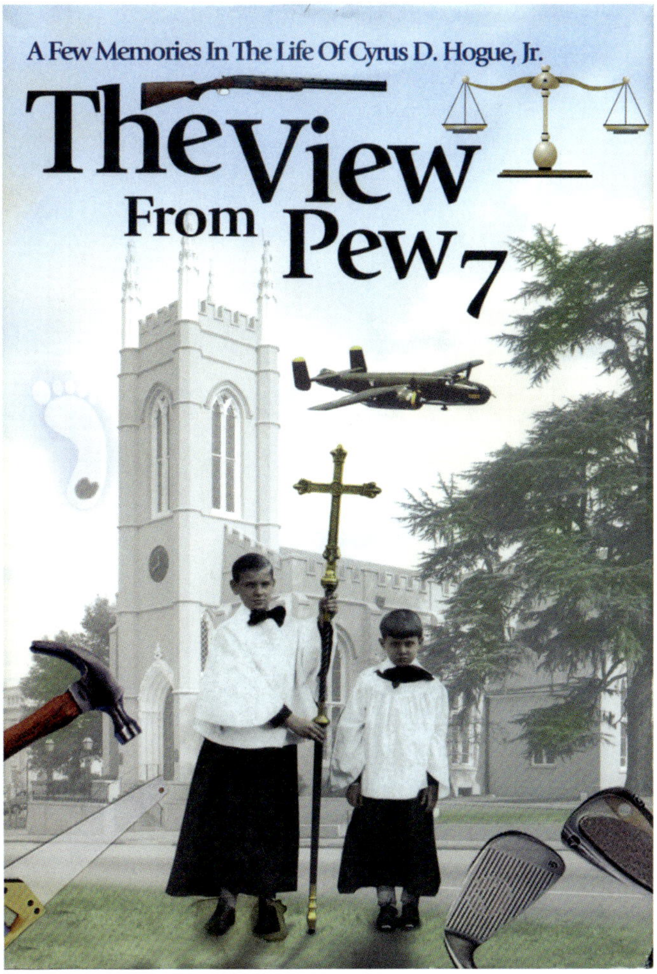

Attorney Cyrus D. Hogue, Jr., did the church proud when he published his memoirs in 2001. "This book details some of the events in a life which always seems to return to Pew #7" he wrote. The boys depicted on the cover are Thomas H. Wright, Jr., and Cy Hogue, in 1930.

The Rev. Mr. Richard Wallace Hogue became rector of St. James Church in 1902, but the first invitation came in February 1901. At the time, he was in Tuscumbia, Alabama — and his references were glowing. Jack Ross, a cotton agent in Mobile, wrote Clayton Giles at St. James: "He was with us before he was ordained, and captured the town - old and young. You will draw a prize if you can get him. Money cuts no figure. He is wedded to his work. He, in my opinion is the most promising young man in the South."

Mr. Hogue declined in May, but was called again in late August. He completed duties in Alabama and began work at St. James 14 months later. "The new rector will arrive by Seaboard Air Line RR tonight on the 12:00 train," reported the *Wilmington Messenger*. "Mrs. Hogue and child will also come with him. They will be guests of Capt. Thomas D. Meares until the Market Street rectory is ready for their occupancy."[304]

A recent graduate of the University of the South, Mr. Hogue used his youthful energy on building the spiritual life of the men of St. James — and strengthening the Order of St. Andrew's. The Rev. Mr. Hogue also created a home for his late brother's son, Cyrus D. Hogue, a brilliant young man who turned 14 in 1902. In 1908, Mr. Hogue left St. James to become rector of Chapel of the Cross in Chapel Hill. The move was advantageous for young Cyrus Hogue, who attended law school and graduated in 1912.[305]

Cyrus Hogue became an esteemed attorney in Wilmington, and the Hogue family remains important to the life of the church. In 2001, Cyrus D. Hogue, Jr., also an attorney, published a memoir: *The View From Pew 7*, a reference to his Sunday morning vantage point at St. James.

In 1904, Mrs. Preston L. Bridgers presented St. James Church with a new organ: a melodious memorial to her husband who died in 1902 at the age of 46. Mr. Bridgers was a merchant, manufacturer, banker — and, for a time, the American consul in Montevideo, Uruguay. Used for the first time on October 23, 1904, the organ was billed as one of the three finest organs in the state, and was "equipped with all the latest improvements." The new features included air furnished by an electric motor, pneumatic tubes, and pipes with double frontage. Seventeen of the pipes faced the congregation and 23 faced the choir. It took mechanics and craftsmen from the Hutchings-Votey Company of Boston several weeks to install the instrument.[306]

Oddly enough, the organ pipes completely obscured a beautiful example of stained glass artistry. Few people remembered the window and when the organ pipes were removed in the 1960s, the surprise was stunning.

James Craft, church organist, chose the style after studying a number of organs across North Carolina. The Bridgers Organ, an air-motivated instrument, was consecrated November 1, 1904. In 1924, the vestry paid H. E. Hodgson and Son of Norfolk $3,000 to electrify it.[307]

Even after the new century arrived, many Wilmingtonians were still fighting the Civil War. Confederate Memorial Day was a full-fledged holiday. Locals frequently refused to sing "The Battle Hymn of the Republic." When Miss Ellen Bellamy was talking her walk, she would cross a street rather than walk by a house where the American flag was flying. And even during the ceremony in which the pulpit Bible that had been

Organ pipes obscured the pretty window, on the north wall of the chancel, for years. Even now, the beautiful glass often goes unnoticed because of the window's position. Recently, renowned stained glass artist Rowan LeCompte cleaned, repaired, and enhanced the window. (Photo by Beatrice Schomp)

confiscated during the Civil War was returned to First Presbyterian Church, Ellen Bellamy spoke aloud from her pew: "I remember the day those Yankees stole it."

St. James Church was no exception. Despite the fact that Union authorities did gather pews from the church yard and the lawn of the Burgwin-Wright House and put them back into the church, animosity continued. Early in 1886, a church committee was appointed to prepare a bill "to be laid before Congress" to reinburse the Parish for use and damage of the church by Union troops during the Civil War. A month later, the Hon. R. T. Bennett introduced a bill in the House of Representatives "for the benefit of the Vestry and Wardens of St. James Parish, of Wilmington, N.C."[308]

Again, on December 15, 1900, U. S. Congressman John D. Bellamy introduced an invoice for "use, occupation, and damage to the St. James Church building by the military of the U.S." The bill was referred to the committee on War Claims, where it apparently died.[309]

Again, in 1904, the wardens and vestry of St. James Parish filed suit against the United States for reimbursement of the cost of repairing the church after Union soldiers turned it into a hospital. "That on or about the 1st day of March 1865, under an order from General Schofield, executed by General Hawley, the church building to said Parish was taken possession of, the pews torn out by a squad of United States soldiers with picks, and the building converted into a hospital.

"The floors and pews were damaged by the rough removal, the walls defaced and injured, and the building left in unclean and filthy condition." Nevertheless, no federal check ever arrived. [310]

In April 1888, St. Agnes Guild hosted a bazaar called "Feast of the Poets." Guild members who participated were: Mrs. E. J. Powers, Mrs. W. E. Storm, Mary Maffitt, Carrie Maffitt, Maggie McPherson, Annie Hargrove, Hattie Whitaker, R. N. Sweet, May French, Susie Price, Sarah Lippitt, Mrs. P. L. Bridgers, Mrs. G. G. Thomas, Belle Thomas, Mollie French, Carrie Price, Mary MacRae, Estella Shackelford, Kate deRosset, Josie Whitaker, Carrie Cazaux, Lizzie Peck, Agnes Daniel, Carrie Myers, Mrs. T. H. McKoy, Mrs. C. H. King, Amoret Cameron, Mamie Burr, Alice Wood, L. Mebane, Josie Myers, Mrs. Rankin, Mrs. J. A. Bonitz, Mrs. W. R. French, Mrs. R. M. Houston, Mamie deRosset, Callie Reid French, Janie Northrop, Mrs. G. W. Kidder, Liliah Brown, Minnie Brown, Ada Schenck, Mal Cowan, Lizzie Waddell, Fannie Watters, Mrs. Graham Davies, Louise Knight, Louise deRosset, Mrs. Dr. Anderson, Mrs. Jane Lippitt, Mrs. Dr. Potter, Mary Vincent, May B. French, Sophy McPherson, Mrs. J. C. Munds.[311]

The cycle of improvements and repairs continued. In 1888 the church was re-stuccoed, organ pipes were installed, the font was moved to the center of the baptistery, and the clock was removed for repairs. Most of the funds came from St. Agnes Guild. In 1889, the side galleries were removed. The following year, the fence around the churchyard had to be repaired after a wayward horse knocked part of it down.[312]

About 1885, a charitable group within the church was born when Alice London Boatwright

Calder (1848-1940) created an unusual way for young people to raise funds. She invited the following children to her home: Alice London Boatwright, Mary Calder, Lizzie Cotchett, Kate deRosset Meares, Eliza Munds, Kate deRosset MacMillan, Keith Calder, Swift Boatwright, Adam Empie, Harry Latimer, John Metts, and Louis Myers. "The zealous young workers" shelled peanuts that were made into a paste that was sold at the Front Street Drug Store. The proceeds went to missionary projects — and the group was known as the Twenty Minute Society.[313]

In July 1891, E. J. Neville Stent, an accomplished New York architect and interior designer, won a $1,000 contract from the vestry to fresco the church. Mr. Stent was of the opinion that "the only proper and desirable style of decoration is fresco painting put on in accordance with designs by a competent artist who has made ecclesiastical decoration a study." His other work includes designs at St. John's Episcopal Church in Detroit; Church of the Epiphany in Washington, D.C.; and at St. James Cathedral in Chicago, where he used an intricate system of stenciling to enhance the existing colors.

In late July, members of St. James were notified that "Mr. Stent and his assistants of New York" would be frescoing the church for five or six weeks. The Rev. Mr. Robert Strange requested that members "remove their prayer books and pew furniture" within days.

St. James was reopened the first Sunday in October 1891. In addition to frescoes, the vestibule was altered by adding new swinging doors and a partition, and removing a closet under the steps. Additional lights and new carpet were installed. The final price was $1318. During this period of time, a north transept was considered for the purpose of additional space and to complete the usual Gothic design of the cross . However consultant J. B. Halcott of Albany, N.Y., the architect of Julian Carr's mansion, Somerset, in Durham, advised against it. Nevertheless, the church now seated about 700.[314]

An old tradition that began to fall away was that of long and spirited bell ringing. Downtown church bells rang for 15 minutes every Sunday to announce each service. In the early 1890s, St. James cut back to just four minutes of bell ringing. Eventually the cacophony was reduced to the tolling of the hour.

On May 16, 1893, the new circular window in the south wall of the transept was opened for "inspection." The window depicts "Our Savior Blessing the Children," and was a gift from Mr. and Mrs. Pembroke Jones in memory of their little daughter, Alice Dickinson Jones, who died in 1890 at the age of four. Jean Farnsworth has also attributed this window to Charles Booth. The Jones window replaced one installed in 1889. E. V. Richards, a Wilmington artist, had decorated the glass of the original window. Richards also designed windows for Fifth Avenue Methodist Church.[315]

In 1893, Mrs. Gaston Meares organized St Mary's Bible class, a group that met every week in the transept of the Church. In 1897, the thriving class was incorporated into St. Mary's Guild. The charter members were: Kate deRosset Meares, Alice London Boatwright, Jean Harriss Delano,

Cammie Lord, Bessie Brock Toon, Mary Polk Davis, Elsa Munds, Lola Martin Taylor, Kate deRosset MacMillan, and Ethel Myers. St. Mary's Guild became known later as St. Mary's Chapter and in 1958 as Episcopal Churchwomen.

The Jones window, a memorial to little Alice Dickinson Jones (1885-1890), was presented to the church in 1893. A gift of her parents, Sarah and Pembroke Jones, the window depicts Christ blessing children. (Photo by Beatrice Schomp)

About 1939, Anne T. S. Bellamy stated that the members of St. Mary's Guild "worked arduously and faithfully in the Five Fields of Service, sewing, participating in the year's bazaars of the Church, serving suppers, operating a successful tearoom, giving financial aid and loving care to children at the Thompson Orphanage, and donating to all worthy causes possible. During these latter years… they have contributed most substantially to the budget of St. James Churchwomen, the Overseas Missions of the Church, and to the work of the Bishop of the Diocese."

Jane MacMillan Rhett, daughter of Kate deRosset MacMillan, added that the tea room "operated for a number of years, entirely through the efforts of the members of St. Mary's Guild. The proceeds from the operation of the tea room were given to the Church at the time of enlarging the Parish House, and the room on the second floor is called the St. Mary's Room, its construction having been paid for by the efforts of this group of dedicated women."

On April 3, 1889, St. James celebrated the 50th anniversary of the 1839 building. The day was extra special for two men: Dr. A. J. deRosset and William C. Lord. Both men were present when the cornerstone was laid — and both were on the vestry.

The anniversary seemed to spark new debates about the pew system, but ownership of seating continued. The doors and hinges had been removed in 1884, ending a lot of inconvenience, but not the proprietary situation. On July 19, 1891, the auction house of Cronly and Morris advertised in the *Star*: "On Wed. 29th, we will sell at 12 o'clock at our office, 15 Princess Street, pew #65, south aisle, St. James Church." [316]

Though the pews were all sold originally to create capital for the building campaign, they were sold subsequently from owner to owner with the exception of a scattered few that were willed back to the church. Eventually, some enterprising members of the church began quietly subletting their pews, a practice that was forbidden by the vestry in September 1893. Though members could be territorial with their sacred real estate, "visitors were always provided with and welcomed to seats." Hospitality aside, not until 1916 would pews be entirely free.[317]

Traffic was so light on Piety Hill during the 19th century that residents were known to occasionally picnic in the street. (Courtesy of Mary M. Wootten)

The chancel looks unfamiliar in this 1882 painting by J. L. Cantwell. As Mortimer Glover said, "The character of the interior has been changed several times." (Photo by John Bankson)

"A Beautiful and Complete and Instructive Chancel"

The intricately carved oak reredos at St. James Church and the stained glass window above it were created in 1891-92. Both were designed by Silas McBee (1853-1924) of Sewanee, Tenn.; Lincolnton, N. C.; and New York City. The carved reredos was financed by Henry Gould Latimer (1845-1925). The Charles Booth stained glass window and bronze relief were underwritten by St. Agnes Guild. The final cost for each, the oak reredos and the window, was around $2,000, the same amount that the St. James rector made in 1884 for an entire year's work. The altar was given in memory of Frederick Lord.

Henry Latimer, son of Elizabeth Savage and Zebulon Latimer, built the imposing residence at 202 South Third Street in 1882-1883. He and his brothers founded the Acme Manufacturing Company, but Henry acted only as an investor. Though Mr. Latimer worked his whole life, he was never known to hold a formal job.[318]

In addition to earning a law degree from Cornell, he was an accomplished artist in watercolors, and an authority on heraldry, genealogy, and botany. He studied painting with numerous teachers, probably one of which was Wilmington's Elisabeth Chant. Latimer's wife, Carria Groot, came to Wilmington from Auburn, N.Y., and taught school with the legendary educator Amy Morris

Bradley. The Henry Latimers lived most of their adult lives in Auburn but kept an apartment in New York City.[319]

Henry Gould Latimer underwrote the cost of the reredos and provided artistic advice to Silas McBee. (Reprinted from *Pictorial and Historical New Hanover County and Wilmington, N. C.*, by William Lord deRosset.)

Mr. Latimer, who was slated originally to finance the window, settled on the reredos instead. But the benefactor provided more than just money. Throughout the reredos project, Henry Latimer shared artistic suggestions with Mr. McBee, particularly urging the use of images from nature. The two artists, both with deep devotion to the church, must have cherished their friendship.

But there is no doubt that the Rev. Mr. Robert Strange provided a holy jump-start to the many improvements made at St. James Church during the period in which he was rector. On November 24, 1891, Robert Strange wrote Henry Latimer. "As both you and I agreed, the chancel window is what we most need to make St. James what it ought to be. I think such a window as you would like to put in, and I should like to see in St. James, would cost about two thousand dollars.

"I think I can get another party to put in a handsome carved oak reredos, running up to the bottom of the window. Knowing what the design of the window would be, the design of the reredos would be made to harmonize; so that we should have a beautiful and complete and instructive chancel.

" (But) I can find no scene in the life of St. James that appeals especially to me."

So the Rev. Mr. Strange looked elsewhere for a subject, and it didn't take long. He simply opened a current magazine and turned to page 686. There in the November 21, 1891, issue of *The Churchman* was an article by William S. Boardman, an American chaplain in Dresden. Boardman described a new painting by Dresden artist Johann Michael Ferdinand Heinrich Hofmann (1824-1911), entitled "The Praying Angel."

"In the painting, 'The Praying Angel,' wrote Boardman, "a lovely female figure, whose face is actually the image of Hofmann's dead wife, stands out boldly from the canvas clad in a simple white tunic, about the lower part of which a light blue mantle falls loosely. The hands are clasped in prayer. The lower part of the figure is lost in fleecy clouds which wreathe themselves about it. All the light seems to come from an aureole of pure gold which surrounds the head of the angel, and descends upon the outspread wings, which are painted in the delicious soft colors which the old masters Perugino and Raphael delight in. The expression of the face is one of pure, rapt devotion mingled with an indescribable sweetness, which is well framed in the golden locks of hair which float about it. The upper background is the sky of night studded with a few stars.

"The picture fascinates the beholder so that having once seen it he must see it again to duly appreciate it. It is the communion of a sinless being with its Maker, whom it addresses without any of the hesitation or reproach which is the fruit of sin and makes contrition a part of our prayers. Reproduced in glass it would make a very beautiful memorial window."

Though few people are familiar with Hofmann's name, almost every child who attended Sunday School in the 20th century saw his work. His many illustrations of the life of Christ have been reproduced in church literature more than those of any other artist. Hofmann's depiction of the face of Christ has given Christians worldwide a visage to carry in imagination. According to author Albert Edward Bailey, Hofmann's Jesus, "while effeminate rather than strong, has elements of beauty that make a strong appeal."[320]

The angel found its way into the window, but Silas McBee gave her a peripheral role in a scene that depicts the resurrected Jesus with the three Marys. Mr. McBee, who designed the window, the reredos, and the bronze relief panels, duly fulfilled Robert Strange's desire, for a large number of artistic improvements were created that are fully integrated, and capable of inspiration for all who were open to them.

But before McBee was ever commissioned, Robert Strange processed the bigger picture of the chancel and came up with a plan. "The design of windows and reredos as a whole could be called The Hour of Prayer," he wrote Henry Latimer. "The window could be … a rose window with this figure on the center and leading features. The

The reredos and altar window were presented to the congregation on November 27, 1892. (Photo by Hugh Morton. Courtesy of Mary M. Wootten)

Silas McBee also used the reredos design for Grace Episcopal Church in Galveston, Christ Church Cathedral in Nashville, and St. John's Church in Hagerstown. Philanthropist Mollie Rosenberg funded Mr. McBee's work in Hagerstown — and Galveston, pictured here. (Courtesy of Grace Episcopal Church, Galveston. Jan Dorsett, historian.)

tempered Eastern light streaming through this window, bringing before us all the lovely figures in rapt devotion would elevate and spiritualize the devotion of the whole congregation."

"This letter will reach you on Thanksgiving Day," Strange concluded in a brilliant moment of spiritual salesmanship. "Could a day be more fitting on which you decide to bestow such a gift on the Church of your childhood to the Glory of God?"[321]

The man chosen to embellish the chancel was a peripatetic church figure who had the ability to function as artist, architect, editor, and writer almost simultaneously. McBee, who sometimes used the return address, "Silas McBee, Carver of Reredos," also installed very similar reredos in Grace Episcopal Church in Galveston, St. John's Church in Hagerstown, Md., and Christ Church Cathedral in Nashville. The carving in Hagerstown, housed in that same church Dr. Drane served before moving to Wilmington, is said to have been previously exhibited at the 1893 World's Columbian Exposition in Chicago. The reredos in Galveston and Hagerstown were funded by philanthropist Mollie Ragan Rosenberg (1839-1917), who also provided beautifications for churches in Richmond and Savage, Md.[322]

McBee also designed (with Arthur Tempest) Christ Church in Houston (1893); St. Luke's Episcopal Church in Lincoln County; and All Saints Episcopal Church in Concord, N. C.

McBee numbered among his personal friends William Howard Taft and Theodore Roosevelt, who once said that McBee "knew the inside of every (political) movement." Mr. McBee was founder of *The Constructive Quarterly.* He also served as editor of *The Churchman*, an august publication, one issue of which found its way into the St. James cornerstone in 1840.

McBee also authored a book in 1911 entitled *An Eirenic Itinerary*, in which he espoused his views on the unity and discordance of Christian churches. "But where the integrity of the Church is at stake," wrote the wise man, "difficulties and dangers are invitations to action, rather than warnings to be heeded by running away."[323]

During the installation process for the reredos, and "super altar" as one person called it, McBee was the houseguest of the Rev. Mr. and Mrs. Robert Strange. At the time, they were living in the Market Street rectory. According to Mrs. Strange, the carving was done in McBee's New York workshop by Swiss carvers. Nevertheless, it is probable that Melchior Thoni, a native of Switzerland who was the lead carver for the Nashville reredos, also carved the St. James work.[324]

Melchior Thoni grew up in Breinz, where he herded cattle and goats. Thoni, like many herders, passed the time by "one hand carving," or what we would call whittling. He held the wood in one hand and the knife in the other. Thoni's talent was quickly apparent and his father sent him to a master carver named Bauman to be tutored. In 1869, Melchior Thoni and the rest of his family moved to America. Their dreams were shattered, though, when they realized they had purchased barren farm land in Grundy County, Tennessee.[325]

Thoni then moved his family to Sewanee, Tenn., where he became a janitor at the University of the South. It was there that he met Silas McBee, who was a student at the time. In the early 1880s, Thoni moved his family to Nashville where, along with his brother and brother-in-law, he created the first carousel in the United States. The "flying jenny," as they called it, featured carved "horses, roosters, ostriches, deer, and chariots." Thoni spent five years hauling the carousel to fairs and amusement parks.[326]

Thoni then took a job at the Edgefield and Nashville Manufacturing Company where he supervised six to eight carvers. It was during this period of time that the reredos at St. James Church and the reredos at Christ Church Cathedral in Nashville were created. Thoni's cousin, Peter Schild, created some of the more intricate figures in the Nashville reredos.

After studying McBee's work, Jane Iredell Meares Williams executed these carvings at her home at 118 South Fourth Street. (Photo by her grandson, Robert M. Williams, Jr.)

Melchior Thoni's mode of carving is a European style known as Tirol-Bavaria. According to Vic Hood, it features "stippled background highlights" that create "texture with hundred of shadow pockets." Human figures done in this style have large heads and narrow faces. Distinctive facial features include eyes with no pupils and high foreheads.

McBee himself accompanied the reredos to Wilmington and spent 10 days installing it. "I shall never forget the visit of that gifted and interesting man," wrote Mrs. Strange. "I used to go over to the church with him constantly to watch him work. He explained the instructive and inspiring symbols of the carving — the wheat for the bread, grapes for the wine, oaks for strength, passion flower for sacrifice, the alpha and omega for birth and death, the lowly flower – and the Acanthus, reaching upward for the Resurrection.

"He prayed so earnestly every morning at the Chancel rail before beginning his work — I could not but feel it would ever be a blessing and inspiration to the many worshippers who would kneel before that altar."[327]

amazed the crowd.

Henry Latimer's mother, Elizabeth Savage Latimer, officially presented the reredos to the church. As a young woman, Mrs. Latimer made her special mark on Wilmington, and on the Latimer House at 126 South Third Street, by forgoing fine plaster moldings in her new house so that she could use the money to purchase freedom for a Wilmington slave family about to be separated by a sale. [331]

The new additions prompted the following announcement in the *Wilmington Messenger*: "The Sexton has been directed to leave the church door open and free to all visitors. The recent additions to this handsome church are worth a visit."[332]

A few years later, Silas McBee also designed a bishop's chair, sometimes called a bishop's throne, for St. James Church. Col. William Lord deRosset commissioned the chair and presented it in memory of his father, Dr. Armand J. deRosset, Jr., (1807-1897) on June 8, 1898. DeRosset's death had brought sorrow to many in and outside the parish. The *Diocesan Journal* recorded the words of the Rev. A. A. Watson when he noted deRosset's long service: "I suppose that the oldest of us does not remember the time when he was not a prominent figure in Diocesan Councils."[333]

Like the Bishop's Chair at St. James Church, the altar window at Church of the Good Shepherd is a memorial to Dr. A. J. deRosset, Jr., who was generous to both churches. (Photo by the author)

The Robert Rufus Bridgers Building

Meanwhile outside the church building, 1892 was also a big year. The local press heralded the news: "Widow and heirs of Hon. Robert R. Bridgers to erect a memorial building in commemoration of him. It is to be a handsome and costly two story structure." A sacred memorial seemed fitting: Robert Bridgers's "heirs" included Mrs. Burke Haywood Bridgers, who was Bishop Strange's daughter, Helen.[334]

Robert Rufus Bridgers (1819-1888), a Tarboro native, was an attorney who served in the N. C. General Assembly and the Confederate Congress. He went on to realize greater fame and fortune when he was elected president of the Wilmington and Weldon Railroad in 1865. Two years later, it was R. R. Bridgers who sold Wilmington and Weldon stock to the William Walters Group in Baltimore, thus creating a business alliance that would alter the history of New Hanover County. Later, Henry Walters, William's son, would collect railroads with the relative ease of a toy collector amassing a curio cabinet full of china dolls. The Atlantic Coast Line Railroad was the result, and the headquarters was placed in Wilmington.

R. R. Bridgers eventually served as an executive with several railroads. Bridgers also helped Henry Walters create the Fayetteville Cut-Off, a million-dollar railroad line to Tokay Plantation, Mrs. Pembroke Jones's family's vineyard. The connections produced and endured. Tokay became the largest vineyard east of the Mississippi — and Sarah Wharton Green Jones eventually became Mrs. Henry Walters.

Bridgers purchased the William B. Meares lot, a parcel that ran from Front to Second Street, along Chestnut Street. His business acumen was further exhibited when he a procured a federal government loan to build a post office, about 1873. Eventually, R. R. Bridgers sold the improved real estate to the U. S. Government. The Bridgers post office was razed when the Romanesque post office was constructed from 1889-1891. In turn, it was demolished in 1936 and the present post office replaced it.[335]

Today the name Bridgers is also known in the St. James neighborhood for the grand house R. R. Bridgers's daughter-in-law, Elizabeth Haywood Bridgers, built at 100 South Third Street in 1905. Currently known as the Graystone Inn, the house was billed in 1912 as "one of the handsomest houses in the state."[336]

The Bridgers family approached the vestry with architectural plans for the new building in hand. The firm of Valentine, Brown, and Company served as the builders. Unfortunately, the name of the architect has been lost, even though we know the fee he charged: $250. It is possible that the

Atlantic View, owned by the Manning family, and by John Hazard Hanby, was a summer playground for many members of St. James. The Fisherman's Wife gift store now sits near where the striped tent was located in this 1900 image. (Robert M. Fales Collection, New Hanover County Public Library.)

design was by architect John H. Hanby, because Hanby was called in later to make alterations when consultants James F. Post and James Walker recommended five-foot buttresses for support.[337]

John Hazard Hanby and his brother, Joseph H. Hanby, were natives of Virginia's Eastern Shore who came to Wilmington by way of Civil War service at Fort Fisher. In later years, John Hanby lived at 15 North Fifth Street, in a house built by James F. Post. Hanby also owned the Atlantic View Hotel, on the west side of Airlie Road near the bridge, at Wrightsville.

From 1883 until 1894, John Hanby was Supervisor of Buildings for the Atlantic Coast Line, a firm dear to the Bridgers family's heart. Additionally, he built the Fishblate-Jennewein House at 318 South Front Street and the Fishblate-Bellamy-Boney Cottage at 315 South Lumina Avenue. He also repaired the foundation and floors of St. James Church in 1888, just four years before the Bridgers Building was erected.[338]

The proposed building site was just east of the church — and the old frame building, Society Hall, was in the way. Society Hall, or Guild Hall, had accumulated a rich history all its own in less

This 1914 photograph illustrates the juxtaposition of the buildings prior to the Upjohn addition. The stained glass window on the upper floor of the Bridgers Building marks what is now the north wall of the Bishop Wright Room. (Courtesy of Janet K. Seapker and the New Hanover County Public Library.)

than sixty years. Originally the property and the building were owned by the Ladies' Working Society, which had purchased the land from John Swann in 1834, a transaction that would eventually evoke a lawsuit.

Though Society Hall was the setting of sewing thousands of "articles of their own manufacture," the hall was the site of innumerable other church functions. With money raised from fairs, concerts, and plays at Society Hall, the women of the church continued to support the St. James Home. In 1885, they also raised $238.55 through an art exhibit for "graveyard renovation." The churchyard was subsequently surveyed by J. C. Chase and the stones were righted and cleaned.[339]

Society Hall served as the church itself from the time the old building was dismantled until the new building was inhabitable. Then from March 1840 until April 1841, New Hanover County Circuit Court was held in Society Hall. One of the more famous trials that occurred there was that of Solomon Tater, a man of mixed race who was tried for murder and acquitted. Society Hall was used also as a station for voting polls and as the venue for numerous concerts and lectures.[340]

Over time, several schools met in the old building including the school of Miss Hetty James and Miss Kate Burr, a girls' academy that occupied the building from about 1867-1879.

The R. R. Bridgers Building and the Lenten choir are framed by the Wilmington Fire Department headquarters (15 South Fourth Street) on the left and the new Donald MacRae House on the right in this photo taken about 1905. (Courtesy of Edward F. Turberg.)

"We went to school in the 'Society Hall' where the Parish House in now," said Minnie Brown, about 1930. "We girls with one of our teachers formed the choir whenever there was a morning service in the church."[341]

Society Hall had also been the site of the Holy Innocents Day celebration for many years. The holiday, which occurs on December 28, was set aside as a children's celebration and a large Christmas tree was always part of the hall's yuletide décor.[342]

The church made at least an attempt at selling the building. "For sale: the frame building immediately in rear of St. James Church. Society Hall (or Old Guild Hall) to be disposed of. Apply at once to H. A. Burr or Thomas D. Meares."

By July 20, 1892, Society Hall was gone. Even so, there still was not enough room for the new building, unless boundaries of the churchyard were changed.[343]

In April 1892, at least twenty graves had been moved to make way for the construction of the Bridgers Building. Among other horrors, one set of remains, resting since 1750, got citywide attention when a reporter for the *Wilmington Messenger* learned of the activity. "...but strange to say, the hair on the head was in a perfect state of preservation. It was cut short and no doubt was that of a man's." Three days later, the antiquity of the place was brought home again when workmen unearthed a copper cent six feet underground. It was dated 1794.[344]

The 1892 Parish House, or Bridgers Memorial Building, was first opened for parishioners' inspection on November 27, 1892, the same day that the new chancel was dedicated. The building cost about $9,000 and contained classrooms and guild rooms. There was no cloister leading to the new building at that time. The cloister, a memorial to Mrs. M. E. Bridgers and her children, would become a welcome reality in 1912.

The Parish House guild rooms served several groups: St. Agnes Guild; Woman's Auxiliary; Knights of Temperance; and St. Andrew's Brotherhood, a men's group that should have had a boost from the visit of Silas McBee. He was national vice president of the organization.[345]

Bridging the Century

In 1892, the auction of pews was discontinued at St. James, but that did not do much to alter seating habits or pride in a family's wooden territory. Almost fifty years later, Mrs. Amelia Harlow would write, "Five generations have now continuously occupied the pew owned by my grandfather, Thomas W. Brown." Mrs. Harlow also stated that among others, the Boatwrights, the Thorpes, Mr. Thomas H. Wright, and Miss Marie Walker "occupy the pews owned by their ancestors when the church was first built."[346]

By 1897, the entirety of St. James Church was valued for insurance purposes at only $20,000. What happened on December 11, 1899, gave the church and the insurance agent a fright. A fire started before dawn in the choir room when some rags and paper ignited. What could have been the demise of the 1839 building righted itself when the first flames burned through lead pipes. Water poured out and the fire turned to thick smoke that was discovered by sexton John Knight when he arrived at church at 6 a.m.

John Knight's duties as sexton extended to the landscape. "The lawn is growing quite prettily now," stated the *Morning Star*, "and is kept in excellent trim by Mr. John Knight, keeper of church and grounds. Arrangements are now being made for lowering the wall and iron fence on the Third Street side of the grounds about St. James."[347]

The year 1905 brought two important real estate transactions to St. James. The church sold the city block, 330' by 396', that was once the site of the St. James Home to Thomas P. Bagley for $12,000. Profit from the sale was added to the existing St. James Home Fund, and renamed the Armand J. deRosset Memorial Fund. Income from the new fund was tagged for promotion of religious and charitable works. The deRosset Fund would lend significant support to the Church of the Good Shepherd until it reached financial independence in the 1940s. Following that, the fund was used to help St. Andrew's on-the-Sound. St. James Parish also acquired additional property in 1905 when businessman Thomas H. Wright contributed a house and lot on South Sixth Street close to the existing Good Shepherd property.

Little Chapel on the Boardwalk was formed in 1907 as a joint venture of St. James Church and First Presbyterian Church. Just as the trip from Wrightsville to Third Street was arduous in 1835 when Lebanon Chapel was built, the journey from Wrightsville Beach to downtown Wilmington was still a long hot ordeal in 1907. Not only was the round trip by beach car a lengthy one, *you had to leave the beach.*

The chapel's quite literal name was coined by businessman Thomas H. Wright back in the days when a boardwalk served as the sidewalk at Wrightsville Beach. The first Little Chapel was located on South Lumina Avenue, near the present site of St. Therese Catholic Church. Until the

A service at Church of the Good Shepherd, about 1946. (Courtesy of Church of the Good Shepherd and NHCPL)

Church of the Good Shepherd, 2004. (Photo by the author)

The beautiful old baptismal font from St. James with its clean lines and gleaming white marble still adorns the Church of the Good Shepherd. (Photo by the author)

This image depicts the ground-breaking ceremony for the 1911-1912 Church of the Good Shepherd building. By that time, the recreational hall (white building in background) had grown to include an upstairs bowling alley. (Courtesy of Church of the Good Shepherd and NHCPL)

The charming Chapel of the Good Shepherd was dismantled in 1911, but the framing was reused in a building that still stands on the southeastern corner of Eighth and Wooster streets. (Courtesy of Church of the Good Shepherd and NHCPL)

1930s when Waynick Boulevard was widened, the chapel was so close to the water that Walker Taylor III fished out the window when he was a boy. Services at first were conducted by Presbyterians in July and Episcopalians in August.

Though Mount Lebanon Chapel was usually closed to the public from 1924 until 1973, St. Andrew's on-the-Sound provided a seasonal church home for many Episcopalians. In 1951, St. James relinquished its portion of the title to Little Chapel to the Wilmington Presbytery. "It (the title) is to be sold and process applied to construction of a new building," reported the vestry. The Presbytery, in turn, sold the old site to the Wrightsville Beach Lions Club. The congregation quickly obtained several lots on the corner of North Lumina Avenue and Oxford Street where they built a new church, designed by Charles H. Boney.[348]

During the early years of the 20th century, the soundfront home of William ("Willie Gus") Wright, Jr., was often the site of St. James Sunday School picnics. Mr. Wright, a jocular law clerk, was the son of esteemed attorney William Augustus Wright. The elder Wright took a low profile at St. James Church, preferring to serve by quietly lending substantial financial stewardship. He was generous both to the church and to Episcopal rectors, who received checks "to keep the domestic wheels a'going." In town, the William Wrights were occupants of the Hill-Wright-Wootten House next door to St. James Church. And they lived just a stroll away from Lebanon Chapel in the summertime.[349]

William Augustus Wright (1807-1878), a brother of Dr. Thomas H. Wright, was a quiet financial angel to the clergy. He lived next door to the church in the Hill-Wright-Wootten House. His summer home was on the north side of Airlie Road, now the property of Agnes Rankin Beane. (Reprinted from *The Cape Fear Club.* Edited by Leslie N. Boney, Jr. Historical Sketch by James L. Allegood.)

In those days, there was no emergency hospital care for residents of Wrightsville Sound. Owing to this and the Wright brothers' large families — and number of friends and distant relatives they hosted during the summer, an amazing number of St. James members were either born or died at their Wrightsville residences. They include Thomas Wright Strange and H. Russell Latimer, who were born at Mount Lebanon — and Mary Wright Giles who died at Lebanon. In fact, "Col. Atkinson was born August 15, 1855, at the summer residence of his grandfather, the late Dr. Thomas H. Wright, on Wrightsville Sound," and died August 22, 1899, at a house on the property of William A. Wright.[350]

The expansive William Wright tract on Airlie Road, now the home of Agnes Rankin Beane,

St. James history took place on both sides of Airlie Road. On the south side of the road, there was Mount Lebanon. On the north side, there was Gabriel's Landing, the William A. Wright residence that was the site of many church parties and a vacation spot for the Atkinson family. (Courtesy of New Hanover County Public Library)

was perfect for events like springtime baseball games and May Queen coronations. Most of the participants rode toward Wrightsville Sound on the beachcar (trolley), then were met near what is now the intersection of Airlie Road and Oleander Drive by horse-drawn or mule-drawn wagonettes. Sometimes as many as six wagonettes were engaged to carry parishioners on the short bumpy ride that ended close to "Miss Lou's Curve," (Airlie Curve) named for the wife of William Wright, Jr., Louisa Gabriella Holmes Wright.

At the 1902 picnic, attendants Cynthia Rountree and Jane Iredell Meares watched as Adair McKoy crowned Fannie Murchison May Queen. The baseball players that year included Kenneth Burgwin, John Murchison, Fred Hamme, Victor Grainger, Jr., Frank Williams, Henry Nash, and Theodore Kingsbury. They were all romping across the same ground that had been the Colonial era home of Gabriel Johnston, the Royal Governor who shifted power from Brunswick to the new town of Wilmington (1739/40). Had it not been for Governor Johnston, St. James and not St. Philip's might be the ruin today.[351]

Another Wrightsville Sound-St. James connection happened that year when Mr. J. E. Hatch was employed to paint the interior of the church and "work over" the windows. Many members of St. James had already seen Mr Hatch's artistry — at Airlie. He was Mrs. Pembroke Jones's favorite

"On the Roof of Saint James"
by Mark Levy

"On the roof of Saint James
On Easter's glad morn,
We sing of the Saviour
In Bethlehem born,
Whose story of wonder,
By sages foretold,
Was known in God's temple
Of marble and gold.

"His life of denial,
Rejection and death,
His rising again
With life's glorious breath,
Was known to the prophets
Long ages ago,
As Israel's right oracles
Blessedly show.

"So we meet with the children
Beside the bell-tower,
And sing in His honor
At Easter's glad hour,
On the roof of Saint James
Over Wilmington town,
Where the streets to the river
Cape Fear runneth down."

On April 2, 1904, Mark Levy, a recent convert to Christianity, published this poem in the *Evening Dispatch*.

"Waken Children of the King" is St. James's own Easter hymn. (Courtesy of UNCW)

painter and he was called upon frequently to mix batches of pearly gray paint that Sarah Jones (Walters) preferred for garden ornaments. The eagles that used to adorn the old Airlie gates were always painted her special color. Mr. Hatch also painted the enormous ballroom at Airlie, an amazing feat since the ceiling was sky blue and the color deepened seamlessly down the walls until it became a rich midnight blue.[352]

Men and Boys

During the Rev. Mr. Hogue's tenure (1902-1908), an unusual number of juvenile pranks occurred. Not since 1879, when "a number of white boys" got into the habit of tampering with the vaults in the churchyard — "lifting the lids and otherwise disturbing the dead," had so much mischief taken place at St. James.[353]

On one occasion in 1905, the organ wires were cut. "Think it was the choir boys," reported the vestry secretary. In 1906, a "trainer" was hired for the boys of St. James, but apparently that didn't solve the problem for, in 1907, Mr. Hogue sent five boys to reformatory school. The congregation provided full and partial scholarships and were kept apprised of the urchins' progress.

"All are doing well," reported the *St. James Parish Record*, April 14, 1907. "One writes in a recent letter: 'It would be a good thing if all the boys I used to run with could come here.'"

But even reformatory school wasn't enough. A year later disturbances by "loafing young men and boys" necessitated the hiring of a church policeman for four weeks." Within months, the Rev. Mr. Hogue took his leave of St. James to go to Chapel Hill, where most likely he would see some of those rambunctious boys again.[354]

Dr. William H. Milton conducted his first service at St. James Church on October 7, 1909. Remembered as an extraordinary teacher and a missionary clergyman, Dr. Milton "always believed that the church's first and foremost duty was to get outside of itself," according to Walker Taylor III.

"I don't think Dr. Milton used the word 'centrifugal,' but he said the church cannot look inward. It must look outward. He was one of the founders of our modern national church and our first field secretary of the National Church. He took a sabbatical leave of absence, courtesy of Victor Grainger, to work as Field Secretary for the national Episcopal church."

"I remember his great teachings," continued Mr. Taylor. "One of the many things he taught us was his great theory of 50/50 giving. For every dollar you give to the church, 50 cents has to go outside to somebody else and 50 cents stays inside.

"You know these church pledge envelopes? Dr. Milton had them cut in half. There were two sides, a red side and a black side. Each person had to determine, of his or her contribution, how much went for missions and how much stayed at home. It wasn't decided by a hierarchy, or a governing board, or the vestry. It was decided by each individual family so Dr. Milton had to constantly preach — and the net result of that was that the congregation was more generous."[355]

William H. Milton was a charter member of the National Council of the Episcopal Church. According to the Rev. Mr. Mortimer Glover, because of Dr. Milton, St. James "assumed a position of national prominence and leadership in the church, and became known as a great missionary parish." Milton initiated the first Every-Member Canvass at St. James Church in 1912. Soon it became a

St. James conducted services at St. Philip's periodically during the years that James Sprunt owned the church ruins. In addition, the Colonial Dames held a picnic at Brunswick Town every year. Here, about 1910, the speaker, Col. Alfred Moore Waddell, addresses the crowd from atop a table. Bishop Strange is seated on the ground beneath the second window from the left. (R. V. Asbury Notebook, Courtesy of LCFHS)

national tradition. Dr. Milton also organized one of the first parish councils.

Bishop Darst said that Dr. Milton, as the first field secretary of the national church, was "overcoming obstacles, changing indifference into zeal, and lifting the eyes of men to fairer visions."[356]

Paticularly from 1880-1920, the women's organizations thrived. Bazaars abounded, both at the church and beyond. For instance, in 1901, St. Cecelia's Circle hosted a benefit in the parish house that featured guessing games; a vote for the most popular boy and girl (Amoret Lord and Dougald McMillan); a Chinese exhibit that was prepared by Charlie Sing, a local laundryman; and lots of homemade ice cream.

A play, "Love and Mushrooms," plus eleven tableaux enlivened the audience in 1898. Florrie Maffitt, Nessie Cotchett, Jane Meares, and Helen and Robert Williams were just of few of the St.

James players. At other times, music was the only treat. Mary Lily Kenan and Mrs. W. G. Elliott put on a vocal concert in 1893.

Many bazaars took place in the homes of parishioners. Smilax covered the banisters of many a house that was decked out for a St. James tea. Another sort of fund-raiser took place at the elegant Orton Hotel in 1907. It was reported that the "decorations were pretty in extreme," perhaps adding to a spirit of liberality: Enough funds were collected in one night to employ a District Nurse for one year.

In 1911, Charles Lamb and Co. replastered the church interior and decorated it. At the same time the chancel floor was replaced with hardwood. In addition, a carved hardwood chancel frontal was installed just in front of the pews.[357]

Fundraisers and benefits were manifest in another way in 1911-1912, when St. James built Church of the Good Shepherd at 515 Queen Street. According to former AIA archivist, Tony P. Wrenn the building was designed by Hobart Upjohn and George W. Conable, and is "an adaptation of the English Gothic country church." The little church was and is the jewel of Dry Pond.[358]

It is probable that the stained glass windows of St. James's nave were the models for those in the mission church. Though larger and finer, the vertical windows of St. James are reminiscent in design to the windows at Church of the Good Shepherd. Architect George W. Conable trained under the firm of Barney and Chapman, of which one of the principals was J. Stewart Barney. Barney drew the plans about 1902 for Pembroke Jones's palatial hunting lodge at what is now the Wilmington subdivision of Landfall. In the following years, Mr. and Mrs. Barney and the Joneses traveled in the same social circles in Newport and the spent time together at Airlie, a place where St. James stalwarts George Rountree, Thomas H. Wright, George B. Elliott, and Bishop Strange were frequently entertained.[359]

The fine clerestory (left) and chancel windows (right) probably predate the other stained glass at St. James. The c. 1871 chancel windows have been moved from their original position. ***Photos by the author (left) and Beatrice Schomp (right).***

Mount Lebanon Chapel: A Mission of St. James Church

Lebanon Chapel continued to be used regularly during summer months as St. James East, from the Civil War until about 1903. Many people who worshiped there were members of the Carolina Yacht Club, the second oldest "boat racing" club in the U.S. Despite rapt interest, they forwent racing on Sundays, but made up for it with conversations "over the backs of pews."

The Rev. Mr. Alfred Watson led many services there, and successfully led a campaign to pay the $1,000 insurance premium on the building by a special offering. Layman Clayton Giles also conducted services at Lebanon. Giles was assisted during the 1870s and 1880s by St. James communicants Joshua Grainger Wright, William B. Giles, J. W. Atkinson, and Charles D. Myers. All of them at various times served as supervisors of the chapel and graveyard. Later, in 1900, Lebanon neighbor William A. (Willie Gus) Wright, Jr., took charge of Lebanon. But that was about the time a big change was afoot in the neighborhood.[359]

By 1900, the Airlie residence was poised for its greatest alterations. Owner Sarah Jones would eventually transform the dwelling from a gracious house to a 39-room mansion with many surrounding structures. The amazing new construction doubtless brought gawkers, and at the same time, it created an enhanced sense of proprietorship.

Mrs. Pembroke Jones purchased another parcel of land in the long process of amassing 155 acres for Airlie. This piece had been Bradley land and formed an easement from the road to Lebanon Chapel. When the Bradleys owned it, they encouraged use of the easement, but the Joneses sought to limit access to the chapel and the graveyard. Their action outraged those who had relatives buried there. The "Pembroke Jones's new gate" became a testy subject.

The vestry of St. James sought local legal opinions that, not surprisingly, favored Jones. But in the end, public outcry and criticism from cousins caused the flamboyant businessman to mellow. He announced that the gate would be left open when the owners were not in residence. When they were at Airlie House, a key was left at the gate to give access to those on horseback or in carriages. He also created steps on each side of the fence so pedestrians could pay homage to the dead.[361]

"I have a great affection and sentiment for the … Graveyard at the Chapel, for some of those who in my boyhood days gave me much happiness rest there," wrote Jones to the Vestry and Wardens of St. James. "My son was baptized in the Chapel," he added.[362]

By 1903, Pembroke Jones had been named "custodian" of Mount Lebanon Chapel and given vestry approval "to improve and repair without cost to the vestry." By that time, Airlie was roaring

Bishop Darst (Photo by Wootten-Moulton Studio. Courtesy of UNC at Chapel Hill Library.)

information, had a lot of experiences, and so on, but the fundamental grounding in the liturgy of the church, the theology of the church, the hymns of the church, the meaning and importance of it all came when I was 8,9,10,11,12 – in the Lenten Choir."[372]

In 1915, Thomas Darst, a native of Virginia, was consecrated bishop of East Carolina. In his first official address, he mentioned the new vibrant spirit within the diocese and gave credit to former bishop Robert Strange and to Dr. Milton's Every Member Canvass. Bishop Darst was known for his attention to missionary detail, as evidenced in his personal door-to-door campaign to help establish St. Andrew's on-the-Sound. He also took great interest in the restoration of St. Thomas Church in Bath, a building known as a "diocesan shrine." During his 30-year period as bishop the diocese made great strides to promote evangelism and "spiritual awakening." Bishop Darst was awarded honorary doctorate degrees from five institutions of higher learning, including Duke University and Virginia Seminary.

On October 25, 1965, the Rt. Rev. Thomas H. Wright, Walker Taylor III, and Canon Charles M. Guilbert dedicated a memorial plaque at the Episcopal Church Center in New York to the Rt. Rev. Thomas C. Darst. The plaque, placed at the entrance to the East Carolina Room, offices of the General Convention of the Episcopal Church, reads: "Thomas Campbell Darst, D. D., third Bishop of the Diocese (1915-1945). Leader in "The National Campaign." Chairman of "The Bishop's Crusade.'"

On July 14, 1916, Mr. and Mrs. George B. Elliott presented a children's Sunday School room to the church as a memorial to their daughter. Elliott was general counsel for the Atlantic Coast Line Railroad. Mrs. Elliott, a sister of Mrs. Pembroke Jones, chose the firm of Rhodes and Underwood as the building contractors. In addition to his work at St. Andrew's on-the-Sound, U. A. Underwood was Mrs. Jones's primary contractor at the Airlie mansion and the supervising architect for the Beane residence at 1005 Airlie Road.[373]

Dr. Milton's rectorship spanned a period of 25 years. When he had been at St. James for nine years, the vestry gave him a very modern and significant gift: an automobile. Streetcars had made suburbs possible, but cars made them popular. Dr. Milton's term of office was to be the last period of time in which most of the members of St. James Church lived in the neighborhood we now know as the Historic District. Changes came slowly in those days and whoever found a place and did their job well could stay in that place for a very long time.

"Victor Grainger, my grandfather, was senior warden of St. James for about forty consecutive years, said Walker Taylor III. "Along with Robert Strange, he was one of those deeply involved members of St. James who actually lived close enough to walk to church — and he stopped by there

Katie and J. V. Grainger are pictured in 1938 at their 50th wedding anniversary party. Mr. Grainger was one of the longest serving senior wardens in St. James's history. Mrs. Grainger gave the lights in the church in his memory. (Courtesy of Walker Taylor III)

daily. The Grainger residence was at 813 Market Street and every morning Victor Grainger walked to the Murchison Bank at 201 North Front Street where he was president."

Jean McKoy Graham, another of Mr. Grainger's grandchildren, concurred. "He stopped by St. James every morning to pray at the altar," she said in 2004.

"J.V. Grainger was also one of the last senior wardens to serve in that capacity for decades," said Walker Taylor III. "In modern days this would be considered the 'old boys' network,' because of the permanence, But the fact of the matter is that the vestry was annually elected at St. James. There was only a one-year term and there were no nominees. And there was a list of all eligible men, only men, who would serve as officers at that time. And every year the congregation elected them.

"Growing up, I never knew anyone but my grandfather ("Papa") to be senior warden. In those days, Dr. Milton, his best friend, used to give the youngsters written exams pertaining to the catechism. I was only twelve years old, but it seems like yesterday.

One of the questions is, "Who's the head of the Church?" And of course the right answer is "Jesus Christ."

I wrote down "J. V. Grainger."

Dr. Milton promptly called me into his office and said, "Walker, why did you put down J. V. Grainger?"

And I said, "Well if I had said, 'Papa,' you wouldn't have known who I was talking about."

The same stability that applied to senior wardens also described the usher situation. For decades, George B. Elliott and J.V. Grainger were ushers and took up the collection down the middle aisle. Peter Browne Ruffin served on the north aisle and Robert Strange passed the plate on the south aisle.

The Era of the Great War

World War I brought changes to St. James: Almost one/sixth of the church's communicants served in the armed forces. Seven clergymen from the Diocese of East Carolina also went to war.

Lt. Frank Lenox Williams (on the right) poses with his brother, Robert M. Williams, in what probably was his last photo. He lost his life in World War I. The Williams brothers stand near the Williams-MacMillan House at 118 South Fourth Street. (Courtesy of Robert M. Williams, Jr.)

Out of those 97 participants from St. James, only one was immediately known to be a victim of warfare: Lieutenant Frank Lenox Williams. Later, victims of mustard gas would join the ranks. The Rev. W. H. Milton, D. D., honored the 96 survivors and eulogized Lt. Williams on January 5, 1919. During a sermon entitled "The Great Adventure," Dr. Milton compared going to war with Abraham's journey of faith, and noted the selflessness of obedient service and the perspective war lends to western materialism. He concluded his tribute with the words of Frank Lenox Williams's commanding general.

"I am distressed to learn of the death by wounds of Lieutenant Williams. He did splendid work over here, and would soon have gained his captaincy; in fact, I had it in my mind to promote him as soon as we got him into a rest area for reorganization. His record was splendid, his courage unquestioned, and he died a glorious death…His development under trying circumstances was marvelous and he gave every promise of a splendid future. He has sacrificed his life in the greatest and most Christian cause that has ever confronted liberty and humanity."[374]

In 1919, Pembroke Jones died. The son of a Navy captain and a young mother who died in childbirth, he was raised by his aunt, Mrs. Platt K. Dickinson. In his will, Mr. Jones included a bequest of $5000 to the church, and willed pew 49 as a "visitors' pew," in memory of Alice H. Dickinson. His regard for visitors reflected an earlier time at St. James when ushers were known to have been employed simply to "seat strangers."[375]

In 1919, the old rectory was sold to Dr. J. B. Cranmer for $16,000. The Cranmers subsequently donated $10,000 to St. James to create a Children's Chapel as a memorial to their daughter, Alice Meade Cranmer, who was an Episcopal nun in the order of St. John the Baptist. Distraught after her sister was killed in a fire, she entered a convent in Mendham, New Jersey, in 1937. They gave her a new name to go along with her new life: Sister Alice Madeline. Sister Madeline died in 1951 and was buried in New Bern.[376]

In August 1919, the vestry paid $14,000 for the M. J. Corbett house on the northeast corner of Fourth and Orange streets. It would serve as the rectory until the Thomas H. Wright house at 110

"Our Roll of Honor."

Harris Percy Alderman
Joseph Creth Angel
William Mayo Atkinson
Louis de Keyser Belden
Emmet Hargrove Bellamy
Hargrove Bellamy
Charles Young Bidgood
Charles Ormond Butler
Hugh Courtney Calder
Richard Willard Cantwell
Paul Langley Cantwell
Robert Calder Cantwell
Edgar Parmelee Cardwell
John Carter
George Thomas Clark
Emory Coffin Cotchett
Louis Myers Cotchett
John Hill Cronly
Robert Dickson Cronly
Moses Ashley Curtis
Robert Cowan Davis
Louis Poisson Davis
Junius Davis
Greene Fenly, Jr.
William Fenly
Allen Garthright Fechtig
Robert Wesley Farmer
Albert Gore
Milton Gore
Fairfax Heiskell Gouverneur
Charles Stedman Grainger, Jr.
Isaac Bates Grainger
John Ernest Grant
Richard Hatch Grant
Paul Fitzsimmons Hammond
Edward Manning Hardin
Andrew Howell Harriss
Andrew Howell Harriss, Jr.
George Latham Harriss
John Ferguson Harriss, Jr.
George Edgar Haskett
Charles Urquhart Hill
Charles Dunlap Hogue
Edward Hall Holmes
James Hall Holmes
Joseph Ward Hooper
Charles Raymond Humphreys
Joseph Nicholas Jacobs
George Everard Kidder
Empie Latimer
Herbert Russell Latimer
Charles James LeGrand
Charles Drayton Lodor
Eugene Willet Van Court Lucas
Dorsey Warfield Lynch
Sydney Gardner MacMillan
William Dougald MacMillan, III.
Louis deRosset MacMillan
Douglas Hart McKoy
Nelson MacRae
George Folger Meares
John VanBokkelen Metts
William Hammond Milton, Jr.
Julian Walker Morton
William Capers Munds
Louis del'Aigle Munds
Frederick Lord Munds
David Reid Murchison
John Reid Murchison
Donald MacRae Parsley
Henry Bose Peschau
Albert Fraser Perry
DeBrutz Cutlar Poisson
Edmond LaFayette Prince
William Franklin Register
Harman Chadbourn Rorison
John Chadbourn Rorison
Edward Draper Savage
Henry Russell Savage
John Franklin Smith
William Lincoln Smith, Jr.
Reston Stevenson
Robert Strange
Thomas Wright Strange
Arthur Hammond Styron
George Thomas Swain
John Douglas Taylor
George Lynch Tillery
James Luther Toon. Jr.
John Piper Watters
Justin Smith White
FRANK LENOX WILLIAMS
Robert Marshall Williams

Madeline deRosset
Virginia Lee Milton, Jr.
Lucy Atkinson Murchison
Dorothy Nash

Names in Italics—"Over-Seas" Service.
Black letter Capitals—"Died on the Field of Honor."

Roll of Honor (From "The Great Adventure," by the Rev. William H. Milton, D. D., St. James Church. January 5, 1919.) (Courtesy of the Lower Cape Fear Historical Society)

North 15th Street was secured in 1964. Since 1972, the church has provided an allowance for housing.

In the fall of 1922, plans were announced for an addition to the existing parish house. The building had already been altered twice, in 1912 and 1922. "The new parish house of St. James Church, for which final plans and specifications are being prepared by Hobart Upjohn, of New York, one of the foremost church architects of the country, will be ready for activities of the church not later than next fall," heralded the local paper. "The building will be placed in front of the present parish house, facing Market Street."[377]

The first building phase began in May 1923 when cemetery space was again diminished to make way for a new building. But this time there were protests. Church fathers defended their stand and cited proper procedure: a notice was posted on the church door for 30 days before the work began. But that didn't stop the grumbling when fourteen graves were moved from the location now occupied by the Upjohn building.

The bones were exhumed by black men who worked for the Woolvin-Andrews Company. Each body was placed in a small casket that was reburied near the southern boundary of the churchyard and each headstone was carefully replaced. James Woolvin and at least one vestryman were always in attendance. Most of the dead who were moved had died around 1800.[378]

The committee in charge of the Upjohn addition included George B. Elliott, Thomas H. Wright, O. H. Lippitt, J. V. Grainger, and W. D. MacMillan. Hobart Upjohn was the grandson of

Richard Upjohn, who was, in effect, the first president of the American Institute of Architects. Among other buildings, Richard Upjohn designed famous Trinity Church on Wall Street; St. Mary's Episcopal Church in Burlington, N.J.; and Christ Church in Raleigh — a church-architect link created by Bishop Ives in 1848. Most if not all of the vestry members had met with Upjohn during the construction of Church of the Good Shepherd, in 1911-1912.[379]

The spire of First Presbyterian Church looms between the Savage (on left) and Latimer houses. The two churches are not only good neighbors, but entwined for perpetuity through myriad family connections. (Photo by William J. Boney, Jr.)

Hobart Upjohn owed his first name to the Rt. Rev. John Henry Hobart, Adam Empie's old friend and the father-in-law of Levi Silliman Ives. Bishop Hobart's fondness for and allegiance to Gothic Revival architecture had results that sweetened Richard Upjohn's professional life. Grandson Hobart Upjohn had many ties in North Carolina, the primary one being with wealthy mill owner Moses Cone, in Greensboro. Upjohn kept a satellite office there for twenty years.

Over time, Hobart Upjohn designed Temple Emanuel, First Presbyterian, Holy Trinity, and Grace Methodist — in Greensboro. In Raleigh, he served as architect for eight buildings on the NCSU campus, including the Frank Thompson Gymnasium — and additions to his grandfather's design, Christ Church. In Chapel Hill, he designed the Sprunt Memorial Church, and the new Chapel of the Cross. Following his work at St. James, he designed Wilmington's First Presbyterian Church building (1927-1928), following the 1925 fire that destroyed the congregation's third edifice."[380]

The Rt. Rev. Thomas C. Darst, flanked by the Rev. William H. Milton, dedicated the new Parish House after ceremonies that included special music, and a series of tableaux that illustrated "The Church at Work." The first tableau addressed the early church and featured Mrs. Julian Morton,

This much-used photo of St. James Church from Fourth and Market streets was taken by 12-year-old Edward (Ned) Wootten on May 30, 1937. Ned Wootten was a grandson of the Rev. Edward Wootten. (Courtesy of Mary M. Wootten)

author and photographer Hugh Morton's mother, as "Mother Church." The second illustrated church growth, with Mrs. Harmon Rorison, Marjorie Willard, and Mrs. Hugh Calder. The final tableau "starred" Emma Williamson, Marjorie Willard, Ruth Pleasants, Monimia MacRae, Mrs. Harmon Rorison, Mrs. Edward M. Hardin, Leila Wootten, and Josey Wright.[381]

But what mattered most to Miss Ellen Bellamy was the origin of a stepping stone Mr. Upjohn incorporated into the building. "The stone you step on as you come down from the Great Hall is a stone taken from my grandfather Harriss's lot. It was ours!"[382]

Dr. Milton's many ties to the national church brought some interesting speakers to St. James. In 1928, the Church Army, a charitable and evangelistic organization associated with Anglican and Episcopal churches, visited Wilmington and held an evangelistic service at St. James. At the conclusion of the service, an altar call was made and members and nonmembers were encouraged to accept the Christian way or to rededicate themselves to the way of the Lord. On that occasion, a twenty-year-old woman named Louise Dick knelt at the altar and made a pledge to God. That decision and its result were recounted 76 years later by her son, Richard Gwathmey. "The defining thing about Mama was her faith. Her deep, deep devotion to, and her close relationship with Jesus

THE VESTRY

1940

Mr. J. V. Grainger, Senior Warden
Mr. George B. Elliott, Junior Warden
Mr. W. B. Thorpe, Treasurer
Mr. R. D. Cronly, Clerk

Dr. J. B. Cranmer
Mr. Stone C. Pulliam
Mr. Harmon Rorison
Mr. Peter Brown Ruffin

Mr. Robert Strange
Mr. George G. Thomas
Mr. Frederick Willetts
Mr. Thomas H. Wright

Members of the 1940 vestry did not deviate much from the dress code of the day. (Courtesy of UNCW.)

This photo was taken at the home of Lizzie Winston Broadfoot at 217 Forest Hills Drive, about 1943. Mrs. Broadfoot liked to "round up" St. James girls for the G.I.s who were regular visitors to St. James. Front row, left to right: George Boylan, unknown, Peggy Moore, Daisy Lee Woodbury, unknown. Middle row: Lizzie Winston Broadfoot, unknown, unknown, Ann Dunn. Top row: Rosalie Oliver, unknown, Cornelia Broadfoot, unknown, Mary Wright Holland, unknown, unknown, Frances Thornton. (Courtesy of Margaret Moore Perdew)

they packed the pews at Third and Market. But their weekend break from the monotony of military life was not over. After the service, without fail, each of them enjoyed some of the best food around when various parishioners hosted them for Sunday dinner.[392]

Meanwhile, Walker Taylor was in the Merchant Marine and had an unexpected meeting with Hobart Upjohn, architect of St. James's Great Hall and Wilmington's First Presbyterian Church. Mr. Upjohn was a grandson of Richard Upjohn who designed Trinity Church in New York.

"During World War II, I went to church at Trinity Church, Broadway and Wall Street one time, and there was a handsome man on the front door wearing a morning coat and I was wearing a sailor suit and he greeted me and said, 'My name is Hobart Upjohn and what's your name, young man?'

"I said, 'Walker Taylor,' and he just about dropped because he and my grandfather, Victor Grainger, and the other grandfather, Col. Walker Taylor, had been good friends. Both my grandfathers were dead by that time."

There were at least three "blackbirds baked in a pie" in this 1932 St. James kindergarten production, directed by Mary Graham and Louisa Howard. The children are: (bottom row) Nell Trask, Fred Block, William Ross, Joe Morrison, and Laurence Sprunt; (top row) Fred Poisson, Francis Van Landingham, Blanche Bolles, Rockwell Poisson, and Shirley Finkelstein. (Courtesy of Cape Fear Museum)

Moore, and Beverly George to start a new kindergarten. The rector helped them establish a curriculum similar to one at the Calvert School of Baltimore. A program for reading readiness prepared the students for public school while regular participation in services at the Children's Chapel gave them early church training. The school was a great success. Even though the program initially cost the church money, it was quickly repaid. The kindergarten also contributed $2,000 to the 1955 building campaign.[398]

The first director was Eleanor Snyder who was followed soon after by Margaret Y. Moore, who was recruited by Mr. Glover. In August 1952, St. James announced Miss Moore's resignation as director of the school. "She has made our kindergarten outstanding among the educational institutions of Wilmington. The long waiting list we have every year is testimony to the regard in which it is held."

The kindergarten group in the Elliott Room was photographed about 1957 when "Miss Peggy" (Peggy Moore Perdew) was director. (Courtesy of Margaret Moore Perdew)

Members of the kindergarten enjoyed an annual trip on the Atlantic Coast Line Rail Road. Here Margaret Willetts (left foreground), Alex Murchison (right, in bow tie), Janice Hall (collar with white lace), and Robbie Little (in hat) take a ride on the rails in 1957. Since 1997, Margaret Willetts has been director of the kindergarten she attended.

The Easter parade of young people on their way to the Great Hall with mite boxes is a reminder of the story of the widow's mite found in Mark 12: 41-44. This photo features Jean Graham, Jane Woodbury, and Horace Hamilton. (Courtesy of Jean McKoy Graham)

Here, about 1954 are Mary Atkinson and Julia Barfield (left to right foreground.) Mrs. Mamie Thomas, legendary children's teacher, and Hugh MacRae II, a longtime steady force within the church, accompany the girls. (Photo by William C. Barfield, Courtesy of Julia Barfield)

The Lenten Choir, about 1930, included these members (left to right): Foreground: Hugh MacRae II. Row 1 - #4 Weddell Harriss, #5 William Ross, # 7 Bob Williams, #8 Lem Doss, #9 Donald Parsley. Row 2 - #2 Jack Preston, #3 Julian Morton, #4 Frank Ross, #6 Pat Preston. Row 3 - #7 Ann Burr, #8 Walker Taylor III, #10 Billie Sidbury. (Courtesy of Hugh MacRae II)

Peggy Moore left her position to become Director of Religious Education of Grace Chapel Parish in Jacksonville, Fla., where she established a kindergarten. Virginia Lynch became director, but left two years later when the Atlantic Coast Line Railroad moved its heaquarters to Jacksonville. Miss Moore returned to work at St. James where she directed the kindergarten for many more years. She is still known affectionately to her "children" as "Miss Peggy."

In 2001, Peggy Moore Perdew reminisced about her church school career. "I don't know how I happened to drift into kindergarten work except that during the war, I used to be around a lot of children. Hannah and Bishop Wright's children and my sister, Florence Dunn's son Jack were such good friends. Those little kids: I was just always very fond of them. And so I ended up directing the kindergarten at St. James and they were really very happy years."[399]

In the 1940s, many members of St. James expressed outrage that city government planned to narrow the plazas on Third Street and create an oil tanker truck route. During that period and for years after that, large petroleum hauling trucks spewed blackened exhaust as they sped down South Third Street. The trucking companies and the Wilmington City Council knew there would be opposition, but they did not expect the likes of W. A. Townes and George B. Elliott of St. James

Members of the 1956-1957 kindergarten posed near the rails at Union Station. Members include Julie Boatwright, Elizabeth Brown, Rachel MacRae, Margaret Willetts, Mary Scott, Kitty Ward, Miriam Broadfoot, Janice Hall, Dottie Crouch, Barbara Bear, Bobby Broadfoot, Alex Murchison, Herbert Harriss, Randall Broadfoot, and Robert Little, Jr. The teachers include (left to right, ends) Margaret Groover, Mildred Lawther, Virginia Lynch, Gibbs Holmes, and Peggy Moore. (Courtesy of the Wilmington Railroad Museum.)

Church.

Writing on behalf of the vestry, they stated their case aesthetically, then added a plea for safety. "A collision between any one of these loaded trucks and another truck or another motor car might well result in a horrible conflagration that would sacrifice our people and our property." Despite the vestry's eloquent pleas, business prevailed. The plazas were narrowed and the sooty tankers rumbled down Third Street for decades.

The little altar in the children's chapel was an honorarium to children's church teacher, Mamie Thomas. The painting, a recent addition by local artist Martha Williams, is copied from a fresco. The cross was a gift from Mary M. Wootten. (Photo by Beatrice Schomp)

This painting by Wilmington artist Neal Thomas depicts the bishop's consecration from the vantage point of the church balcony. The painting won an award at the ninth annual exhibit of NC artists. (Courtesy of J. Robert Lane, Jr., photo by J. Robert Warren)

The Rt. Rev. Thomas H. Wright

From the author's interviews with the Rt. Rev. and Mrs. Thomas H. Wright, in 1988, 1991, and 1992.

Thomas Henry Wright, the son of John Maffitt and Josie Whitaker Wright, was born in Wilmington on October 16, 1904. He was baptized at St. James Church. Tom Wright was only fourteen months old when his father died of blood poisoning. He continued to live at 207 Nun Street with his older siblings, Laurens and Josie Wright.

As a young boy, Tom Wright attended Miss Annie Hart's School behind St. John's Lodge. He and his close friends, Fred Dick, Donald MacRae, and Devereaux Lippitt, had the run of the downtown neighborhood, and often played football in the yard of the Donald MacRae House, now the St. James Parish House.

In 1920, Peter Browne Ruffin moved to Wilmington from Hillsborough when his mother, Annie Gray Ruffin, married his stepfather, James Laurence Sprunt. According to the late Mr. Ruffin, interviewed in 1992, he and Tom Wright "became friends straight away. The Bishop was a very popular young man. We were and are devoted friends." In 1924, when the Laurence Sprunt family moved into the Governor Dudley mansion, Peter Browne Ruffin and Tom Wright would play spirited sets of tennis in the lower garden of the backyard at 400 South Front Street, just a block's walk from Bishop Wright's home.

This photo was taken in 1905 or early 1906 when Laurens Wright (on right) was still wearing a mourning band for his father. (Courtesy of Allan T. Strange)

Tom Wright also found a good friend in Scotty Robertson, the church organist. Mr. Robertson's warmth and devotion had a tremendous influence on the boy. So did Robert Strange, superintendent of the St. James Sunday School for thirty years. Another man who spent time with the fatherless boy was his uncle, Thomas H. Wright. Young Tom Wright served as a ribbon boy at the wedding of his uncle and Eleanor

Gilchrist in 1914. Mr. Wright also took him to Christmas parties at Airlie where Mr. and Mrs. Pembroke Jones, and Henry Walters, president of the Atlantic Coast Line, would give toys to all the young guests. Tom Wright's favorite Airlie treat was a full coat of mail presented to him when he was twelve.

After Miss Annie Hart's School, he went to Tileston and then to New Hanover High School, where he was president of the first senior class. During the summer, he would help his uncle, Thomas H. Wright, host Children's Night at Lumina. Tom Wright would take a streetcar that natives always called the "Beachcar" to Wrightsville Beach and help supervise the children who were dancing with instructor Leonora Cantwell to the music of a band from the Oceanic Hotel. Then young Tom would pay 50 cents to spend the night at the Carolina Yacht Club.

The Rev. Frank Wakefield, a recruiter for Sewanee School, came to Wilmington just as Thomas Wright was considering the question of college. Sewanee, also known as The University of the South, has often been called the "Oxford of America." Mr. Wakefield announced that the school had one unused partial scholarship and that St. James Church had been given authority to choose the recipient.

St. James, under the leadership of Dr. Milton, chose Tom Wright. The young man's uncle, Thomas H. Wright, also made him a formal education loan of $600. He spent four years at the small, distinguished university during which he played a banjo with a woman's face painted on it and worked as an assistant librarian to help pay his expenses. He also found time to serve as president of the student body and Sigma Nu, the fraternity he pledged "because brother Laurens had." Tom Wright also managed the school's basketball team. Even with a full schedule of extracurricular activities, he managed to make good grades and returned to Wilmington with a diploma and enough money to pay his debt to his uncle. When he met Thomas H. Wright to give him the $600, the older man smiled and simply tore up the note.

His brother Laurens had obtained an excellent job with the Standard Oil Company and after several promotions, became head of Standard Oil for North and South Carolina. Laurens Wright was probably the reason that a drawing of St. James Church was featured in a nationwide Standard Oil advertisement in 1925. Laurens Wright quickly found his sibling a job that would urge him toward a higher vocation.

"I walked the line. My entire job was to walk up and down the gas line from the ship to the tank and make sure there were no leaks. I walked up and down that line for a year carrying a screwdriver and a flashlight. I learned to negotiate the rope ladders to the ships so that I could get a bite to eat and I befriended a watchman who delighted in serving coffee that stood at attention in the cup. Walking that line one night, I decided I had had enough of the business world.

"Up until that time, I had not had a thought of going into church work. As I began to think through all my happiest, most meaningful memories, I realized that they had all happened in one

Church and commercial business transpire simultaneously in this photo of Bishop Hunley Elebash's investiture on October 3, 1968. Presiding bishop John E. Hines was the consecrator. (Courtesy of Church of the Good Shepherd and New Hanover County Public Library.)

place: St. James Church. So I decided on the ministry.

"Just after I made my decision, Mr. Goodlett Thornton, who was president of Wilmington Savings and Trust, told me he had been watching me and thought I would make a good banker. When I told him of my plans, he replied, 'All my life I have wanted to go into the ministry. Go and you won't regret it.'"

Tom Wright then attended Virginia Theological Seminary in Alexandria for three years. Once again he was elected president of the student body. He found the other students to be "much more normal" men than he expected and particularly enjoyed the friendship of John Bryant, a Princeton-educated handsome blond who scoured the papers to find news of large, upcoming debutante parties in the newspapers. When the parties were well in progress, Tom Wright and John Bryant would drive up in *Josephine*, Tom Wright's ancient Model T which he found in an "abandoned state. It had sides, but no top. The valets did not enjoy parking it." Nevertheless, the two young men proceeded to gracefully crash the parties, smoothly conversing their way through crowds of people they had never seen before and meeting lots of pretty girls in the process.

He earned extra money by working at camp in the summers, and teaching swimming in the cold waters of Maine.

Tom Wright was entered in the 1928 issue of "Who's Who in America" because he was one of two young men selected to represent the USA at the "World Christian Student Federation Meeting" in Gizat, Holland. The other man was Pitney van Husan who later became president of Union Seminary in New York City. At the evening ball given for them in Holland, Tom Wright was the guest of the Queen's daughter, Juliana, which was "an event for a country boy from North Carolina."

Mr. Wright was ordained to the diaconate in St. James Church in 1929. Bishop Thomas Darst then sent him to Lumberton to serve five churches: Maxton, Laurinburg, Red Springs, Whiteville, and Lumberton. He stayed there one year.

Subsequently, he was sent to Chapel Hill to be the full-time minister for the university. He was the first Episcopal chaplain to serve the campus of the University of North Carolina. He lived in the parish house, but had to take baths at the "Tin Can," the school's old gym. His quarters consisted of a bedroom with a single bed. An adjoining room served as a tiny dormitory for the co-captains of the football team, a situation that put the minister in contact with plenty of students.

"These were some of the happiest times of my life. They treated me wonderfully. I had the help of two great men who came to Chapel Hill anytime I needed them. One was Coleman Jennings, whose family owned diamond mines in South Africa. Coleman, who was one of the world's greatest laymen, gave half of his income away every year to boys who were not able to finance their own education. The other was Alexander Zabriskie, the Dean of Virginia Seminary."

While at Chapel Hill, Tom Wright, Alexander Zabriskie, and Coleman Jennings helped organize what became an annual retreat for 25 ministers. Their two-week meetings were held at various places including a fully staffed estate in New Hampshire and an oceanfront cottage at Wrightsville Beach. Businessman Thomas H. Wright put up eight of the ministers at his beach house, which was located where the Station One condominiums now stand.

During the three years Tom Wright served as Episcopal chaplain to the University, eight students opted to become ministers. Two of them were later elected bishops.

From Chapel Hill, the young minister moved to New York City to work for the National Council of the Church as Secretary of College Work. Collegiate ministry was considered the "Church's newest mission field" and it was the Rev. Mr. Wright's job to see that churches were built and staffed in college towns all over the United States. For two years he lived in a fifth-floor walkup apartment at 12th and Broadway. It was the time of the Great Depression and it was not unusual for him to return to his apartment after work and find a "sleeping homeless person on every single stair step."

In New York, Tom Wright was offered three jobs. He chose an offer from Lexington, Virginia, and became the minister of Robert E. Lee Memorial Church as well as chaplain to Washington and Lee and Virginia Military Institute. The handsome young prelate had a challenging job, loads of friends, and a lovely 1812 Rectory in which to live. After five years in Lexington, he was as happy with his single life as could be humanly possible — until one night when he had an almost blind date with Hannah Knowlton of Charlotte.

Mr. Wright and Miss Knowlton had actually met before at a party in the Bishop's House in Wilmington. The Rt. Rev. Thomas Darst had hosted the occasion. She was the daughter of James Woolcott and Marie Knowlton of Knowlton, West Virginia, and Charlotte. Her great-grandparents had been married by Ralph Waldo Emerson, who was a cousin of her father's. A year after their first meeting, Tom Wright was passing through Charlotte and called an old friend who arranged a blind date for him. When Tom Wright arrived at the front door of the Knowlton home, Hannah recognized him. They disagreed as to whether he recognized her. Nevertheless, he would never forget again. The next morning a dozen roses arrived, with a proposal soon to follow. On December 1, 1937, they were married.

The bride was fourteen years younger than the groom, a fact reflected by their cars. He drove a black Pontiac, the "sedate sedan" as she called it. She loved her Carolina blue Ford convertible. Hannah's presence never went unnoticed. John N. Camp, Jr., of Franklin, Virginia, reminiscing fifty years later said , "Having been a cadet at V.M.I., and a Baptist, I knew immediately the weapon that gave Episcopalians the advantage: Hannah! As she drove around Lexington with the top down on her beautiful convertible, every cadet envied the Rev. Mr. Wright. Her smile and enthusiasm matched her beauty and still charms us all."

Another former V.M.I. cadet who vividly remembers the minister's taking a wife is Bruce B. Cameron, who noted that Hannah was younger at the time than many of the students and lots of them whistled as she passed by in her convertible.

Eventually both cars were sold and they settled on a compromise vehicle: A black Pontiac with red leather seats and a convertible top that, of course, was black for funerals.

In 1941, the young couple moved to San Francisco when Wright was called as Dean of Grace Cathedral. Dean Wright was in the pulpit delivering a sermon on December 7, 1941. A government official interrupted the service to whisper the news about Pearl Harbor to him. After a brief prayer, the worshipers were sent home. The war created special challenges in San Francisco with hundreds of young wives anxiously passing the time, waiting for news from their husbands who were fighting overseas. Hannah decided that the church ought to do something about it and after making funding and hospitality arrangements on Nob Hill, she organized teas for all the ladies.

On Christmas morning, 1942, Dean Wright took the Choir School for Boys to San Quentin. The outstanding vocalists performed for the prisoners as part of a special holiday service. The men acted very disrespectful at first. Dean Wright suffered their insolence for a few minutes. Finally, in anger he addressed their misconduct saying, "These young boys left their homes to be with you this Christmas morning! Can't you be quiet and give them your attention?" The prisoners settled down a bit and the boys began to sing again. Soon the audience fell completely silent and eventually some of the prisoners even cried.

While at Grace Cathedral, Dean Wright was often in the chapel when strangers came by to pray or just to meditate. He befriended many of these people. One was a ragged looking gentleman who lived in a nearby home for elderly men. He told the young Dean that he existed on a mere $30 a month. He had been raised in a bleak orphanage in Bristol, England, where one of his few pleasures was hearing the ringing of the cathedral church bells. The old man showed enormous interest in plans Dean Wright divulged concerning the building of a bell tower at Grace Cathedral and the need for a benefactor.

A short time later, Dean Wright learned of the man's true identity. He was Dr. Nathaniel T. Coulson, a wealthy retired dentist and real estate entrepreneur. Dr. Coulson eventually underwrote costs for the church bells, went to England to watch over the casting, and hired a steamship to take them to San Francisco.

In 1991, Bishop Wright recounted an emotional experience which happened during his years in San Francisco. "One of the most remarkable stories that I can remember while the war with Japan and Germany was progressing was going to my early service in Grace Cathedral and finding a whole row of English sailors at the outer rail. They had come from the British ship *Orion,* which had been bombed during the Battle of the Coral Sea. Almost all were on crutches or wore bandages or showed some sign of having been in a battle.

"After communion they told me their story. The whole front end of the ship had been blown away. The carpenters of the crew had replaced the woodwork with a makeshift front end but it could not stand the pressure going forward and so had to back all the way across the Pacific. Because it was so slow it couldn't travel with any of the convoys and so they never expected to make it — for they felt sure the Japanese would blow them up. But the Lord had been good to them. They were safe in San Francisco and the first thing they and their chaplain wanted to do was to thank God.

"Their chaplain was Gerald Ellison who as time passed became a leading churchman in England, bishop of Chester, and later, bishop of London. We visited the bishop and his wife in both places. Once when they were in Boston for a General Convention, we had a dinner party to honor them. We were very good friends."

During his wartime stay in San Francisco, Dean Wright performed an average of eight to ten weddings a day, primarily hastily planned generic services for sailors. However, one wedding he performed was anything but routine. Charlie Soong, Madame Chiang Kai-Shek's brother, decided he wanted to be married in Grace Cathedral. Charlie was the youngest son of a man who was converted to Christianity through the ministry of Fifth Avenue Methodist Church while he was a cabin boy on a ship docked at Wilmington.

"There was such planning," recounted Bishop Wright. "There were big committees and little committees and all the proceedings were very polite and took many hours. I performed the religious part of the wedding first and then the state wedding proceeded outside the rail. The church documents were signed at the altar and the state documents, outside the rail. *LIFE* magazine photographers were all over the place. The crowd took up the whole cathedral: 5,000 seats. Afterwards, there was a big reception and I was placed in the seat of honor. I delivered a blessing in English and they clapped. We were served twelve courses of food. When they served us soup with whole chicken feet, I would just as soon have had a less conspicuous seat."

" John Craine, my first assistant in the Cathedral in San Francisco, became the bishop of Indianapolis. I went to Indianapolis to do the Lenten preaching for him one year. In those days all large churches had Lenten services with different preachers each week. I did this many times, but I would only do it one week each Lent. I preached many years in Trinity Church in New York. I preached in almost all of the big New York churches during the year: St. Thomas, St. James and St. Bartholomew's.

"On this particular week, we had done what I usually did — preach each day at 12 noon. They didn't take up a collection except the last day which was Good Friday. I had finished the service and was packing my vestments for my return plane trip home. I noticed that the treasurer of the church, a layman, was placing the offering in a bank bag. Before I finished he called to me. He had a check in his hand and he said, 'Read this.'

"The check was made out to the church, of course. After the words, 'In the amount of,' it said, 'One million dollars.' It was a personal check and I immediately asked if it was meant to be a joke.

" ' Not at all. This man's checks are always good. Read the signature.'

"It was signed, 'Eli Lilly.'

"Of course the check was good and the contribution of the pharmaceutical king of Indianapolis went to good purposes throughout the world."

After San Francisco, Dean Wright was rector of St. Mark's Church in San Antonio, Texas. With 10,000 parishioners, it was the largest Episcopal church west of the Mississippi and the biggest congregation in the country, outside of New York City. The Wrights were there for only two years before he was called to return to North Carolina to become Bishop of East Carolina.

Dean Wright was notified of his election as bishop by Atlantic Coast Line president Champion McDowell Davis. It was May of 1945 and World War II was still raging so very few people had access to telephones. But Mr. Davis always had a phone and used it to inform Tom Wright that he had been elected in an unprecedented single nomination and unanimous vote. At the age of 41, he was also the youngest bishop ever consecrated by the Episcopal Church. The committee of three who met in New Bern consisted of Mr. Davis, Bryan Grimes, and R. I. Johnson, a nominee as bishop of Africa.

Bishop Wright's Consecration

"*There were cakes and apples in all the Chapels.*" - Rev. Richard Harris Barham (1788-1845)

George T. Clark, crucifer; Laurence Gray Sprunt, flag bearer; Mortimer Glover, Mary Wright Holland (Cantwell), Eugie Watters (Stillman), Nancy Lynch (Ball), Leonora Cantwell, Fred Willetts. (Photo by Hugh Morton. Courtesy of UNCW.)

Here, the new first lady of the diocese takes a turn serving punch at her husband's reception. To the right, looking into the camera, is Jane Rhett, who hosted a cooking program during the pioneer days of local television. Mrs. H. M. Roland, and author and historian Lewis Phillip Hall appear on the left. (Photo by Hugh Morton. Courtesy of UNCW.)

The Rt. Rev. Darst, Presiding Bishop Henry St. George Tucker, and the Rt. Rev. Thomas Henry Wright, in 1945. Bishop Wright would mingle business acumen with the spiritual aspects of his new position when he created The Episcopal Foundation of the Diocese of East Carolina. (Photo by Hugh Morton. Courtesy of UNCW.)

The church, as it appeared in this 1945 photo, featured dominant organ pipes, Mortimer Glover facing east at the altar, and an array of ladies' hats. (UNCW)

Mortimer Worth Glover was rector of St. James for a record period of time: from 1936 until 1964. Possessed of an encyclopedic mind and a dignified presence, he stands truly tall in the annals of parish history. Here he speaks with Lily Taylor Groover during the reception. George Gornto, church treasurer, is on the far left. His son, Dean Gornto, now serves as church adminstrator. (Photo by Hugh Morton. Courtesy of UNCW.)

Children's procession: (Photo by Hugh Morton. Courtesy of UNCW.)

The five Thomas Henry Wrights in this 1952 photograph are all descendants of Capt. Thomas Wright (1714-1771), who owned a pew in the old St. James Church building. Bishop Wright and his first cousin, businessman Thomas Wright (holding his grandson) stand at the center. The bishop's son (far left) became vice-president of Princeton University. The baby, Thomas H. Wright III, is the son of businessman and preservationist Thomas H. Wright, Jr. (far right). Throughout the first 275 years of St. James's history, no other family has been so active for so long a time as the Wrights. (Courtesy of James Knowlton Wright)

and tenure, established enormous influence. He managed to build up the institution of the church as well as minister to the individual.

"He always had an uncanny knack to turn things around. In small churches, he had the power of appointment because the diocese supplied the money for the ministers' salaries. He was very persuasive in convincing a disgruntled congregation that they actually liked their minister. I studied Bishop Wright carefully and when I became bishop, I tried to repeat the things he had said to congregations who were trying to oust their ministers. I tried to say the same words he said and use the same expression he had used and when I was through talking, someone in the room would invariably stand up and say, 'We know this man. We don't like this man, and we want him out of our church.'"

In the month of September 1951 alone, Bishop Wright visited St. Mark's Church and St. John's Church in Wilmington; Holy Trinity , Fayetteville; Holy Cross, Aurora; St. John's, Bonnerton; held separate meetings in New Bern, Beaufort, Morehead City, Holly Ridge, Goldsboro, Jacksonville, Fayetteville, and Havelock; conferred with members of St. James and St. Andrew's on-the-Sound; performed two weddings; a baptism; officiated at a clergy conference at Camp Leach; dedicated a rectory in Washington, N. C.; and delivered a talk on WMFD radio in Wilmington[400]

The Bishop and Hannah still managed to maintain an active social life and keep up with scores of close relatives in Wilmington. They had a particularly close relationship with Mr. and Mrs. W. S. R. Beane. Bill and Eleanor Wright Beane were good to the Wrights. And the Bishop and Hannah gave the Beanes, who were older parents, peace of mind when they agreed to adopt their daughter, Agnes Rankin Beane, if anything happened to them before she became of age.

The Bishop and Hannah always reserved Palm Sunday as a very special time for the Wright family, who trooped perennially from 510 Orange Street to St. James. "Palm Sunday was Dad's Sunday at St. James. We walked to church together, as a family. He spoke on Palm Sunday and on Easter Sunday he would sit there with us. The rest of the year, he was away on the weekend," said one of his three sons, Jim Wright.

The Rt. Rev. Thomas H. Wright and his wife, Hannah, relax on the beach at Honolulu during a General Convention. (Photo by Fannie G. Taylor. Courtesy of James Knowlton Wright.)

Over time, Bishop Wright received four honorary doctorates. They were awarded from the University of North Carolina, Washington and Lee, Sewanee, and Virginia Seminary. Even after retiring, he was busy speaking, baptizing babies, conducting weddings and funerals, and keeping a heavy social calendar.

Bruce Cameron, a codeveloper of Figure Eight Island — and currently Wilmington's foremost businessman and philanthropist, commented on the bishop's place in town. "He has meant a lot to more people than anyone I can think of around town. Locally, there are people who consider that they are living in sin unless the Bishop performed the wedding ceremony and are afraid of where they might be headed if he isn't scheduled to perform their funerals."

"I had an agreement with him on Figure Eight Island that he could come over anytime he wanted to and fish if he would pray away the hurricanes."[401]

Hannah Wright created her own ministry by touching people with the God-given warmth of her own personality. She was, for the most part, enormously popular, perhaps because of some advice she got not long after moving to Wilmington. A caring friend took her aside and said, "If you have anything bad to say about anyone at St. James, just go into a closet and talk to yourself – because they are all related." But when her beliefs and the desire to please friends and relatives clashed, she had little trouble taking the less socially acceptable road.

One of her bravest moments came in the 1970s when she was in her 60s. Integration, though legislated, had not yet reached Wrightsville Beach. Feeling compassion for local impoverished black children who had few diversions, she transported carloads of ecstatic youngsters to her summer home on Water Street. She walked them over to the ocean and led them back to her soundfront house for swimming in Banks Channel. Despite blistering criticism, she persevered, happy and confident that she was doing "the Lord's work."

Bishop Wright died in 1997 and Hannah followed in 2001. The remains of both were interred in the chancel.

Walker Taylor was made an honorary Doctor of Canon Law by Berkeley Divinity School at Yale in 1973. Bishop Strange and the Rev. Dr. Tom Milam graduated from Berkeley Divinity School.

One of the Bishop's Recruits

Walker Taylor III saw Bishop Wright through the eyes of an adoring friend and layman. "He was very popular with his fellow bishops, but the striking thing about this man was his special relationship with the laity. He was often called a 'layman's bishop,' Mr. Taylor said. "He was an ecumenical figure, greatly loved by people of other persuasions as well as his own flock."

"I was just amazed to see the scope of Bishop Wright's labor, the versatility of his ability. He had that quiet voice, full of conviction, and was able to bring unity and support for the diocese. He was a good administrator, firm in overseeing the clergy, and made tough decisions. A bishop's life is not easy. His job was much like a traveling salesman's: on the road, all the time. The Bishop spent thirty years in an automobile, and took a thousand flights."

"But it was his personal charisma that many will remember. A bishop has little legal authority, so he must lead by example and by the power of his personality." Walker and Bishop Wright worked together on the "Mutual Responsibility Commission" of the General Convention. This was a worldwide effort to bring together the churches of the Anglican Communion, for unity in mission. Almost a hundred dioceses in the Episcopal Church joined the effort, and became linked with dioceses in other Anglican churches abroad.

In 1957, Fannie Grainger Taylor became the first woman ever elected to the vestry of St. James Church. (Portrait by Henry J. MacMillan. Courtesy of Victor G. Taylor)

In 1968, Lucille Murchison Marvin conveyed the Murchison House at 305 South Third Street to the Diocese of East Carolina. She included an endowment for maintenance. Mrs. Walker Taylor, Jr., (the first woman ever elected to the vestry of St. James), gave a little chapel there "because the Bishop didn't have any place of worship for himself." Walker also had an office in the building.

"I assisted Bishop Wright when he went up to the national church," said Taylor. "He was chairman of all our missionary work around the world. I went to work for him, followed him, went to New York and worked full-time for our missions overseas.
The Presiding Bishop appointed me as a layman on his staff at national headquarters."

Walker's job entailed work for the churches in the South Pacific, South America, and East Africa. "We would meet in conferences and I was trying to understand the work of the church in those places. I went to some forsaken dioceses, visited leper colonies, saw the impoverished condition of the clergy, and the needs of their schools and hospitals. I went there to make it real so that I could communicate to the church at home what we were doing abroad, and get funds, moral support, and the involvement of congregations." The Mutual Responsibility Commission established new structures for the Anglican Communion including the Anglican Consultative Council . [402]

Later, he was assigned to work with the domestic missionary districts of the church. His "territory" included Wyoming, South Dakota, Montana, Nevada, Utah, and Western Kansas. These dioceses worked to improve the living conditions of Native Americans and all those of

In 1965, Walker Taylor received a pearl-laden cross at St. Peter's Theological School, near Guadalcanal in the South Pacific. The cross was a gift for Bishop Wright, who passed it along to Bishop Elebash, who, in turn, gave it back to Walker. The World War II events associated with John F. Kennedy and PT-109 happened near this spot. (Photo by Bill Page of St. Mary's Church, Kinston.)

underprivileged backgrounds. Walker was a deputy to six General Conventions, was elected to the boards of many agencies and seminaries, and nominated as president of the House of Deputies.

"With bishops like Wright," Taylor said, "laymen were much stronger in the governance of the church. Nowadays lay leadership revolves constantly, which leaves the clergy in charge. Men like J.V. Grainger, George Elliot, Bob Strange and Peter Browne Ruffin were permanent figures. They exercised great influence in all church affairs, in harmony with the clergy." St. James has had more members elected to the Executive Council of the Church than any other parish in the United States. The list includes Dr. Milton, Mrs. Henry J. Macmillan, George Elliott, Bishop Wright and Walker Taylor. Champ Davis from St. John's Church was another member of the Executive Council from Wilmington. Mr. Davis was largely responsible for the election of Thomas H. Wright, rector of St. Mark's, San Antonio, as the fourth bishop of the Diocese of East Carolina.[403]

This photo of the Hill-Wright-Wootten House was taken shortly before the house was destroyed. (Courtesy of Mary Wootten)

The Changing Scene

In the 1950s, St. James fell in with a general trend and demolished a valuable old structure in the name of "progress." The 18th-century Hill-Wright-Wootten House at 11 South Third Street had been home to banker John Hill, William Augustus Wright and his survivors, and the Jewett-Wootten family. The four-story building boasted wrought iron grillwork and slate floors on the entrance porch, three small stained glass windows, a continuous three-story solid mahogany banister, and fireplaces in every room.[404]

From 1830 until 1878, William A. Wright was man of the house. Wright, the brother of Dr. Thomas H. Wright, was a local land baron, attorney, and president of the Bank of Cape Fear. For almost forty years, he served, without pay, as counsel for the Wilmington and Weldon Railroad, a service rewarded by the naming of a locomotive. William Wright also made the introductory speech when Jefferson Davis came to Wilmington in 1863, and handled the estate of Confederate spy Rose Greenhow when she drowned off Fort Fisher.[405]

During Wright's residency, there was a one and a half-story house behind the Wootten House and kitchen where blacks lived. It is thought that Prince Wright, a one-armed ex-slave who played the violin, once lived in the house. Prince played for parties and almost certainly played at St. James.

Milton Hall. (Photo by Charles H. Boney)

Boney, in 2004. "The several Gothic arches facing west are the bold and predominant feature of the façade and they give a rhythmic background to the adjoining lawn and quadrangle."[411]

Mr. Boney, a recipient of the Gold Medal Award from the City of New York, modeled the pinnacles on the west wall after a similar design at St. Alban's Cathedral. The relationship of the cloister is "similar to the south side of the nave of Salisbury Cathedral in England." He gave special attention to the connection with the Donald MacRae House, and created a bonus feature of an all-weather canopied access to the cloister.[412]

The stained glass window in Milton Hall, located in the Children's Chapel, was designed by the Willet Company of Philadelphia, a firm that was also responsible for the clerestory windows at neighboring First Presbyterian Church. The stained glass depicts scenes of Jesus's early life in glass that is refreshing in its clarity and color. The Children's Chapel window was a gift from Lillian Maxwell Bellamy in memory of Emmett Hargrove Bellamy. Mr. and Mrs. Bellamy were the parents of St. James parishioners Lillian Bellamy Boney and Mary Bellamy Koonce. [413]

At the same time, as a safety measure, the brick sidewalks around the church, on South Third and Market streets, were covered with concrete. There were many parishioners who mourned the loss of charm.[414]

The view from the Cloister Garden is teeming with architectural elements. (Photo by Charles H. Boney)

In 1964, Rachel Cameron Camp donated the Cloister Garden, a project that turned a "quagmire" into a beautiful space. Previously, the only "landscaping" in the area consisted of Cherokee roses that grew along the cloister. "They had heavy brambles," said Peggy Moore Perdew, who remembered them from the days of her childhood. "We made sure we didn't get near them." The thorns may have been symbolic, but the plant was bleak most of the year.[415]

The new space, sometimes known affectionately by others as "Rachel's Garden," was dedicated as a children's garden on Easter Sunday, 1964. The inscription, written by Mrs. Camp, reads: "A Garden, dedicated to the glory of God whose living presence may be discovered through children who gather here. April 5, 1964."

Charles Freeman Gillette (1886-1969), of Richmond, designed the space. An apprentice under Boston landscape architect Warren Manning, Gillette had a distinguished career that spanned more than 50 years and included notable work at the Virginia executive mansion; Woodrow Wilson's birthplace in Staunton, Virginia; Washington and Lee University; and the University of Richmond. During the Great Depression, as part of a federal and locally funded project, Charles Gillette landscaped the area around Greenfield Lake.

Katherine Shaw gave the St. Francis Garden as a memorial to her husband, William Shaw. The space now serves as a final resting spot for many. (Photo by Ronald G. Abrams)

In 1982, Katharine Shaw offered to create a garden north of the Cloister Garden known as the St. Francis Garden. The space was dedicated in 1984 to the memory of Mrs. Shaw's husband, William. The area was graced with a statue of St. Francis of Assissi — and a fountain. Both were made in Vicenza, Italy, the birthplace of St. Francis. Following a vesty vote in 1984, the area became known as the St. Francis Memorial Garden. Since that time, ashes have mingled with consecrated earth to create a blessed place for those who mourn.

Rachel Cameron Camp envisioned the Cloister Garden as a place the children of St. James could call their own. (*Photos by Beatrice Schomp)*

Artist Jack Berkman's interpretation of Third and Market streets, about 1972. (Courtesy of Bob Jenkins. Photo by J. Robert Warren.)

Happy Days

By 1965, St. James Church had needed a new organ for some time. Helen Messick Willetts, a church member and an organist, used to substitute for Mr. Robertson. " The first time I played," said Mrs. Willetts, "he took me in to show me about the organ and there was a screw driver and a butcher knife and you had to put them in different places to keep the organ from making unattractive sounds."[416]

The process took about one year, from vestry approval to the completion of installation, a process that took about six weeks. Moving the organ to the balcony was not without controversy. Most parishioners couldn't remember a time when the choir and the great pipes of the organ were not part of the chancel scene. "It was a major upheaval," said Dotty Harriss Weathersbee. "My father (Andrew Harriss) said, 'If the Lord intended for that organ to be in the balcony, he would have turned our ears the other way.'"[417]

The new St. James organ was a proud product of Casavant Freres, a famous old company in Saint-Hyacinthe, Quebec. Casavant created some of its best organs during this period because it was a time in which Bostonian Lawrence Phelps was employed as tonal director. Phelps, an organ designer and a scholar, incorporated techniques from centuries-old organ designs from Germany and France to bring new quality to American organs. The result was an instrument that could "focus, project, and color the sound."

Lawrence Phelps also designed several hundred other organs while working for Casavant Freres, including ones for Myers Park Presbyterian Church in Charlotte; St. Andrew's Episcopal Church in Wellesley, Mass.; Grace Episcopal Church in Providence, R.I.; Anglican Church of St. John the Divine in Vancouver, B. C.,; and First Church of Christ Scientist in Boston.

The dedication service, held on the evening of June 6, 1966, included a prayerful promise that the organ be used "for the interpretation of the great masters of music" and for the "development of faith and the ennobling of life." Guest organist John S. Mueller, of Salem College, showed off most if not all of its 1633 pipes playing the music of Handel, Bach, Pachelbel, Walond, and other composers.[418]

Thomas Ustick Walter designed and engineered St. James Church so beautifully that the building has continued to reveal its strengths in new ways through the years. Before the organ was moved from the chancel to the balcony, the Rev. Mortimer Glover, along with others, was worried that the balcony supports needed augmenting. "We got an engineer to come down here and see how we could get the supports for the organ because it's heavy and needs thousands of pounds to support it. So the next time I saw him he said he found out that we're not going to have to do that. We found

This 1966 picture of Easter crucifer Kenneth Murchison Sprunt, Jr. also showcases the bronze relief in which Jesus' birth and death are depicted. (Photo by Hugh Morton. Courtesy of Betsy Long Sprunt)

that in the present church, built back in the 1800s, there are four pillars and the organ can sit on those pillars that go from the loft all the way down into the ground. Those original pillars are strong enough to support the organ.

"We continue to find out things like that about St. James Church. It's well built." By that time, the entire church was unaware that the organ sat in the rear balcony prior to 1885.[419]

Another reminder of the quality of the 1839 building's original materials came when termites were discovered in the 1960s. The floors were already damaged and the rector dreaded the architectural surgery that would almost certainly be required to rectify the problem. The floors and joists of the Parish House had just been repaired at great expense when the church problem was discovered.

Glover reminisced about the process in 1989. "We didn't know how in the world we were going to do it — take all that pine and all those joists out. But of course we had to. We took up the flooring and they went down to get the joists, but found that termites hadn't eaten them. They were heart pine and the termites had just tunneled over them, just as they do on the ground. They were eating the flooring but the joists were just as they were over 100 years ago."[420]

St. James was a leader in "Festival Sunday in Church" during the early days of the Azalea Festival. (Courtesy of Cape Fear Museum)

The N. C. Azalea Festival presents a good example of St. James Church's work with the community. A hefty percentage of its leaders have been members of St. James Church, many of them vestrymen. During the festival's early years, members of the church enjoyed watching the parade from the church lawn. "At St. James Episcopal Church," said one eyewitness, "members of the congregation were sitting out in front of the building before 8 a.m. Benches from the Sunday School served as seats for the early risers." About 1954, the church's youth groups used the occasion as a benefit and sold seating on the lawn.

St. James took a leading role in "Festival Sunday in Church," an effort to bring tourists into worship services. St. James hosted interesting and distinctive events, usually at St. Philip's Church. At the 1962 service, Bishop Wright officiated and Cotesworth P. Lewis, the rector of Bruton Parish in Williamsburg, delivered the sermon. The Hanover Singers from New Hanover High School sang, and ministers B. Frank Hall and Randolph Gregory, Presbyterian and Baptist respectively, assisted.[421]

Though many women contributed their work, the fine needlework art of St. James was spearheaded by sisters Eugenia Watters Stillman and Rosalie Watters Carr. (Photo by Beatrice Schomp)

The beautiful needlework at St. James comprises one of the more recent adornments in the chancel. In the mid-1960s, Rosalie Watters Carr and her sister, Eugie Waddell Watters Stillman, first got the idea for the needlework project. Mrs. Stillman had already created needlework pillows for St. Paul's Church in Wallingford, Conn. When the sisters decided to make two needlepoint cushions in memory of their mother for St. James, they first visited Robert Mazaltov and Son, Inc., in New

York, for materials and advice. Expenses were always donated, as was the labor: work that four decades ago would have cost $2 a square inch. The project grew, and, years later, the church owns a handsome collection of artistic stitchery. The volunteers' names are listed on a plaque on the chapel wall.

The year 1972 brought changes to the diocese and to St. James Church. William Ludwig Dols, Jr., a Baltimore native who had been rector since 1964 resigned. The Rev. Mr. Robert Cook took over as new rector of the church. And Bishop Wright announced his retirement, a move that prompted a small avalanche of mail. The following letter, dated March 1, 1972, is one example.

"Dear Bishop:

"I have learned from Leslie Boney of your forthcoming retirement at the end of this year. The members of the Diocese of East Carolina are indeed fortunate to have had the benefit of your warm compassion, wise counsel, and complete dedication to God and his Church for so many years.

"Speaking for the men and women of the Army, I wish to thank you for your selfless efforts on behalf of our Nation's military personnel, and particularly for your visit to Vietnam in February 1967. Your dedication to the cause of world peace, the warmth and understanding you brought to our troops during your numerous trips to the field, and the personal example you set for the chaplains with whom you met - - all won for you our deepest respect and admiration.

"With warm personal regards,

"W. C. Westmoreland, General, United States Army, Chief of Staff"[422]

On June 15, 1972, the Rev. Robert Daniell Cook, a native of Reading, Penn., became rector of St. James Church. A graduate of the University of the South at Sewanee, Tenn., and the Virginia Theological Seminary, Mr. Cook had most recently been rector of St. John's Church in Huntington, W.Va.

One of the major developments during his ministry was the lengthy introduction of a new Book of Common Prayer, a potentially divisive and painful process which, Mr. Cook believes, became a healthy experience for St. James. During his tenure a parish Christian Education program was expanded and strengthened as the teachers each year developed and wrote their own curricula. The Christian Education room in the new building was dedicated in honor of the Cooks.

After 20 years of service in St. James, Mr. Cook announced his retirement from the active parish ministry, and he and his wife, Ann, left for a year of volunteer work around the country with Habitat for Humanity. The Cooks, however, chose to stay near St. James and Wilmington, their adopted hometown, and now live a shell's throw away from the Atlantic Ocean at Wrightsville Beach.

During the 1970s, once again, the graveyard required maintenance. Generous financial assistance came from the Kenan family, and from Elizabeth Winston Broadfoot. The space was landscaped anew, and many gravestones were repaired.

Saving Mount Lebanon Chapel

But another church property had been easier to ignore. By 1972, little Lebanon Chapel was a sacred wreck. Simple lack of use took a great toll, not to mention occult groups and more innocent youthful gatherings that occurred there after dark. Vandals ripped windows away from the frames, gouged holes in the doors, destroyed the pulpit, and hammered the 50-year-old organ. They completed their defilement of the little temple by covering the floors and pews with litter and excrement. Neither was the cemetery considered sacred: vandals dug up graves, removed ironwork and shrubs, razed plot walls, damaged large tombstones and stole smaller ones.[423]

In the meantime, the Rev. Herbert Aman, rector of St. Andrew's on-the-Sound, was diagnosed with a heart condition. His doctor prescribed regular exercise, so Mr. Aman began taking daily walks through Airlie. "He saw the chapel and it touched him," said John C. Drewry, a vestryman at St. Andrew's. "Herb was unbelievably moved by it and began trying to get it restored. He called me to see what we could do."[424]

Like many people, John Drewry had assumed Mount Lebanon reverted to the owners of Airlie, Corbett Package Company, after St. Andrew's was built. Once again, the deed was discovered. Soon after a committee was named that included Judge James C. Fox, Victor G. Taylor, Rt. Rev. Thomas H. Wright, Sadie Dizor Webb, Waddell Corbett, and the Rt. Rev. Hunley A. Elebash. In addition, the Rev. Herbert L. Aman; the Rt. Rev. Thomas Henry Wright, retired bishop of East Carolina and a great-grandson of Dr. Thomas Henry Wright; Maxine Dizor; and John C. Drewry were great leaders in the battle to procure funds and materials to save the building.

All the while, Herb Aman led the way. He campaigned for funds, sought the best craftsmen, and negotiated for the lowest price. "We are considering restoring Old Lebanon Chapel," he wrote more than once, "and would like to have an estimate from you."

And once again, there was confusion over ownership. The Lebanon deed was researched, but not before plans were being made. Mr. Aman explained: "Mrs. Akers (the Joneses' granddaughter) said she would turn the property over to us if we can't find where it still belongs to the church. She seemed to think it had already been turned over. We haven't decided yet whether to put the property in the name of the Diocese or St. Andrew's."

But soon the deed emerged and everyone was again aware that St. James Church owned the chapel and the 6 1/2-acre tract of land on which it sat. Then Herbert Aman, acting on behalf of St. Andrew's on-the-Sound, submitted an application for a building permit to "repair institutional," for a cost of $10,000. Though some emergency mending was already in motion, official restoration didn't begin until September 13, 1973.

Some of the craftsmen and laborers who helped restore the chapel include Ivey Lewis, Steve

Collins, J. P. Craven, E. M. Smith, Tommy Reaves, Bob Baker, Douglas Baker, Jimmy Sidbury, Kenneth Braxton, Ed Frederickson, Jimmy Mathews, L. D. Register, Ed Merritt, Buddy Hayes, Ronnie Long, Johnny French, Tim Long, L. D. Register, and J. Gainey.

Those who made monetary donations toward the restoration were: Corbett Lumber Company, Mount Lebanon Chapter ECW, St. Andrew's, Emma Woodward MacMillan, Mr. and Mrs. E. C. Chewning, Mr. and Mrs. Julius T. Herbst, Daisy G. Hutaff, Oliver C. Hutaff, Mrs. J. H. James, Mrs. J. Winder Hughes, Mrs. Fred Dick, Mrs. Haskell Rhett, Elizabeth L. and Thomas H. Wright, Jr., Mrs. J. Holmes Davis, Mrs. Pomeroy Nichols, Maxine Dizor, Mrs. Lillian B. Aman, Mr. and Mrs. Edward Moore, Mrs. Marie DeRosset Clark, the St. James ECW, Mrs. Nixon Jones, Penelope S. Baker, Mrs. O. D. Landis, Mr. and Mrs. Donald Sneeden, Jack Sneeden, Mrs. Richard Wetherill, the Bishop Wright Chapter of the ECW at St. Andrew's, Mr. and Mrs. M. J. Fountain, Jr., and Mrs. A. B. Blake.

During the restoration, the women of St. Andrew's on-the-Sound organized a Lebanon Chapter, dedicated to preserving the chapel. The group still exists and donates annually to Lebanon's preservation.

Workmen attempted, as much as possible, to recreate the chapel as it was in 1835. One of their first jobs was to remove "two small rooms which were added to the rear of the Chapel on either side" of the chapel for the Jones-Pope wedding in 1912, to protect the bridesmaids from the weather. Damaged timbers were replaced through the generosity of the Corbett Lumber and Godwin Lumber companies. Local boatbuilder and woodcrafter Julius Herbst created some of the church furniture. And plasterers recreated the look of the old smooth walls. [425]

It is possible that the present pews are the third ones to sit in Lebanon. Pembroke Jones, probably about 1912, gave the original Lebanon pews to St. Matthew's A.M.E. Church. Another set of pews replaced those but were damaged during the period of vandalism. The present pews were made from virgin Airlie timber, under the supervision of Airlie overseer W. A. Taylor, for the Parish Hall at St. Andrew's before they were moved to Lebanon during the restoration. One piece of wood each was used for the length of them. The pews were finished in Sanford.[426]

The Alper family, owners of Queensboro Steel, donated and installed a steel rod to strengthen the structure and Watkins Hardware provided the paint.

A Raleigh firm, Stained Glass Associates, restored the chapel windows. At least 62 panes were broken and four of the windows were bowed out from pressure caused by roof problems. Stained Glass Associates saved and recovered as much original glass as possible from the windows, chapel floor, and grounds, then created matches to fill the voids. "We find that we can match the old glass extremely well with the same texture and color of the glass that was originally leaded into the building," wrote Robert J. Wysocki, owner of the company.

During the restoration process, Mr. Wysocki carried each window back to Raleigh in its

A detail from one of the Salem windows at Mount Lebanon Chapel. (Photo Courtesy of Fred Newber)

original wood frame mounting. "It would be best for us," he wrote Mr. Aman. "Then as we complete our work we could mount them into the wood frames that have already been indexed for them and then return them and mount them into the property."[427]

Heavy-duty wind bars were added to reinforce and protect the windows. When the work was complete, the windows were guaranteed against 75 miles per hour wind but not against flying debris.

Elizabeth Labouisse Wright, wife of businessman and preservationist Thomas H. Wright, Jr., contributed two pre-Raphaelite style stained glass windows that once graced Salem Chapel. Mrs. Wright is the great-great-granddaughter of Duncan Cameron, who built the chapel. The windows were a portion of the improvements made to the chapel by Paul Cameron (1808-1891), Duncan's son, about 1884. The stained glass artist is unknown but it is thought that they were made in Europe.[428]

The original windows were part of a larger window design — a triptych inscribed with the words: "In Memory of Duncan Cameron who built this Chapel and Dedicated it to the Service of his Lord and Savior." Mrs. Wright and her sisters gave the central part of the window to St. Matthew's Church in Hillsborough.

Stained Glass Associates of Raleigh installed the Fairntosh windows for a total of $647. 20. They reconstructed each window and created the borders. Then they painted leaves and rosettes within the borders.

Other church furniture arrived from Fairntosh, the home now of Terry Sanford, Jr. "Recently we visited a plantation chapel in the Durham area at Fairntosh and they were telling us that some pews were going to be moved to Wilmington," wrote Robert J. Wysocki, in 1973.

"Are these pews being moved to Airlie Garden? If so, there was one or two other items of interest in the old plantation chapel that perhaps would be helpful at Airlie because of the wood carving and the period, time and style of the carving in the wood itself."[429]

The side windows and several pews from Salem Chapel at Fairntosh Plantation were moved to Mount Lebanon Chapel during the 1974 restoration. The center portion of the triptych was installed at St.Matthew's Church in Hillsborough. The windows were part of Salem Chapel alterations wrought by Paul Cameron following the death of his father, Duncan, in 1853. (Courtesy of N. C. Department of Cultural Resources.)

When it came to their attention that repairs were being made to the chapel, two sisters, one in Memphis and one in New York, donated two original alms basins, engraved THW, that had been given originally to the chapel by Dr. Thomas Henry Wright. The two women could have been Marie Grainger Phillips of Memphis and Catherine G. Grainger of New York.[430]

When finally Mount Lebanon Chapel was rededicated, on April 4, 1974, Bishop Thomas Henry Wright, a great-grandson of Dr. Wright, led the service. It was the first official church use of the building since 1923. The service included a baptism for Allison Ligon Bundy, the first such occasion at the chapel in fifty years. The Rev. Herbert Aman, who had fought so hard for Lebanon's restoration, pleaded with the congregation: "Ask God to take care of this chapel. Ask him in your prayers and you will see, it will be done."

"Although Lebanon Chapel was started by communicants of St. James Church, Wilmington, the indications are that the affiliation of its people and their descendants were, and still are, connected more with St. Andrew's Church, Wrightsville, than with any other Episcopal Parish," wrote Bishop Wright in 1972. The statement was true at the time, but now St. James has taken a more active role.

Although Mount Lebanon Chapel has been electrified, the delicate building has been spared such invasive improvements as central heating and air conditioning. Cypress trunks supported the building for 169 years but were replaced in 2004 for reasons of safety. Mount Lebanon is still one of the oldest and least altered structures in New Hanover County.

When Bob Cook was rector, Edward F. Turberg made alterations to the existing Murchison-Curtis Memorial Chapel. The space, a gift from Fannie Murchison Curtis and Jennie Murchison in memory of their parents, is located in the northeast corner of the church. It was created after the organ pipes were moved in 1966. Mr. Turberg also created a situation where *Ecce Homo* could be seen, could be protected, and could still remain in the vestry room, its home since being moved from the chancel.

Dotty Harriss Weathersbee was the first woman to be a layreader in St. James Church. "I saw an item in the Grapevine with the heading, 'S.O.S.' They were recruiting layreaders, but they were expecting men. Again, in 1979, they ran the same thing. I signed up — and it is the joy of my life," said Mrs. Weathersbee in 2004.

In 1979, St. James celebrated its 250th anniversary. One long lasting project was the creation of a number of banners that were designed by John Parker. Though the banners were made by the ladies of St. James, Mr. Parker did all the research and provided the details for the congregation. Mr. and Mrs. Parker, both artists, have contributed much to the church life of St. James.

The banners created in 1979 enliven this image of the transept. (Photo by Beatrice Schomp)

More Recently

The kindergarten of St. James Church continues to thrive. A few years after Peggy Moore Perdew retired in 1967, Linda C. Hicks began work as a teacher. Eventually she became director, retiring in 1997. At that time, Margaret Willetts, an alumna who was one of "Miss Peggy's" pupils, became director. "It is fascinating work and all our children are good children. These days, we rarely say 'no.' We just stop undesirable behavior and redirect it."

St. James Kindergarten continues to operate as a separate financial entity. The budget is now a quarter of a million dollars a year.

Another upheaval occurred in 1993-1994 when the organ was out of commission for six weeks. It could hardly have happened at a worse time for, during that period, the church lost one of its great leaders. St. James organist Candy Williams recalls, "Unfortunately, we had just begun the actual restoration and were bringing in an electronic organ - a rented toaster - when the Rev. Mortimer Glover passed away. It was one of the biggest funerals we had had at St. James in ages and would include a choir. I had only a few minutes to adjust to the temporary appliance before the funeral prelude began. I am still grateful to Mortimer Jr. and wife Eugenia for their graciousness!"

The Rev. Mr. Charles von Rosenberg came to St. James in 1994 and was rector for four years before becoming the Bishop of East Tennessee. (Courtesy of the Diocese of East Tennessee.)

The Rev. Mr. Charles vonRosenberg was rector of St. James from 1994 until 1998 when he was consecrated bishop of East Tennessee. Though his tenure was short, significant things happened.

He led the campaign to open the homeless shelter of Good Shepherd Ministries; called the first two women to serve on the clerical staff of St. James; oversaw negotiations to purchase the fire station property that is now the site of Perry Hall; and instigated the repositioning of the altar.

"We moved the altar away from the church wall, in response to the spirit of inclusion emphasized by liturgical renewal, which - in turn - reclaims ancient church tradition," said Bishop vonRosenberg in 2004.[431]

But when it came time to make the change, Charles vonRosenberg had the good sense to call on a heart-of-pine pillar of the church: Allan T. Strange. In his own words, Mr. Strange tells the story:

"You know, things don't change fast at St. James and when they do, there is usually a lot of resistance. So the last year I was senior warden here –1997, Charles vonRosenberg said, 'There's one more thing I want you to do before you go off the vestry.'

"And I thought, "OK...."

And he said he wanted to move the altar.

"'I said, "Well you have lost your mind! I am not going to do it.'

"He said, 'Yes you are.'

"The altar was right up against that wall. It was hard to move around back there. John Parker, who was on the vestry at that time, drew the new plan. So I got everything arranged. We got the carpenters, the material, whatever permits we needed.

Rick Willetts (left) and Allan Strange pose at the Diocesan Convention in Wilmington, about 1997. Mr. Strange served as senior warden for three different rectors. (Photo by the author)

"So we waited. Then I announced it at the annual meeting which was on December the 7th. I said, 'And there's one more thing. Today is Pearl Harbor Day and I'm going to drop a bomb on you.'

"We waited another month, and the new vestry voted unanimously. One Monday we started work and by the following Sunday it was ready to be used. All we had to do was move it out, and make some small alterations. (The steps were put in later when we saw how they were needed.)

"But then I ran into a friend in a store somewhere the following Monday after that first service and I said to him, "Did you see Charlie behind the altar?

"And he said, "Was he *behind* the Altar?"

"All that worrying about what everyone would think — and he didn't notice. Didn't even notice."[432]

After Charles vonRosenberg was elected bishop of East Tennessee, Dr. James Sloan led the Search Committee that selected the Rev. Ronald George Abrams. Elected unanimously by the vestry, Rev. Abrams began work at St. James on October 30, 1999.

A native of Long Island, N.Y., Mr. Abrams was baptized, confirmed, and ordained a priest at St. George's Church, in Hempstead, N.Y. He graduated magna cum laude from Long Island University before receiving his Masters of Divinity degree in 1982. Before his arrival at St. James, he served as assistant rector at St. Mark's Church in Westhampton, N.Y.; rector of St. Ann's Church in Bridgehampton, N.Y.; and rector of Holy Trinity Church in Fayetteville.

From 1999 until 2004, Ronald Abrams has reestablished the presence of St. James Church at

Artist Chip Hemingway's painting of St. James evokes the familiar words, "Light from Light." Mr. Hemingway of BMS architects was also the supervising architect for Perry Hall. (Courtesy of the artist)

Lebanon Chapel. Multiple services are held during the summer months and special holiday events at the little church have proved popular. A growing endowment fund helps assure that the sacred property will remain in good condition.

The Light-a-Fire Campaign provided more than $4 million dollars for construction of the new multipurpose building. On Palm Sunday 2000, Rev. Abrams officiated at the groundbreaking for Perry Hall, the new multipurpose building. The building is a memorial to Marie and Albert Perry whose family, through the Perry Foundation, gave generous support for its construction. Herb McKim of BMS Architects of Wilmington designed the new space. Mr. McKim has a long and distinguished history as an architect, having designed many structures in Wilmington as well as the Kenan Laboratories building and the Morehead Laboratories building on the campus of the University of North Carolina at Chapel Hill — and Cox and Dabney halls on the campus of North Carolina State University. McKim studied elements of the existing St. James structures and carefully crafted a new space that blends as perfect as is humanly possible considering the inflationary nature of building expenses.

According to George C. (Chip) Hemingway, project architect for Perry Hall, the building process held a big surprise. "We demolished the old Wilmington city fire department headquarters to accommodate the addition. Perry Hall would be the fourth building built on that site. Before it became the Wilmington fire department headquarters (three fire stations had been constructed there) the site had been part of a Colonial graveyard. As we began excavating for the new building artifacts from the old graveyard began to emerge. One artifact in particular was the highlight of the excavation process.

"It started when I received a call from the job superintendent stating that the he'd unearthed an old drainage line. Our office is a block away so I went down to investigate. It turned out to be a preserved coffin with the occupant, until now intact and at rest. The backhoe had cut the coffin open and unknowingly sent part of it to the dump. The occupant's blonde hair and denim sailor's uniform were clearly visible. The casket was made of lead and conformed closely to his body. The top-side even had a viewing window.

"He must have been a man of prominence because the caskets of that time were usually wood. He was exhumed and removed from the site by the mortuary. The work continued. His presence has stayed with the construction crew and and with me to this day."

The church has now over 1700 members and an annual budget in excess of a million dollars. Two rectors currently assist Rev. Abrams with pastoral and ministerial duties. They are Lynn Peterman, and Thomas Milam. Cookie Cantwell serves as Youth Group Coordinator. David Williams is director of music. Candy Williams, his wife, continues to be the organist. Carol Gaither is Director of Christian Education. Jane Roberts is parish coordinator and Jan Hincke is financial secretary. Linda Bialaszewskis is parish secretary. Deanes Gornto is parish administrator.

In 2003, members of St. James, for the most part, either jeered or cheered the results of the General Convention at which an openly gay man was elected bishop.

In 2004, St. James Church celebrated its 275th anniversary. Projects included a picnic at St. Philip's Church; a fundraiser for Good Shepherd Ministries; a parish quilt; restoration of the reredos and stained glass; and publication of a history.

This is a charcoal rubbing by J. Fred Newber of the St. James gravestone of Francis Wilkinson and her infant son. Both died in 1788. (Courtesy of J. Fred Newber)

Church member J. Fred Newber did tracings of select gravestones in the churchyard. The graves of well-documented patriot

Celebrating 275 Years

The Rev. Mr. Ron Abrams and the Rt. Rev. Henry N. Parsley. June 6, 2004, at the 275th anniversary celebration. (Photo by Beatrice Schomp)

The Rev. Mr. William Ludwig Dols, Jr., served St. James from 1964 until 1972. (Photo by the author)

The Rev. Mr. Robert Daniell Cook served St. James from 1972 until 1994 — a period of tremendous change. (Photo by Bea Schomp)

Mary Broadfoot (with flag) takes part in the Memorial Day concert at St. James, 2004. (Photo by Logan Wallace, Courtesy of the *Star News*.)

Perry Hall architect Herb McKim, parish administrator Dean Gornto, Mary Gornto, and Catherine McKim have all given years of service to St. James. Mrs. Gornto was the first woman ever elected senior warden at St. James. (Photo by the author.)

Dorothy Taylor. (Photo by Logan Wallace, Courtesy of the Star News.)

Jean McKoy Graham and son-in-law Bob Rapp. (Photo by the author.)

Walker Taylor IV and his wife, Amy. (Photo by the author.)

Bea Cochran Schomp and Susan Taylor Block pose during the 275th celebration at St. James, June 6, 2004. Ms. Schomp is the granddaughter of Claude Willard Sprouse, former Dean of Grace and Holy Trinity Cathedral in St. Louis. The Rev. Dr. Sprouse died in 1952, just after being elected President of the House of Deputies at the General Convention.
Susan Block is an eighth generation descendant of the Rev. Mr. Alexander Stewart, an author, SPG missionary, and the rector of St. Thomas Church, in Bath, N.C. from 1754-1771.

Graebner, rector of St. Matthew's Church in Hillsborough; Charles Pollock, historian of St. Philip's Church in Southport; Elizabeth Oldham, archivist of the Nantucket Historical Foundation; Fletch Coke, archivist of the Diocese of Tennessee; and Jean Farnsworth of Philadelphia, noted stained glass authority — all have provided valuable help.

J. Fred Newber has passed along information, images, and interesting interpretations accumulated over many years of observation. His documentation of stonemasons' art in the churchyard is a treasure.

Other members of St. James who have been valuable sources of information include Cy Hogue, Mary Ann Hogue, Tom Grainger, Agnes Rankin Beane, Mary M. Wootten, Dotty Harriss Weathersbee, Ethel A. Taylor, Margaret Moore Perdew, Jean McKoy Graham. Florence Moore Dunn, Robert Lane, Robert Warren, Raymond Williams, Hugh MacRae II, Bryan Broadfoot, Dean Gornto, Ann Flint, Jocelyn Strange, Kenneth M. Sprunt, Betsy Long Sprunt, Cornelia Broadfoot, Peg Rorison, Si Cantwell, Virginia Callaway, and Beth Harriss Sprunt.

Others who have been helpful include stained glass artist and historian Rowan Lecompte, Bruce B. Cameron, Jr., Nancy Latimer, Terry Sanford, Jr., John Bankson, Ed Frederickson, John C. Drewry, Lossie Gardell, George Evans, Wood family authority Donald Koonce, Marie Ashworth, E. L. Nunn, Jr., Charlotte Magee, Donna Moore, Anne Russell, Diane C. Cashman, Christine Leahy, Sue Boney Ives, and Michael Whaley — to name only a few.

As usual, booksmith Suzanne Nash Ruffin has been exactly the editorial medicine this manuscript needed. Book designer Jane L. Baldridge has again delighted me with her art, her reason, and her spirit.

On a personal note, I wish to express gratitude to my husband, Frederick L. Block, whose great enthusiasm and interest in this project has made it even more fun. His loving encouragement fuels my writing fire.

St. James Church, 2004.

About the author

Historian Susan Taylor Block was born in Wilmington in 1951 and graduated from the University of North Carolina in 1973. She is the author of a number of books and inscriptions, including *The Wrights of Wilmington; Van Eeden; Wilmington's Confederate General: William MacRae; The Character Factory: A History of the Boys' Brigade; Along the Cape Fear; Cape Fear Lost; Cape Fear Beaches; Wilmington Through the Lens of Louis T. Moore; Airlie: The Garden of Wilmington; and Belles and Blooms: Cape Fear Garden Club and the N. C. Azalea Festival.*

"It is that strange disquietude of the Gothic spirit that is its greatness; that restlessness of the dreaming mind, that wanders hither and thither among the niches, and flickers feverishly around the pinnacles, and frets and fades in labyrinthine knots and shadows along wall and roof, and yet is not satisfied, nor shall be satisfied." John Ruskin, *The Stones of Venice*. (1937 St. James Church scene by Wilmington artist William Whitehead. Courtesy of J. Robert Lane, Jr. Photo by J. Robert Warren.)

Abbreviations

ECU: East Carolina Univeristy.
IBK-LHM-EFM: Ida Brooks Kellam, Leora Hiatt McEachern, and Elizabeth F. McKoy. Indexed highlights of vestry minutes and records of St. James Church.
MMW: Mary Malone Wootten
LCFHS: Lower Cape Fear Historical Society archives.
NHCPL: New Hanover County Public Library.
SAOTS: Saint Andrew's on-the-Sound
SHC: Southern Historical Collection. (U.N.C.)
SJC: St. James Collection. A tremendous archive that was once housed at the church is now at the University of North Carolina at Wilmington. Carroll Jones catalogued the collection and has served as curator during this project.
SJL: St. John's Lodge No. 1
UNC: University of North Carolina
UNCW: Special Collections at Randall Library, University of North Carolina at Wilmington.
WRC: William Reaves Collection at the New Hanover County Public Library.

Select Bibliography

Addresses Delivered Under the Auspices of the N. C. Society of the Colonial Dames of America, 1900-1926. Lawrence Lee Library. LCFHS.

Anderson, Jean Bradley. *Piedmont Plantation: The Bennehan-Cameron Family and the Lands in North Carolina.* Durham, 1985.

Barnhill, Edward Stanley. *The Beatys of Kingston.* 1983.

Bedford, Steven McLeod. *John Russell Pope: Architect of Empire.* Singapore, 1998.

Bingham, Emily. *Mordecai: An American Family.* New York, 2003.

Bishir, Catherine W. *North Carolina Architecture.* (Photographs by Tim Buchman.) Chapel Hill, 1990.

Block books and deed transfer records. New Hanover County Courthouse.

Boney, Leslie N., Jr., ed. (Historical sketch by James L. Allegood.) *The Cape Fear Club.* Wilmington, 1984.

Burke, James. "Charles Baldwin, A Likely Joe." Wilmington, 2004.

__________. "Proceedings of the Wilmington and Raleigh Railroad: May, 1838."

Bolles, Marie Louise DuBrutz Reston. (Memoirs) LCFHS.

Burnett, David. Longleat: *The Story of an English Country House.* London, 1978.

Burr, James G. *Sketch of St. James Parish: Wilmington, N.C.* New York, 1874.

Cain, Robert J (editor). *Records of the Church of England in North Carolina (1699-1741).* Raleigh, 1999.

Calder—Lazarus Letters. LCFHS.

Campbell, Walter E. *Across Fortune's Tracks: A Biography of William Rand Kenan, Jr.* Chapel Hill, 1996.

Carolina Yacht Club Collection. LCFHS.

Cashman, Diane Cobb. *Cape Fear Adventure.* Woodland Hills, Ca., 1982.

___________. *Headstrong: the Biography of Amy Morris Bradley (1823-1904), A Life of Noblest Usefulness.* Wilmington, 1990.

Cashman, Diane Cobb. Videotaped interview with Henry J. MacMillan. LCFHS.

Clitherall, Eliza Burgwin. "Diary of Eliza Burgwin Clitherall." SHC. UNC.

Cochran, Hamilton. *Noted American Duels and Hostile Encounters.* Toronto, 1963.

Davies-Rodgers, Ellen. *The Great Book: Calvary Protestant Episcopal Church; Memphis, Tenn. (1832-1972.)* Memphis, 1973.

deRosset, William Lord. *Pictorial and Historical New Hanover County and Wilmington, N.C. (1723-1938).* Wilmington, 1938.

Drane, Robert Brent. "An Address delivered in St. James Church, Wilmington, N.C., at the interment of Dr. Thomas Henry Wright." (NCC, UNC)

___________________. *Sketch of St. James Parish.* New York, 1874.

Empie Papers. Manuscripts and Rare Books Department, Swem Library, College of William and Mary.

Empie, Adam, D.D. "A Discourse Delivered before the Masonic Societies." Wilmington, 1824.

Empie Papers. LCFHS.

Empie Papers, Schaeffer Library, Union College.

Empie Papers. U. S. Military Academy, Special Collections and Archives Division.

Empie, Adam, *Discourses on Immersion and Infant Baptism.* Printed by Bruff and Repiton, Williamsburg. 1829.

____________, D.D. *Sermons on Various Subjects: Written and Preached at Different Places and Times During his Public Ministry of Forty-Four Years.* New York, 1856. Valentine Museum, Richmond.

Fales, Robert Martin. *Wilmington Yesteryear.* (Edited by Diane Cobb Cashman). Wilmington, 1984.

Farnsworth, Jean M. "*Identifying Stained Glass Windows by Charles Booth in Philadelphia.*"

Fonvielle, Chris E., Jr., *Fort Anderson, Battle for Wilmington.* Mason City, Iowa, 1999.

___________________., *The Wilmington Campaign.* Campbell, Ca., 1997.

Franz, Captain Rod, U. S. Navy, "Antebellum Episcopalians in North Carolina. 1996. LCFHS.

Fulham Papers. Lambeth Palace. (Courtesy of Bishop John Kirkham.)

Gadski, Mary Ellen. "The History of the deRosset House." 1978.

Giles Collection. SHC. UNC.

Glover, Mortimer W. "The Mission of the Good Shepherd." LCFHS.

Goode, James Moore. *Architecture, Politics, and Conflict: Thomas Ustick Walter and the Enlargement of the United States Capitol, 1850-1865.* Michigan, 1994.

Gunter, Carol S. *Carolina Heights: Preservation of an Urban Neighborhood in Wilmington, N.C.* Wilmington, 1982.

Henderson, Archibald. *Washington's Southern Tour.* Boston, 1923.

Hicks, Eugene C. *Hicks, Ward, Wright, Yonge, and 7812 Descendants.* Wilmington, 1982.

Hogue, Cyrus Jr. *The View From Pew 7: A Few Memories in the Life of Cyrus D. Hogue, Jr.* Wilmington, 2001.

Holder, Bill. "Memoir of Melchior Thoni." *The Nashville Tennessean Magazine.* November 16, 1947. (Courtesy of Tennessee State Library and Archives.)

Hood, Vic. "History of Carving: Melchior Thoni. *Carving Magazine.* Vol. 1.

Johns, John. "Wilmington During the Blockade." *Harper's New Monthly Magazine,* 1866. Vol. 33. NHCPL.

Lee, Lawrence. *The History of Brunswick County, North Carolina.* Charlotte, 1980.

Lee, Lawrence. *The Lower Cape Fear in Colonial Days.* Chapel Hill, 1965.
London, Lawrence Foushee, and Sarah McCulloh Lemmon, eds. *The Episcopal Church in North Carolina, 1701-1959. Raleigh, 1987.*
Lossing, Benson J. *Pictorial Field-Book of the Revolution.* New York, 1855.
Mason, Lockert, M.D. "Separation and Reunion of the Episcopal Church, 1861-1865: The Role of Bishop Thomas Atkinson of the Diocese of N. C." Lower Cape Fear Historical Society Bulletin, Vol. 37, 1. Oct. 1992.
McKoy, Elizabeth F. "Old St. James Church." St. James Collection, LCFHS.
Adelaide Meares Papers. Special Collections. William R. Perkins Library, Duke University.
Memorial of the First Presbyterian Church, Wilmington, N.C. (1817-1892). Richmond, 1893.
Meredith, Hugh. *"An Account of the Cape Fear Country, 1731,"* Edited by Earl Gregg Swem. Swem Library, College of William and Mary.
Minutes of St. John's Lodge No. 1. (Courtesy of Mervin Hogg.)
Moore, Louis T. *Stories Old and New of the Cape Fear Region.* Wilmington, 1999.
Neale, Robert S. *The Bank of Cape Fear.* Wilmington, 1999.
Newspaper files (NHCPL): *Star News, Chronicle, Messenger, Advertiser, People's Press.*
Newber, J. Fred. "The Vigilant Angels of St. James Parish." Wilmington, 2004.
Oates, John A. *The Story of Fayetteville and the Upper Cape Fear.*
"One Hundredth Anniversary Commemorating the Building of St. James Church." Wilmington, 1939.
William Reaves Collection. Indexed and chronicled by Kenneth Davis. NHCPL.
Repiton—Lamb Papers. East Carolina Manuscript Collection. Joyner Library, ECU.
Ruffin, Virginia Bellamy. Historical Scrapbook. LCFHS.
Russell, Anne. *Wilmington: A Pictorial History.* Norfolk, 1981.
Russell, Anne, and Margorie Megivern (with Kevin Coughlin). *North Carolina Portraits of Faith.* Wilmington, 1986.
St. Andrew's on-the-Sound Archives. Wilmington, N.C.
St. James Collection. UNCW.
St. John's Lodge # 1 minute books. Wilmington, N.C.
Saunders, William L., ed. *The Colonial Records of North Carolina.* Raleigh, 1886-1890.
"Scheme for raising a fund for building an academy in the Town of Wilmington." Giles Collection. SHC. UNC.
Schenck, Nicholas." The Diary of Nicholas Schenck." LCFHS.
Seamen's Bethel records. LCFHS.
Sprunt, J. Laurence. *The Story of Orton Plantation.* Wilmington, 1958.
Sprunt, James. *Chronicles of the Cape Fear River.* Wilmington, 1992.

Stamp Defiance Chapter of the D.A.R. Scrapbooks. LCFHS.
Joseph Gardner Swift, *The Memoirs of Joseph Gardner Swift,* Worcester, MA, 1890.
The State, November 1981.
Upjohn, Richard. *Upjohn's Rural Architecture.* New York, 1852.
Athenaeum of Philadelphia Archives.
Watson, Alan D. *Society in Colonial North Carolina.* Raleigh, 1975.
__________ *Wilmington, North Carolina, to 1861.* Jefferson, N. C., and London, 2003.
Weisiger, Minor T., Donald R. Traser, and E. Randolph Trice. *Not Hearers Only: A History of St. James Episcopal Church, Richmond, Va. (1835-1985.)* Richmond, 1986.
What God Hath Wrought: A History of the Little Chapel on the Boardwalk (1907-2002).
Wilmer, Richard H. *The Recent Past from a Southern Standpoint: Reminiscences of a Grandfather.* New York, 1887.
Winslow Family Papers. Quincy Historical Society. Quincy, Mass.
Wrenn, Tony P. *Wilmington, North Carolina: An Architectural and Historical Portrait.* Wilmington, 1984.
Wright-Scott Letters. LCFHS.

Endnotes

[1] John F. Woolverton, *Historical Society of the Episcopal Church.*

[2] Hugh Meredith, "An Account of the Cape Fear Country, 1731." Edited by Earl Gregg Swem. Swem Library, College of William and Mary. Robert J. Cain (editor), *Records of the Church of England in North Carolina (1699-1741.) Raleigh, 1999.*

[3] Lawrence Lee. *The Lower Cape Fear in Colonial Days.* Chapel Hill, 1965.

[4] Charles M. Andrews, *Colonial Folkways.* New Haven, 1921.

[5] Colonial Office, America and the West Indies: 5/293, Public Records Office, London. IBK-LHM-EFM, SJC, UNCW. Robert J. Cain.

[6] Terry H. Jones, Catholic Community Forum.

[7] Edward Stanley Barnhill, *The Beatys of Kingston.*

[8] Lawrence Lee. *The Lower Cape Fear in Colonial Days.* Durham, 1965. Book of Remembrances, UNCW. Claude Moore, "Our Heritage." (LCFHS)

[9] William L. Saunders, *Colonial Records,* Vol. III, p. 623.

[10] Graves, "Land Grants of New Hanover County." IBK-LHM-EFM, SJC, UNCW.

[11] Robert J. Cain. Dobbs Collection, SHC, UNC. Colonial ministers data from the Brown

Library, Washington, N.C. Saunders, *The Colonial Records of N. C.* Raleigh, 1886. LCFHS.

[12] Robert J. Cain.

[13] J. G. Burr. *Sketch of St. James Parish: Wilmington, N. C.* New York, 1874. (J. G. Burr, listed on the title page as "a member of the Vestry," incorporated interviews with the Hon. Hugh Waddell and N. C. Governor Henry T. Clarke in his history of the church.)

[14] Lawrence Lee, *The Lower Cape Fear in Colonial Days.* Chapel Hill, 1965.

[15] Robert J. Cain.

[16] Burr.

[17] Ibid. *Colonial Records*, 754. *State Records*, XXIII, 190.

[18] *Star News*, March 30, 1930.

[19] Burr.

[20] Burr. Fulham Papers, Lambeth Palace. (Courtesy of the Rt. Rev. John Kirkham)

[21] Moore family files, LCFHS. Lee, *The Lower Cape Fear in Colonial Days.*

[22] Walter Clark, ed. *The State Records of N. C.* XXII. Wilmington, 1994.

[23] Louis T. Moore files, NHCPL.

[24] Lawrence Lee. *The Lower Cape Fear in Colonial Days.* Chapel Hill, 1965. Book of Remembrances, UNCW. Vestry Minutes, SJC, UNCW.

[25] Walter Clark, ed. *The State Records of N. C.* Volume XXIII, p. 537; Vol. XXII.

[26] "The Diary of Nicholas Schenck." LCFHS. UNCW.

[27] "Minutes of the Town of Wilmington, County of New Hanover, State of N. C. The Property of the Commissioners of the Town." (Note: A house sat also sat in the middle of Orange Street between Third and Fourth streets. The Rev. Dr. M. B. Grier lived there in 1859, and said that the lot "pushed itself out into Orange Street. But it had a good right to be there, for it was built long before Orange Street was laid out." – *First Presbyterian Church* (1817-1892).

[28] *Addresses Delivered Under the Auspices of the N. C. Society of the Colonial Dames of America – 1900-1926.* Lawrence Lee Library, LCFHS. William B. McKoy, in a speech delivered May 14, 1914, states that the Brunswick Church was built with locally made brick despite faulty statements that the brick came from England.

[29] J. Fred Newber, "The Vigilant Angels of St. James Parish." Wilmington, 2004. SJC. UNCW. *Addresses.* William B. McKoy, speech to the Colonial Dames, May 14, 1914. LCFHS.

[30] "Contents of St. James Episcopal Corner Stone," (with notes by Dr. Robert Brent Drane) – courtesy of Louis T. Moore, George Thomas, and the Rt. Rev. Thomas H. Wright. Special Collections, UNCW.

[31] "Andrew Jackson Centre." Carrickfergus, Northern Ireland.

[32] Castle Dobbs Papers, Reel 2. Southern Historical Collection, University of North Carolina.

[33] New Hanover County Deed Book DBD, page 248. (McEachern files)

[34] D. Helen Rankin and E. Charles Nelson (editors*), Curious in Everything: The Career of Arthur Dobbs of Carrickfergus, 1689-1765.*

[35] Elizabeth F. McKoy, "Old St. James Church." LCFHS. Rouge Dragon Pursuivant, The College of Arms.

[36] Stamp Defiance Chapter Scrapbooks, Daughters of the American Revolution. LCFHS. Desmonde Clarke, *Arthur Dobbs Esquire, 1689-1765.*

[37] *Colonial Records*, 23, page 535; 25, page 391. McEachern files, UNCW. Lee, *Lower Cape Fear.*

[38] Lee, *Lower Cape Fear.* "*One Hundredth Anniversary Commemorating the Building of St. James Church.*" Wilmington, 1939.

[39] *Colonial Records,* VI, page 552. *One Hundredth Anniversary booklet. Addresses,* William B. McKoy.

[40] Andrews, *Folkways.*

[41] *The State Records of North Carolina.* Edited by Walter Clark. Vol. XXIII, Wilmington, 1994. p. 535.

[42] Desmond Clarke, *Arthur Dobbs Esquire (1680-1765).* Great Britain, 1958.

[43] Fulham Library, Lambeth Palace. London. (Courtery of the Rt. Rev. John Kirkham)

[44] *Star News,* June 18, 1939. (Article contains the reference to the *South Carolina Gazette*, April 27, 1765.) William L. Saunders, Editor. *Colonial Records of N. C.* Wilmington, 1993. Volume VII, p. 3.

[45] Saunders.

[46] Saunders. Lawrence Lee. *The Lower Cape Fear in Colonial Days.* Chapel Hill, 1965.

[47] Fulham Papers, Lambeth Palace. Courtesy of the Rt. Rev. John Kirkham.

[48] Hamilton Cochran, *Noted American Duels and Hostile Encounters.* Toronto, 1963.

[49] Fulham Papers, Lambeth Palace. (Courtesy of the Rt. Rev. John Kirkham.)

[50] Burr.

[51] Lee. Burr. Benson J. Lossing, *Pictorial Fieldbook of the Revolution.* New York, 1860.

[52] Fulham Papers, Lambeth Palace. (Courtesy of the Rt. Rev. John Kirkham.)

[53] Elizabeth F. McKoy, "Old St. James Church." Lower Cape Fear Historical Society. Vestry minutes, March 13, 1812. IBK-LHM-EFM, SJC, UNCW.

[54] Lossing. James Sprunt, *Chronicles of the Cape Fear River.* Wilmington, 1992.

[55] Lawrence Lee, *A History of Brunswick County.* Charlotte, 1980.

[56] Ibid. *Virginia Gazette*, March 21, 1766.

[57] Lawrence Lee. *Colonial Days.* Chapel Hill, 1965.

[58] "*One Hundredth Anniversary Commemorating the Building of St. James Church.*" Wilmington, 1939. Notes by J. G. Burr.

[59] Robert D. Bass, *The Green Dragoon.* New York, 1957. Lee, *Colonial Days.*

[60] Bass. Lee.

[61] Bass, *The Green Dragoon.* Lee, *Brunswick County.* Christopher Hibbart, *Redcoats and Rebels.* New York, 1990.

[62] Johann David Schoepf, *Travels in the Confederation (1783-1784).* Philadelphia, 1911. (Translated and edited by Alfred J. Morrison.) Robert I. Vexler and William F. Swindler, editors, *Chronology and Documentary Handbook of the State of N. C.* Dobbs Ferry, NY, 1978.
[63] Louis T. Moore, *Stories Old and New of the Cape Fear Region.* Wilmington, 1999. Archibald Henderson, *Washington's Southern Tour.* Boston, 1923.
[64] *National Encyclopedia of American Biography.* 1897, Volume 7. (McEachern files) Sprunt Monograph No. 4, 1908.
[65] *One Hundredth Anniversary booklet.* Wilmington, 1939. (Excerpts from Memoirs of Col. James G. Burr, 1874.) *Addresses Delivered under the Auspices of the N. C. Society of the Colonial Dames,* William B. McKoy, speech to the Colonial Dames, May 14, 1914. LCFHS. *Memorial of the First Presbyterian Church, Wilmington, N.C. (1817-1892).* Richmond, 1893.
[66] *Memorial of the First Presbyterian Church.*
[67] New Hanover County Deed Book N, page 352; D, 402. Drane. (McEachern Files)
[68] Burr.
[69] Thomas Wright, May 13, 1816. Wright/Scott correspondence, LCFHS. Emily Bingham, *Mordecai: An Early American Family.* New York, 2003.
[70] Schaffer Library, Union College: Special Collections.
[71] Ibid. Adam Empie Papers, Manuscripts and Rare Books Department, Swem Library, College of William and Mary.
[72] Schaffer Library, Union College Special Collections.
[73] St. James Collection. UNCW, Special Collections.
[74] Rev. Adam Empie, D.D., *Sermons on Various Subjects.* New York, 1856. Valentine Museum.
[75] Ida Brooks Kellan, *St. James Parish Register.* Wilmington, 1958.
[76] "*Diary of Eliza Burgwin Clitherall.*" Southern Historical Collection. University of North Carolina. Ledger, SJC. UNCW. Assorted vestry minutes, 1820 until 1900, SJC, UNCW.
[77] Meares Collection, Perkins Library, Duke University.
[78] St. James Collection. UNCW. MS#169, Box 5, File 2. Assorted Empie records within the St. James Collection, UNCW.
[79] St. James Collection. UNCW. MS#169, Box 5, File 2. Vestry minutes, March 13, 1812. IBK-LHM-EFM, SJC, UNCW.
[80] Vestry Minutes. January 12, 1813. IBK-LHM-EFM. SJC. UNCW.
[81] The Rev. Dr. R. B. Drane and J. G. Burr, *Sketches of the Parish.* New York, 1874.
[82] Louis T. Moore, *Stories Old and New.* James Laurence Sprunt, *The Story of Orton Plantation.* Dobbs Papers, Carrickfergus, N.I.
[83] *The University of North Carolina (1776-1799),* compiled by R. D. W.Connor. Edited by Louis

R. Wilson and Hugh T. Lefler. Chapel Hill, 1953. James Laurence Sprunt.

[84] Ibid. David Stick, *Bald Head: A History of Smith Island and Cape Fear.* Wendell, 1985.

[85] "Scheme for raising a fund for building an academy in the Town of Wilmington," Giles Collection. SHC. UNC.

[86] Joseph Gardner Swift, *Memoirs.* Empie papers, LCFHS.

[87] Diocesan Minutes, NHCPL. Ellen Davies-Rodgers, *The Great Book.* Arthur Howard Noll, *History of the Church in the Diocese of Tennessee.* New York, 1900.

[88] The will of Dr. Samuel Green, proved 1771. Will book C, page 117. (Elizabeth Brown King Collection)

[89] Wright-Scott Letters. LCFHS. Eugene Hicks Collection, NHCPL.

[90] Catherine W. Bishir, *North Carolina Architecture.* Chapel Hill, 1990. Hicks.

[91] *Jackson Daily News,* January 21, 1979.

[92] "The Rev. Edward Winslow," handwritten document, 1840. Ida Brooks Kellam Genealogical files, LCFHS. Quincy Historical Society. Wright Family Collection. Joseph Caldwell Huske, *A Brief History of St. John's Episcopal Church.*

[93] Diocesan records of the City of New York. Trinity College Archives.

[94] Pat Fenoff, Hudson Church, NY. Vestry minutes, IBK-LHM-EFM, SJC, UNCW. Church Rector Records, SJC, UNCW.

[95] *Wilmington Herald,* May 28, 1851. NHCPL.

[96] Ida Brooks Kellam and Leora Hiatt McEachern, *St. James Church Records.* LCFHS.

[97] Elizabeth McKoy's notes, St. James Collection. LCFHS.

[98] Robert Johnston Miller. "The Robert J. Miller Letters, 1813-1831." Edited by D. L. Corbitt. *N. C. Historical Review* (October 1948). *The Episcopal Church in N. C., 1701-1959.* Edited by Lawrence Foushee London and Sarah McCulloh Lemmon. Raleigh, 1987.

[99] Church Rectors. SJC. UNCW.

[100] SJC, UNCW.

[101] Diocesan Journals, NHCPL. Vestry Minutes, SJC. UNCW. E. C. Hicks, *Hicks, Ward, Wright, Yonge, and 7812 Descendants.* Wilmington, 1982.

[102]U. S. Military Academy Archives. Swift, *Memoirs.* *Cape Fear Recorder,* May 15, 1819. (Compiled by James H. McKoy, LCFHS)

[103]*St. James Parish,* Burr.

[104] Adam Empie, *Sermons on Various Subjects Written and Preached at Different Places and Times, During his Public Ministry of Forty-four Years.* New York, 1855. (Valentine Museum)

[105] St. James Collection, UNCW. The Wright-Scott Letters, Lower Cape Fear Historical Society.

[106] The Wright-Scott Letters, Lower Cape Fear Historical Society. Emily Bingham, *Mordecai: An Early American Family.* New York, 2003.

[107] Louis T. Moore, *Stories*. Wilmington, 1999.
[108] Giles Family Papers, SHC, UNC. Interviews with Lossie Dizor Gardell.
[109] "A Tribute to Oakdale." Oakdale Cemetery Company. Wilmington, N. C. 1991.
[110] Leora Hiatt McEachern and Ida Brooks Kellam. LCFHS. MacRae Collection, Perkins Library, Duke University.
[111] James Burke, "Charles Baldwin, a likely Joe." 2004.
[112] The Will of Capt. Thomas Wright, LCFHS. David Burnett, *Longleat: The Story of an English Country House* (London, 1978) Crockette Hewlett and Mona Smalley, *Between the Creeks.* (Wilmington, 1971.) James Robert Warren, "History in Towns: Wilmington, North Carolina." *Antiques*, December 1980.
[113] Adam Empie. "A Discourse Delivered before the Masonic Societies." Wilmington, N. C., 1824. (Printed, with notes and appendix, at the office of The Cape-Fear Recorder, for David Smith, Jr.) Schaeffer Library, Union College. (Note: "On December 27, 1812, anniversary of St. John the Evangelist, the officers met at St. John's Lodge...and marched with a band of music to Church where the morning service was read by the Rev. Mr. Empie." From "A Sketch of the Jacobs Family in N.C." LCFHS)
[114] E. W. Timberlake, Jr. "The Rise of Freemasonry in North Carolina." Colin James Hamer, Neith Network Library. *Wilmington Herald*, May 21, 1851.
[115] Minutes of St. John's Lodge No. 1. Book 9. SJL.
[116] Burr.
[117] South Caroliniana Library, University of South Carolina. Schaffer Library, Union College.
[118] Minor T. Weisiger, Donald R. Traser, and E. Randolph Trice; *Not Hearers Only: A History of St. James Episcopal Church, Richmond, Va. (1835-1985).* Richmond, 1986.
[119] Ibid.
[120] Adam Empie. *Sermons.* U. S. Military Academy, Special Collections and Archives Division.
[121] St. James Collection. University of North Carolina, Special Collections.
[122] Author's correspondence with clergy of First Baptist Church in Richmond. Mills Lane, *Architecture of the Old South,* Savannah, 1996. Additional information supplied by Edward F. Turberg.
[123] Union archives. Bishir, p. 234.
[124] Ravenscroft quoted by Thomas H. Wright in letter to Christian Giles, January 1, 1827.
[125] Ibid.
[126] Information about the Ravenscroft portrait supplied by Edward F. Turberg.
[127] Meares Collection. Perkins Library, Duke Univeristy. Alice London Boatwright, as quoted by William Reaves in the Reaves Bridgers Collection. NHCPL.
[128] Giles Collection, SHC, UNC. Vm, IBK-LHM-EFM, SJC, UNC.

[129]). *The Episcopal Church in N. C., 1701-1959.* Edited by Lawrence Foushee London and Sarah McCulloh Lemmon. Raleigh, 1987.
[130] VM, IBK-LHM-EFM, UNCW. "Work of Ladies Society", SJC, UNCW.
[131] Burr, *Sketch of St. James Parish.*
[132] *The Episcopal Church in N. C.*
[133] Ellen Davies-Rodgers, *The Great Book.*
[134] *Diocesan Journal,* May 1832. IBK-LHM-EFM, SJC, UNCW.
[135] SJC, UNCW. James Laurence Sprunt. Ellen Davies-Rodgers, *The Great Book.*
[136] William C. Lord, correspondence. *Diocesan Journal,* May 1837) SJC. UNCW. (Note: William Blaney, a black man who was a communicant of St. James, built a c. 1850 house at 508 South Third Street that is now the home of Haywood and Bill Mason. Mr. Blaney was a painting contractor who probably worked on the 1839 church building.)
[137] *One Hundredth Anniversary booklet, 1939.*
[138] New Hanover County Deed Book L, page 326. Trinity Church Archives; New York City. Scott-Wright Files, LCFHS. Anna Jean Sampson, Giles Collection, SHC, UNC. E. Clowes Chorley, *Quarter of a Millennium: Trinity Church in the City of New York.* Richmond, 1947. Archibald Henderson, *Washington's Southern Tour.* Boston, 1923. (Note: The older Grainger name died out in Wilmington. The J. Victor Grainger family that came later has no known relation to them.)
[139] Ibid.
[140] New Hanover County Deed Book O, page 290. Emma Woodward MacMillan. *Wilmington's Vanished Homes and Buildings.* Raleigh, 1966.
[141] *The State,* November 1981. (Letter from Charles T. Upjohn.)
[142] Jean Bradley Anderson. *Piedmont Plantation. A comprehensive history of the* ***Bennehan-Cameron*** *Plantations.* Durham, 1985
[143] Jean Bradley Anderson. Author's interview with Dr. Brooks Graebner, 2004. Green family papers, courtesy of Elizabeth Brown King.
[144] Richard Upjohn. *Upjohn's Rural Architecture.* New York, 1852.
[145] Diocesan notes, page 26. McEachern Files.
[146] *Wilmington Herald,* June 14, 1851.
[147] Special Collections, Duke University
[148] Luciana Poisson Pickrell to the Rev. Mr. Herbert Aman. May 4, 1974.
[149] Calder Lazarus letters, LCFHS.
[150] J. G. Burr, additions to Dr. R. B. Drane's *Sketch of St. James Parish.* New York, 1874.
[151] Vm. August 14, 1848. IBK-LHM-EFM. SJC. UNCW. Author's correspondence with Charles Pollock, Southport.
[152] *Wilmington Post,* October 12, 1879. Robert B. Drane, "Contents of St. James Episcopal Church

Corner Stone." (Dr. Drane's personal copy was preserved by George G. Thomas, who transcribed Dr. Drane's marginal notes as well.) LCFHS Archives.

153 *Wilmington Advertiser,* November 17, 1837.

154 *Diocesan Journal,* May 22, 1839. IBK-LHM-EFM. SJC, UNCW.

155 *Peoples' Press,* September 27, 1839. NHCPL. *Diocesan Journal,* May 22, 1839. (McEachern files)

156 Repiton-Lamb Family Papers. East Carolina Manuscript Collection. Joyner Library. East Carolina University. Repiton attended the Cumberland Street Baptist Church. It became eventually the Freemason Street Baptist Church. Repiton was greatly influenced by the sermons and life of the minister, Robert Boyte Crawford Howell.

157 Repiton-Lamb Family Papers.

158 Repiton-Lamb Family Papers.

159 James Sprunt, *Chronicles of the Cape Fear River.* Wilmington, 1992. *Advertiser,* November 17, 1837. WRC. NHCPL.

160 James Moore Goode, *Architecture, Politics, and Conflict: Thomas Ustick Walter and the Enlargement of the United States Capitol, 1850-1865.* Ann Arbor, 1995.

161 Ibid.

162Ibid.

163Ibid. 1994. Author's conversation and correspondence with James Moore Goode, 2004. Joseph Gardner Swift, *Memoirs.*

164 The Reverend R. B. Drane, "An Address Delivered in St. James Church, Wilmington, N. C., at the interment of Dr. Thomas Henry Wright; Wilmington, 1861." North Carolina Collection, Wilson Library, University of North Carolina.

165 Letter written July 21, 1851. Giles Collection. SHC UNC.

166 James Moore Goode. Author's correspondence with James Moore Goode, 2004.

167 Images of both churches were furnished to the author by the Athenaeum, with the suggestion that St. James was a scaled down version of one or both the English churches. Catherine W. Bishir, *North Carolina Architecture.* Chapel Hill, 1990. John Henry Hopkins, *Essay on Gothic Architecture, with Various Plans and Drawings for Churches.* Burlington, Vt., 1836.

168 Vestry minutes, Feb. 7, 1839. McEachern files, UNCW. *Wilmington Advertiser,* November 17, 1837. VM, IBK-LHM-EFM, UNCW.

169 William Lord deRosset, *Pictorial and Historical New Hanover County and Wilmington, NC.* Wilmington, 1938. (The Rev. Mr. Mortimer Glover, "Historical Notes of St. James Church.") Author's interview with Walker Taylor III, 2004.

170 Robert B. Drane, "Contents of St. James Episcopal Church Cornerstone." *Wilmington Advertiser,* November 17, 1837. WRC.NHCPL. Vestry circular, April 11, 1845, SJC, UNCW.

[171] March 19, 1839, SJC. UNCW.
[172] *Chronicle*, January 7, 1903. The poem is signed, "A," apparently for Asa Brown.
[173] *One Hundredth Anniversary s Church booklet.* 1939. (Excerpts from Memoirs of Col. James G. Burr, 1874.)
[174] LCFHS archives. Robert S. Neale, *The Bank of Cape Fear.* Wilmington, 1999.
[175] James Burke (compiler and editor), "Proceedings of the Wilmington and Raleigh Railroad: May, 1838."
[176] *Wilmington Advertiser*, April 5, 1839.
[177] The Athenaeum of Philadelphia. James Moore Goode. Beatrice St. Julien Ravenel, *Architects of Charleston.* Charleston, 1964.
[178] Elizabeth F. McKoy, "Old St. James Church." LCFHS.
[179] *Morning Star*, May 25, 1878. McEachern Files. WRC.
[180] Mary Ellen Gadski, "The History of the deRosset House." 1978.
[181] Ibid. (Gadski cites within the deRosset Papers, SHC, UNC: correspondence dated July 22, 1843; August 4, 1843; and December 8, 1844.)
[182]Gadski.
[183] Gadski. Catherine W. Bishir, *North Carolina Architecture.* Chapel Hill, 1999.
[184] "Review of Wilmington, N. C." 17 March 1890 – W. B. McKoy files. Janet K. Seapker, "Wood Works: The Architectural Creations and Personal Histories of John Coffin and Robert Barclay Wood." Lower Cape Fear Historical Society *Bulletin*, XXXIX.
[185] "Ibid.
[186] 'Some Recollections of my life for my children during my confinement with aneurysm," by Dr. Thomas Fanning Wood. Catalogued by Donald Koonce. New Hanover County Public Library. UNCW.
[187] Floor plan design for pews, SJC, UNCW.
[188] Vestry Minutes, Jan. 16, 1840 and March 16, 1840. McEachern files. UNCW. Star, October 21, 1880. WRC, NHCPL. James Moore Goode.
[189] Address of Bishop Levi S. Ives to the 24th annual convention of the Protestant Episcopal Church in the stte of N.C. The Athenaeum of Philadelphia.
[190] St. James Collection, UNCW. Vestry Minutes, Feb. 3, 1840.
[191] Levi Silliman Ives, "Proclamation on the Dedication of St. James Church," 1840. SJC. UNCW.
[192] St. James Collection. Empie papers. UNCW.
[193] Organ file, 23 October 1839. St. James Collection.
[194] Clock files, SJC, UNCW.
[195] *Chronicle*, August 30, 1843. WRC. NHCPL.
[196] St. James Church: 1839-1939, LCFHS. W. L. DeRosset, *Pictorial and Historical New Hanover*

County.

[197] Book of Remembrance, SJC, UNCW.

[198] John E. Kleber, ed. *Kentucky Encyclopedia.* Courtesy of Holt Culpepper, Louisville, Ky. James Grant Wilson and John Fiske, eds. *Appleton's Cyclopedia of American Biography.* Richard H. Wilmer, *The Recent Past from a Southern Standpoint, Reminiscences of a Grandfather.* New York, 1887.

[199] Circular to the Members, April 11, 1845. SJC, UNCW.

[200] *Peoples' Press,* April 1, 1841. NHCPL.

[201] Meares Collection, Perkins Library, Duke University.

[202] Photograph, LCFHS. 19th century image of St. James with the fence intact.

[203] "Notes on Local Churches," compiled by James H. McKoy. LCFHS. (Note: The organ was located in the rear balcony until 1885 when it was moved to the chancel. By the 1960s when plans were made to move it back to the balcony, there was apparently no one alive who remembered it had once been there. See page 201.)

[204] Mary Ellen Gadski, "The History of the deRosset House." 1978. Cape Fear Museum.

[205] Ibid.

[206] Ibid.

[207] *The Commercial,* Feb. 17, 1847.

[208] St. James Collection. UNCW. *Wilmington Chronicle,* May 17, 1848.

[209] Giles Collection, SHC, UNC.

[210] Giles Collection, SHC, UNC. *Wilmington Daily Herald,* December 3, 1856.

[211] Virginia Bellamy Ruffin notebook, LCFHS.

[212] Empie Family Papers, LCFHS.

[213] SJC, UNCW. Emily Bingham, *Mordecai: An Early American Family.* New York, 2003.

[214] Lawrence Foushee London and Sarah McCulloh Lemmon, (William S. Powell), *The Episcopal Church in North Carolina, 1701-1959.* Raleigh, 1987.

[215] William Lord deRosset, *Pictorial and Historical New Hanover County and Wilmington, North Carolina, 1723-1938.* Wilmington, 1938.

[216] University of North Carolina at Chapel Hill Libraries. Documenting the American South, Electronic Edition. Atkinson, "Christian Duty," Wilmington, 1861.

[217] Giles Collection, "Grand Excursion from Ayr." James Allan Wright to Tommie Wright, July 29, 1855. SHC, UNC.

[218] Rev. Robert B. Drane, "An Address Delivered in St. James' Chrch, Wilmington, N. C., at the interment of Dr. Thomas H. Wright." Allan Taylor Strange.

[219] John Reston Giles to Mary Allan Wright, September 26, 1861 (Thunderbolt Battery). SHC, U.N.C.

[220] Giles Collection, SHC, UNC.

221 James Sprunt, *Chronicles.*
222 Tammy L. Colson. "Yellow Jack: Yellow Fever in Wilmington, N.C." UNCW.
223 J. G. Burr, *A Sketch of St. James Parish, Wilmington, N. C.* New York, 1874.
224 Ibid.
225 "The Memoirs of Marie Louise DuBrutz Reston Bolles." LCFHS.
226 J. G. Burr, additions to Dr. R. B. Drane's *Sketch of St. James Parish.*
227 University of North Carolina at Chapel Hill Libraries, *Documenting the American South.* Raleigh, 1863.
228 SJC, UNCW. Empie Collection, LCFHS. London and Lemmon *The Episcopal Church in N.C.*
229 John Johns, "Wilmington During the Blockade," Harper's New Monthly Magazine, 1866. (Volume 33, 497-503). Eugene C. Hicks Collection.
230 James Sprunt, *Tales of the Cape Fear Blockade.* Wilmington, 1960.
231 Johns.
232 Johns. Additional facts supplied by Chris E. Fonvielle, PhD.
233 Johns.
234 Chris E. Fonvielle, *The Wilmington Campaign.* Campbell, Ca., 1997.
235 J. G. Burr's additions to Dr. Drane's work in Sketch of St. James Parish.
236 SJC, UNCW.
237 Burr.
238 Bishop Atkinson's handwritten notes on St. Paul's. NHCPL.
239 Harriet O Jeffress. Vm, December 6, 1870. IBK-LHM-EFM, SJC, UNCW.
240 Alfred Watson to Pres. Abraham Lincoln, April 12, 1865. SJC. UNCW.
241 Burr.
242 Lockert Mason, M.D. "Separation and Reunion of the Episcopal Church, 1861-1865: The Role of Bishop Thomas Atkinson of the Diocese of N.C." Lower Cape Fear Historical Society *Bulletin,* Vol. 37, 1. Oct. 1992. Statement from Dr. Lockert Mason, 2004.
243 Richard H. Wilmer.
244 Lazarus-Calder letters, March 29, 1866. LCFHS.
245 Book of Remembrance, SJC. UNCW.
246 *Star,* April 27, 1886. WRC. *Star,* April 7, 1901. Author's interview with Jean McKoy Graham.
247 John Wheeler, *Reminiscences and Memoirs of North Carolina and Eminent North Carolinians.* Columbus, Ohio; 1884.
248 Wheeler. E. C. Hicks. John H. Wheeler, *Reminiscences and Memoirs of North Carolina and Eminent North Carolinians.*
249 Vm. January 6, 1868. March 3, 1868. IBK-LHM-EFM, SJC, UNCW.
250 NHC Deed Book WW, page 241.

251 *Star*, September 22, 1869.
252 Courtesy of Candy Williams.
253 Vestry Minutes, Nov. 30, 1874. *Morning Star*, July 8, 1876. *Morning Star*, Jan. 10, 1877.
254 *Star*, May 13, 1879, July 22, 1879, April 29, 1883, June 6, 1883. WRC, NHCPL.
255 NHC DB MMM 487-489. June 6, 1875. Marion Potter to the Vestry Wardens and Trustees of St. James Church. SJC. UNCW.
256 NHC DB MMM 487-489. June 6, 1875. Marion Potter to the Vestry Wardens and Trustees of St. James Church. SJC. UNCW.
257 Florence A. Bason, "History of Lebanon Chapel, 1836-1936." LCFHS. Note: In 1887, a small cottage was moved from Lebanon to a nearby neighbor's property.
258 Vm. 1871. IBK-LHM-EFM. SJC. UNCW.
259 Vm. March 7, 1871;March 10, 1871;December 5, 1871. The term hammer-beam is from architectural historian Edward F. Turberg.
260 Vm. May 11, 1869. IBK-LHM-EFM, SJC, UNCW.
261 Star, October 17,1885. VM, 1884-1885. IBK-LHM-EFM, UNCW.
262 *Diocesan Journal*. Diocesan Convention: May 24-27. SJC, UNCW. Beverly Tetterton, NHCPL.
263 Author's interviews with Allan T. Strange, 2003.
264 *Morning Star*, March 30, 1875. WRC. NHCPL.
265 *Charleston News and Courier*, April 15, 1886. WRC. NHCPL.
266 Ibid.
267 Mrs. John D. Bellamy, Jr., Book of Remembrance. SJC, UNCW.
268 Vestry Minutes, Feb. 1874.
269 NHC Deed Book UU, 666. (McEachern) The Rev. Mortimer Glover, "The Mission of the Good Shepherd." (A sermon delivered on November 5, 1967, the 75th anniversary of the Church of the Good Shepherd.) LCFHS. Burr, *Sketch of St. James*. Vestry Minutes, March 5, 1895.
270 Block, *Wilmington Through the Lens of Louis T. Moore*. Wilmington, 2001. (Note: At the turn of the century, the MacRaes sold Wilmington Cotton Mills to John D. Bellamy, Jr. Bellamy brought his son-in-law, J. Walter Williamson, into the business and renamed it Bellwill.The mill closed in the late teens.)
271 *Diane Cobb Cashman. Headstrong: the Biography of Amy Morris Bradley (1823-1904), A Life of Noblest Usefulness*. Wilmington, 1990. Minutes of the Sisterhood of the Good Shepherd, Diocese of N.Y. Wade H. Kempton, Diocese of N.Y.
272 Author's correspondence with Wade H. Kempton, archivist for the Diocese of N.Y.
273 Kempton. *Star*. February 1, 1880. WRC.
274 Author's correspondence with Wade H. Kempton, archivist for the Diocese of N.Y.
275 Ibid.

[276] "The 16th Annual Report of the Sisterhood of the Good Shepherd." New York, 1885. Kempton, Diocese of New York.
[277] Vestry Minutes, April 23, 1889.
[278] Author's correspondence with Wade H. Kempton, archivist for the Diocese of New York.
[279] *Messenger,* April 19, 1892. WRC.
[280] Vm. September 6, 1892. IBK-LHM-EFM, SJC, UNCW. *Morning Star,* November 3, 1892, NHCPL. WRC.
[281] No name, January 26, 1894. Oakdale Cemetery data supplied by director Eric Kozen.
[282] WRC, NHCPL. January 23, 1894. January 26, 1894.
[283] No name, November 23, 1894.
[284] "The 16th Annual Report of the Sisterhood of the Good Shepherd." New York, 1885. This testimonial was recorded by a woman who was presumably a member of St. James Church. The passage was included in the 1885 records of the Good Shepherd Ministry. Wade H. Kempton, Diocese of New York.
[285] Ibid. Vm. November 8, 1892.
[286] *Morning Star,* November 8, 1892. Reaves Files, NHCPL. McEachern Files, SJC, UNCW.
[287] Mortimer Glover, "The Mission of Good Shepherd." 1967. LCFHS.
[288] *Messenger,* February 10, 1895.
[289] *Diocesan Journal,* 17. IBK-LHM-EFMcE SJC. UNCW.
[290] Book of Remembrances. UNCW.
[291] *Messenger,* January 22, 1901. WRC. NHCPL.
[292] "Register of the Professors and Cadets of the Cape Fear Military Academy." Wilmington, 1870. Cape Fear Museum. Glenn Hoffman, *Building a Great Railroad: A History of the Atlantic Coast Line Railroad Company.* Jacksonville, 1998.
[293] Book of Remembrance. UNCW.
[294] Interview conducted in 1975 by Diane Cashman and Jean Poole at the home of Felice Sadgwar and Mabel Manly. Both sisters were nieces of Alexander Manly. They stated that it was their understanding- via family oral tradition- that in 1898, Bishop Strange personally took Manly to the train station so that he could escape the riots. Author's interviews with Clarence Jones, celebrated gardener at Orton, who had relatives among the group gathered in Sprunt's warehouse.
[295] James Sprunt, *Chronicles.* Lower Cape Fear Historical Society subject files. Robert Martin Fales, M. D., *Wilmington Yesteryear.* Wilmington, 1984.
[296] Seamen's Friend Society minutes. LCFHS.
[297] *Star,* August 28, 1902. WRC, NHCPL. *Star,* November 12, 1901.
[298] SJC. UNCW. *Wilmington Messenger,* October 30, 1904. *Southern Churchman,* undated. (Courtesy of Allan T. Strange) *Morning Star,* August 27, 1904.

[299] *Star,* August 26, 1900. WRC, NHCPL.
[300] *Star,* April 6, 1884. Vm, SJC, UNCW.
[301] Book of Remembrances, SJC, UNCW.
[302] *Star,* December 25, 1897. WRC, NHCPL. Book of Remembrances, SJC, UNCW.
[303] *Messenger,* June 18, 1902. WRC, NHCPL.
[304] *Messenger,* October 31, 1902. WRC. NHCPL. Rector's files, SJC, UNCW.
[305] Cyrus Hogue, Jr. *The View From Pew 7: A Few Memories in the Life of Cyrus D. Hogue, Jr.* Wilmington, 2001.
[306] Vestry Minutes, March 8, 1904. IBK-LHM-EFM, SJC, UNCW. Bridgers files, WRC, NHCPL.Wilmington Messenger, October 23, 1904. Edward F. Turberg.
[307] *Star,* February 4, 1924.
[308] *Star,* Feb. 21, 1886. WRC.
[309] *Dispatch,* December 15, 1900. WRC.
[310] No. 11650 *Congressional Records.* SJC. UNCW.
[311] *Star,* April 18, 1888. WRC.
[312] *Messenger*, September 21, 1888. VM, October 9, 1888, November 6, 1888. *Messenger,* March 9, 1889.
[313] Anne T. S. Bellamy, "Adieu, St. Mary's."
[314] VM July 7, 1891, July 24, 1891, August 11, 1891. *Messenger*, October 6, 1891. WRC, NHCPL.
[315] Vm April 23, 1889. IBK-LHM-EFM, SJC, UNCW.
[316] Vm, March 17, 1884. IBK-LHM-EFM, SJC, UNCW.
[317] Vm November 19, 1891. February 7 , 1893, IBK-LHM-EFM, UNCW.
[318] Latimer family papers (LCFHS.) Author's interview with Nancy Latimer, 2003.
[319] Correspondence from Nancy Latimer, January 13, 2004.
[320] Bailey, *The Gospel in Art. USA, 1944.*
[321] Robert Strange to Henry Latimer, November 24, 1891. SJC, UNCW.
[322] Ibid.
[323] Silas McBee, *An Eirenic Itinerary.* London, 1911.
[324] Vic Hood. "History in Carving: Melchior Thoni." *Carving Magazine.* Issue #1. Archives of Christ Church Cathedral, Nashville. Fletch Coke, historian. Bill Holder. "Memoir of Melchior Thoni." *The Nashville Tennessean Magazine,* November 16, 1947.
[325] Vic Hood.
[326] Vic Hood.
[327] Book of Remembrance, SJC, UNCW.
[328] Mortimer Glover stated that McBee and his daughters carved the reredos. (Edward F. Turberg.)

Information on Ashley Hall from the school.

329 William Lord deRosset, *Pictorial and Historical New Hanover County.*

330 Silas McBee to Vardry McBee, October 6, 1894. SHC, UNC. Jean M. Farnsworth, "*Identifying Stained Glass Windows by Charles Booth in Philadelphia.*" Author's interview with Jean Farnsworth in 2004.

331 *Messenger*, November 27, 1892. Reaves Files, NHCPL. McEachern Files, SJC; UNCW.

332 *Messenger*, December 1, 1892. Reaves Files. McEachern Files.

333 *Star,* June 8, 1898. William Reaves Files. McEachern Files. Diocesan Journals, NHCPL.

334 *Messenger*, August 14, 1891. Eugene Hicks.

335 Nicholas Schenck. "*Diary of Nichomas Schenck.*" LCFHS. *Evening Post,* January 29, 1873.

336 Tony P. Wrenn.

337 *Messenger*, August 14, 1891. Vestry minutes, February 21, 1894, March 13, 1894. IBK-LHM-EFM, SJC, UNCW.

338 Tony P. Wrenn.

339 *Chronicle,* December 15, 1847.

340 "The Diary of Nicholas Schenck." LCFHS,

341 Book of Remembrance, SJC, UNCW.

342 March 24, 1841, Ladies Working Society. SJC. UNCW. General minutes, Ladies' Working Society. SJC, UNCW.

343 Vm, May 5, 1892. IBK-LHM-EFM, SJC, UNCW.

344 *Messenger*, April 14, 1892. *Messenger*, April 17, 1892.

345 *Messenger,* November 28, 1891, December 6, 1892, December 14, 1892. WMR.

346 Vm, November 8, 1892. IBK-LHM-EFM, SJC, UNCW. Book of Remembrances, SJC, UNCW.

347 *Morning Star,* June 2, 1898. WRC, NHCPL.

348 Family files, LCFHS. *What God Hath Wrought: A History of the Little Chapel on the Boardwalk (1907-2002).* Author's interview with Charlotte Murchison, 2004.

349 Giles Collection, SHC, UNC. Note: Ironically, William S. R. Beane, a subsequent resident of the William Wright property would also persoanlly subsidize the salary of the local clergy.

350 *Dispatch* August 22, 1899. Giles Collection, June 15, 1839. , SHC, UNC. Interviews with Eleanor Wright Beane. Wright-Beane Collection. The John London family, who had moved from Wilmington to Birmingham, visited the William Wrights on the sound as late as 1907.(*Star,* August 25, 1907.)

351 *Star*, May 18, 1902. WRC. *Messenger,* May 19, 1906. WRC.

352 *Dispatch*, July 24, 1902. WRC, NHCPL. Author's interviews with Fred Hatch, 2002.

353 *Star,* March 36, 1879.

[354] Vm, April 9, 1908. IBK-LHM-EFM, SJC, UNCW.
[355] Author's interviews with Walker Taylor III, 2003.
[356] Foushee and London. *The Episcopal Church in N. C.*
[357] *Dispatch*, August 11, 1911. WRC, NHCPL.
[358] Tony P. Wrenn.
[359] Lebanon Chapel records. Vm, IBK-LHM-EFM.
[360] Vm, IBK-LHM-EFM.
[361] Jones-Bradley correspondence, Lebanon, LCFHS. SJC, UNCW.
[362] SJC, UNCW.
[363] *Morning Star*, October 14, 1923. (WRFiles)
[364] "Leading Society Folks Wed Near Wilmington." LCFHS.
[365] Maxine Dizor, "A Little Girl's Memories." St. Andrew's on-the-Sound archives. Author's interview with Maxine Dizor, 1992.
[366] St. Andrew's on-the-Sound archives.
[367] Maxine Dizor.
[368] Author's interview with Lossie Gardell, 2002.
[369] Author's interviews (1993-2004) with Lossie Gardell, Leslie N. Boney, Jr., and Carl McGowan.
[370] Virginia H. Holland, *Mission Herald* (December 1963). "William G. Robertson Honored at St. James Church, Wilmington." LCFHS. Author's interview with Jean McKoy Graham, 2004.
[371] Author's interview with Dorothy Harriss Weathersbee, 2003.
[372] Author's interviews with Walker Taylor III, 2004.
[373] *Dispatch,* August 23, 1916. WRC, NHCPL. Author's interview with Leslie N. Boney, Jr., 2001.
[374] The Rev. William H. Milton, "The Great Adventure." January 5, 1919, St. James Church. (Lower Cape Fear Historical Society)
[375] Vm, January 5, 1875. Andrew Gardner, usher.
[376] Vestry Minutes, April 9, 1919. (IBK-LHM-EFM. SJC. UNCW) Peggy Moore Perdew, "Notes Taken by Peggy Moore from the Rev. Mortimer Glover."
[377] *Morning Star,* October 15,1922. Edward F. Turberg.
[378] *Morning Star*, May 4, 1923; May 2, 1923.
[379] Charles Upjohn, nephew of Hobart Upjohn. WRC. NHCPL.
[380] Catherine W. Bishir. Charles Upjohn. Edward F. Turberg. (Lifelong St. James member Florence Moore Dunn witnessed the fire. Interviewed in 2001 by the author, Mrs. Dunn said: "And then when I was eight years old, the First Presbyterian Church burned New Year's Eve. It was spectacular but we were absolutely terrified the steeple would come our way. As it turned out, it fell right straight down. We stood on our back porch (on Dock Street, between 3rd and 4th streets.) We had an upstairs back porch and I think Mother made us go in the house and watch out the window."

381 *Morning Star*, March 6, 1924. Edward F. Turberg.
382 Book of Remembrance, SJC, UNCW.
383 Richard Gwathmey, Eulogy for Louise Dick Gwathmey. St. James Church, March 27, 2004.
384 Leonora Cantwell to Margaret Y. Moore, November 19, 1937. Miss Moore was a student at Oldfields. Miss Cantwell's return address was spare, but all that was needed in those days: "L.C., St. James Parish, Wilmington, N.C."
385 Tape of Mortimer Glover, courtesy of Mary Ann Hogue. Transcribed by the author.
386 Author's interview with John J. Ormond, 2004.
387 Book of Remembrance, SJC, UNCW.
388 SJC. UNCW.
389 Vm, June 12, 1940. IBK-LHM-EFM, SJC. UNCW.
390 Ibid.
391 Author's interview with Margaret Moore Perdew, 2004.
392 Vm, 1942, IBK-LHM-EFM, SJC, UNCW.
393 The Rev. Mortimer Glover, "Unfinished Symphony." April 15, 1945, St. James Church. (Lower Cape Fear Historical Society)
394 Vm.:May 13, 1946, October 7, 1946. IBK-LHM-EFM, SJC, UNCW.
395 Bryan Broadfoot. Cornelia Broadfoot.
396 Vestry Minutes, March 8, 1948. IBK-LHM-EFM, SJC, UNCW. Author's correspondence with Meg Davenport, Walker Taylor III, Florence Moore Dunn, and Margaret Moore Perdew, 2004.
397 Margaret Moore Perdew, "St. James Kindergarten." UNCW.
398 Vm, May 31, 1949. IBK-LHM-EFM, SJC, UNCW.
399 Author's interviews with Peggy Moore Perdew, 2004.
400 Bishop Wright's 1951 diary. James Knowlton Wright.
401 Author's interview with Bruce B. Cameron, Jr., 2001.
402 Author's interviews with Walker Taylor III, 2003.
403 Ibid.
404 Emma Woodward MacMillan, *Wilmington's Vanished Homes and Buildings.* Raleigh, 1966. (Article, "Eleven South Third Street," by Mary M. Wootten.) LCFHS family files.
405 "The Yellow Terror and Blockade."
406 *Trinity College Bulletin*, Necrology. Hartford, April 1936. MMW.
407 MMW.
408 Author's interviews with Mary Wootten and Anne Russell, May 2004.
409 Undated *Star News* clipping and family data (Mary Wootten Collection) Hill and Wright Family Files, LCFHS Archives.
410 Undated Star News clipping. (Mary Wootten Collection) Tony P. Wrenn.

[411] Charles H. Boney to the author, March 26, 2004.

[412] Ibid.

[413] Ibid.

[414] Author's correspondence with Walker Taylor III.

[415] Author's interview with Peggy Moore Perdew and Florence Moore Dunn, 2001.

[416] Recorded interview with Helen Messick Willetts, 2003. Interview and transcription by the author.

[417] Author's interview with Dorothy Harriss Weathersbee, 2003.

[418] "Organ Recital by John S. Mueller" and "The Renaissance in Organ Building." (Betsy Sprunt Collection) Casavant Freres Handbook.

[419] Recorded interview with the Rev. Mortimer Glover, 1989. Moderators: Mary Ann Hogue, Bill Grainger, and Joan Grainger. Transcribed by the author. Architectural notes and timelines, UNCW.

[420] Rev. Mortimer Glover interview, 1989.

[421] James McKoy Collection. CFM. (James McKoy originated the idea for Festival Sunday.) St. James *Bulletin,* April 8, 1962. MMW.

[422] Courtesy of James Knowlton Wright.

[423] Bobbie Marcroft, "Mount Lebanon Chapel, Wilmington." *Cross Current,* November 1991.

[424] Author's interview with John C. Drewry. Wilmington, 2002.

[425] Herbert Aman to Waddell Corbett, November 16, 1972. Records, April 7, 1973. SAOTS.

[426] Author's interviews with George Evans, Terry Sanford, Jr., John C. Drewry, Lossie D. Gardell, and the late Carl McGowan. Dates of interviews ranged from 1992-2004. SAOTS.

[427] Robert Wysocki to Herbert Aman, March 14, 1973. SAOTS.

[428] Anderson, Jean Bradley. *Piedmont Plantation. A comprehensive history of the* ***Bennehan-Cameron*** *Plantations.* Durham, 1985.

[429] Robert J. Wysocki, March 1, 1974. Aug. 28, 1973. SAOTS.

[430] St. Andrew's on-the-Sound Archives. Author's correspondence from Victor Grainger Taylor, April 5, 2004.

[431] Author's correspondence with Bishop Von Rosenberg, 2004.

[432] Author's interview with Allan T. Strange, 2003.

Ever Growing – Welcoming new members of the St. James Community

Index

Jim Morton, Easter 1963. This photo was taken by Jim's father, St. James native son Hugh Morton, owner of Grandfather Mountain and one of the nation's most accomplished photographers.

"Again, some people visit old churches because they are the best places to be quiet and at peace. There could be nowhere better if one needs to set one's thoughts in order or to get the measure of some turning point, some joy or sorrow in one's life. From which it follows, of course, that old churches are the best places to pray.

"'You are here to kneel, says T. S. Eliot in his poem 'Little Gidding', 'where prayer has been valid', and some of that validity comes from the sheer length of time that this has been a holy place." – Author Unknown (Photo by John Parker)

Notes

Notes